Counseling
for
Sexual Disorders

RESOURCES FOR
CHRISTIAN COUNSELING

RESOURCES FOR CHRISTIAN COUNSELING

1. Innovative Approaches to Counseling *Gary R. Collins*
2. Counseling Christian Workers *Louis McBurney*
3. Self-Talk, Imagery, and Prayer in Counseling *H. Norman Wright*
4. Counseling Those with Eating Disorders *Raymond E. Vath*
5. Counseling the Depressed *Archibald D. Hart*
6. Counseling for Family Violence and Abuse *Grant L. Martin*
7. Counseling in Times of Crisis *Judson J. Swihart and Gerald C. Richardson*
8. Counseling and Guilt *Earl D. Wilson*
9. Counseling and the Search for Meaning *Paul R. Welter*
10. Counseling for Unplanned Pregnancy and Infertility *Everett L. Worthington, Jr.*
11. Counseling for Problems of Self-Control *Richard P. Walters*
12. Counseling for Substance Abuse and Addiction *Stephen Van Cleave, Walter Byrd, Kathy Revell*
13. Counseling and Self-Esteem *David E. Carlson*
14. Counseling Families *George A. Rekers*
15. Counseling and Homosexuality *Earl D. Wilson*
16. Counseling for Anger *Mark P. Cosgrove*
17. Counseling and the Demonic *Rodger K. Bufford*
18. Counseling and Divorce *David A. Thompson*
19. Counseling and Marriage *DeLoss D. and Ruby M. Friesen*
20. Counseling the Sick and Terminally Ill *Gregg R. Albers*
21. Counseling Adult Children of Alcoholics *Sandra D. Wilson*
22. Counseling and Children *Warren Byrd and Paul Warren*
23. Counseling Before Marriage *Everett L. Worthington, Jr.*
24. Counseling and AIDS *Gregg R. Albers*
25. Counseling Families of Children with Disabilities *Rosemarie S. Cook*
26. Counseling for Sexual Disorders *Joyce and Clifford Penner*
27. Counseling for Conflict Resolution *L. Randolph Lowry and Richard B. Meyers*

(Other volumes forthcoming)

VOLUME TWENTY SIX

Counseling
for
Sexual Disorders

JOYCE J. PENNER, R.N., M.N.
CLIFFORD L. PENNER, Ph. D.

RESOURCES FOR
CHRISTIAN COUNSELING

General Editor

Gary R. Collins, Ph.D.

WORD PUBLISHING
Dallas · London · Vancouver · Melbourne

COUNSELING FOR SEXUAL DISORDERS, Volume 26 of the Resources for Christian Counseling series. Copyright © 1990 by Word, Incorporated. All rights reserved. No portion of this book may be reproduced in any form, except for brief quotations in reviews, without written permission from the publisher.

Unless otherwise indicated, all Scripture quotations in this volume are from The New American Standard Bible, NASB, © The Lockman Foundation 1960, 1962, 1963, 1968, 1971, 1972, 1973, 1975, 1977.

The authors gratefully acknowledge permission to reprint drawings in this book from their volume *The Gift of Sex*, copyright 1981, Word Books. Some drawings have been adapted for use in this book.

Library of Congress Cataloging-in-Publication Data

Penner, Joyce.
    Counseling for sexual disorders / Joyce J. Penner, Clifford L. Penner
      p.   cm. — (Resources for Christian counseling; v. 26)
    Includes bibliographical references and index.
    ISBN 0-8499-0482-X
    1. Sexual disorders—Patients—Pastoral counseling of. 2. Sex
counseling. 3. Sex therapy. 4. Sex—Religious aspects—
Christianity. 5. Pastoral counseling. I. Penner,
Clifford. II. Title. III. Series.
BV4460.8.P45   1990
616.85'830651—dc20   90–46790
                                              CIP

Printed in the United States of America

0 1 2 3 4 9 AGF 9 8 7 6 5 4 3 2 1

ACKNOWLEDGMENTS

We want to express our gratitude to:

Anita Yousoofian and Elise Waltersdorf, our typists, for their perseverance with our ancient word-processing system;

Christy Claxton-Brink and Kathleen Reagan for handling the endless details of this project at the office;

Carol Dettoni for getting the editing process started;

David Sielaff, who really understands computers, for his speedy work and his willingness to stay at the word-processor till late into the night;

Sue Ann Jones, the publisher's editor, for her carefully sensitive and clarifying editing;

Dr. Tom Olschner for his most helpful comments and corrections in the area of his expertise—sexual addictions;

and to Roland Hinz, our special friend and critic, for his investment in making us into real authors.

A special word of love and appreciation to our three children!

Julene, our primary editor, having just graduated from Harvard University and having just completed her honors thesis, was well prepared for the task of polishing her parents' imperfect manuscript. She was relentless in her attention to every detail. At times that was not easy to accept, but her critical eye clearly enhanced the final product and ultimately justified the massive investment in her college education.

Greg's ongoing involvement and consistent interest in our work has continued throughout the years—beginning back in grade school. Now, even when he is off counseling at summer camp, studying Japanese in Osaka, Japan, or continuing his studies in international relations at Georgetown University, his critical perspective and wise input are invaluable!

Kristine's encouraging, helpful, sparkly spirit freed us to focus on our writing tasks. Her computer knowledge—which far surpasses ours—was vital to our survival. Her attention to detail as she prepared the bibliography was her special contribution to this book. That work should stand her in good stead as she begins her high school years.

This indeed was a family project!

CONTENTS

Editor's Preface   ix

Part I: The Framework for Sexual Counseling   1

  1. Sex Is Hard to Talk About   3

  2. The Therapist: Are You Comfortable with
     Your Sexuality?   11

  3. The Christian Component—It Sets You Apart   25

  4. The Marriage: Sex Provides the Lubrication,
     Not the Fuel   38

  5. The Body: Sexual Anatomy and the Physical Response   44

  6. What Is Sexual Therapy?   67

  7. Why Sexual Therapy?   70

  8. Assessment   95

  9. Sexual Therapy   121

Part II: Diagnosis and Treatment   177

  10. Treating Problems Due to Couple Dissatisfaction   179

  11. Treating Problems of Sexual Desire   187

  12. Treating Problems of Sexual Arousal   204

  13. Treating Problems of Sexual Release   216

  14. Treating Problems of Intercourse   248

  15. Understanding and Treating Sexual Addictions   273

  16. The Results of Sexual Therapy   297

Bibliography   301

Notes   305

Index   309

EDITOR'S PREFACE

I BOUGHT MY FIRST COMPUTER from a sex therapist!

About ten years ago, I decided that the time had come to put away my yellow notepads and No. 2 pencils and start writing on a word processor. I had read that most people write faster on a computer, and someplace I had seen research showing that most of us write better when we sit at a keyboard. But I wasn't enthusiastic about making the transition and I knew nothing about computers.

One afternoon I mustered the courage to enter our user-friendly neighborhood computer store. I expected to be confronted by some young computer whiz who probably wouldn't understand my middle-aged hesitation. To my surprise, the salesperson turned out to be a young lady who introduced herself (I think her name was Kathy) and asked my name and what I did for a living.

She seemed delighted to discover that I was a psychologist.

"I'm in that field too," she said, and then identified herself as a sex therapist who was working part time selling computers.

Kathy was knowledgeable as a computer salesperson and she showed all kinds of empathy, warmth, and unconditional positive regard when I mentioned my uncertainties about buying the machine that she eventually sold to me. Since we talked mostly about bytes and floppy disks and hard drives I have no way of knowing if she was equally informed and effective as a sex therapist.

I do know, however, that becoming a competent sexual counselor is not easy and neither is it a task to be undertaken lightly. Often there are feelings of inadequacy, embarrassment, and frustration when an individual or couple takes the courageous step of talking to a counselor about sex. To be effective, counselors need knowledge, sensitivity, and experience if they are to help those who struggle sexually.

Joyce and Clifford Penner clearly have the needed attributes. Their many years of counseling experience, their awareness of sexual issues, their knowledge about sexual dysfunction and therapeutic techniques, and their sensitivity and commitment to biblical standards of morality all combine to give them an expertise in this area that perhaps few Christian counselors can match.

But the Penners have an additional qualification that many good counselors lack. Cliff and Joyce are able to communicate—clearly, accurately, and in a style that is easy to read. Their earlier books have established them as first-rate writers and leaders in the field of human sexuality. This volume on counseling and sexual disorders again demonstrates their capabilities both as sexual counselors and as communicators.

If you have read the introductions to earlier books in this series, you are by now aware of what we seek to accomplish with the Resources for Christian Counseling volumes. When we planned the series, we were determined to find authors who had a strong Christian commitment, impeccable counseling credentials, and extensive counseling experience. We wanted each of the books to be practical and helpful examples of accurate psychology and careful use of Scripture. Each was intended to have a clear evangelical perspective, careful documentation, a strong practical orientation, and freedom from the sweeping statements that sometimes characterize writing in the counseling field. Our goal was to provide books that would be clearly written, useful, up-to-date overviews of the issues faced by contemporary Christian counselors—including pastoral counselors. We have continued to be guided by these standards and as a result, we have seen the appearance of books that many counselors continue to consult on a regular basis. All of the Resources for Christian Counseling books have similar bindings and together they are intended to comprise a helpful encyclopedia of Christian counseling.

Joyce and Clifford Penner were among the first of the potential authors that we contacted. They agreed to write, but the demands of a busy counseling practice prevented them from getting their manuscript completed earlier. As you read through the pages that follow, I suspect you will agree with me that this book is worth the wait. The authors have written a practical and useful volume that can be helpful to Christian counselors for years to come.

I don't know what happened to Kathy, the sex therapist/computer lady. Three or four years after I had purchased my computer I saw her in a coffee shop, trying to control a cup of coffee and program a very active toddler who was up and running! Maybe Kathy has forsaken both computers and sex therapy for motherhood. If she ever goes back to her work as a therapist, however, I hope she is able to first get a copy of the Penners' book. Beginning counselors will find it helpful, but so will pastors, individuals, couples, and those who are experienced in helping people who have sexual problems. Whatever your level of experience, I suspect you too will find this book to be a useful addition to your library.

Gary R. Collins, Ph.D.
Kildeer, Illinois

PART I

THE FRAMEWORK OF SEXUAL COUNSELING

CHAPTER ONE

SEX IS HARD TO TALK ABOUT

WE LIVE IN THE ERA of the post-sexual revolution. Sex is so freely displayed on TV screens and in movies, magazines, and videos that people think sex should be easy to discuss. But dealing with sex on an intimate level—especially when sharing personal problems—reveals that exposure to sexual explicitness has not eased the process of discussion. The sexual revolution has not necessarily made people better informed about how to function as healthy and successful sexual partners. Rather, it has made people more comfortable in viewing sexual activity and hearing sexual terms used boldly. It also has made society more tolerant of a great range of sexual activity. But it has not helped the average married couple, churched or unchurched, experience a comfortable, informed approach to sexuality. Many still lack the tools with which to share the inner struggles of their sexual relationships.

As a result, when somebody comes for counseling about sexual matters, the counselor should expect him or her to show some initial discomfort. It may be the first time this person has ever talked openly about sexual concerns. Some counselees may not even have told their spouses the difficulties they are about to share with the counselor. The discomfort of being in a setting where sex is openly discussed will sharply raise the counselee's anxiety level and insecurity.

COMMON ANXIETIES IN THE COUNSELING SETTING

Sexual Terminology

The counselee's anxiety will come from a number of different sources. Using words that deal with sex is the first common source of anxiety. Often these words have never been spoken—the sexual revolution did not bring good, clear, extensive sex education into most homes. A person may have attended sex-education classes at school, but still may be uncomfortable talking about sex. A father said recently, "We assumed the kids learned about sex just like we did. They picked it up and we didn't have to talk to them about it." Most people do not talk naturally about sexual activities, body parts, feelings or fantasies. They are uncomfortable using their familiar street terms with the counselor, and are unsure of the technically correct terms. For example, men often confuse the vagina with the uterus.

As a counselor, you can quickly relieve a counselee's discomfort. When the person uses street terminology, reflect back that you understand the word used and then use the technically correct term for that word, so he or she has a choice between the slang and the clinical terminology. This not only teaches the correct term, it also lets the client know that you understand the slang used.

Explicit Discussion

Because a sense of privacy appropriately surrounds our sexuality, the counselee's second source of anxiety may be the embarrassment with speaking explicitly. Discomfort with explicitness will show itself in various ways. Some people will openly declare that they feel uncomfortable talking about specific sexual matters. Others wander in conversation and tell stories that are unrelated to the reason they are seeking help. Still others use general summarizing statements to communicate a very specific dilemma. For example, some women are unable to experience an orgasm without fantasizing. These fantasies may vary from violent, exposing, or illicit images, to fantasies of sexual experiences with another man or more than one person at a time. These women may report, "I have difficulty with my thoughts while making love," or, "My mind wants to wander." It is difficult for them to admit to using specific fantasies in order to be orgasmic.

In our society, we learn that sexual matters are acceptably shared in the privacy of the bedroom, or in jokes, or in the movies. The counselor, respecting this natural sense of privacy, carefully guides the client into sharing those explicit details that are necessary to the therapy process. Trust deepens as the counselee becomes comfortable with how the explicit information is handled.

The Counselor's Gender

The counselee may feel uneasy about the gender of the counselor. For example, some women will find it easier to share intimate details with a woman counselor—sharing them with a male counselor could cause high anxiety. Yet, on occasion, it is less threatening for a woman to share with a man, particularly if she had a close relationship with her father and experienced distance from her mother. Similarly, some men may share most easily with other men. But some men are used to sharing personal, intimate information only with women; they find it is more natural to share specifically with women, because they feel less vulnerable.

It is difficult to set an all-encompassing guideline as to gender in the counseling setting. A competent helper will be able to determine with whom the explicitness can be most readily shared. Sometimes a referral to a counselor of the opposite sex may be necessary. Yet most of the time you will be able to help the counselee past the difficulty, and thus connect effectively and specifically.

Reporting Unacceptable Behavior

Discomfort will most certainly arise when the counselee reports behavior that is generally viewed as immoral, indecent, illegal, or socially

5

inappropriate or unacceptable. This will be particularly evident in a Christian setting, whether that be in the office of a pastor or a Christian counselor. The reporter of this unacceptable behavior or these forbidden thoughts will continually check for clues to see how the information is being received and whether it is safe to continue. The discomfort will initially come from the person's own feelings of shame, remorse, or guilt about the activities, but can be exaggerated or eased by the nonverbal as well as verbal messages from the counselor.

Talking About Sex

Often there is anxiety or unsureness about the appropriateness of talking about sexual matters at all. We experienced an example of this while giving a lecture series at a Christian school to a group comprised primarily of pastors and seminary students. We were surprised when the leader who had invited us to his institution stood up after our first presentation and raised the question as to whether it was acceptable for us to be talking about these explicit sexual matters in a public forum. His ambivalence was evident.

Similar concerns may cause many individuals and couples to be long overdue in seeking help, because they view it as inappropriate or unchristian to discuss their intimate, sexual lives. Permission-giving may be necessary by a pastor, religious authority, or Christian mentor. We have on occasion invited the client's religious mentor to join us for a session because we knew the explicit permission granted by the authority was needed.

Exposing Secrets

More secrets exist in the sexual realm than in any other area of life. When people come for sexual help, they will need to reveal some of those secrets, and some individuals may find this difficult to do, because we have all been taught that it is wrong to tell secrets. This exposure of secrets, whether they are about fantasy, pornography, adultery, inadequacy, or desires, may bring intense discomfort. A person's public image may be at stake if abuse is involved, since it needs to be reported to authorities. Thus, the danger of sharing that secret is very real. Fear about the spouse's reaction also is realistic. Hence, because of anxiety, some people will have difficulty sharing sexual details.

Sharing Common Problems

Some counselees may find it difficult to talk about their sexual situations because they believe what they have to share is unique to them as individuals or couples. They feel terribly embarrassed by their problems. There is great relief in discovering that they are not alone. As you, the therapist, reflect back to them an understanding of their situation, they become aware that others have struggled with similar difficulties. This reflection and familiarity with their struggle diffuses the heaviness and intensity they have felt. Sometimes the details *will* indeed be unusual or unique to a specific individual and not something that even the counselor will have heard before. When this is the case, their uniqueness should not be announced to the counselees. Rather, it is important to reflect what you hear and to gather as many details as possible. You may then call on an expert for advice in the area of the difficulty that was shared. The expert might be an experienced sexual therapist, urologist, gynecologist, or other professional. In addition to aiding the counselee, you will have further educated yourself about specific difficulties.

Being Vulnerable

Because sex is very private and very personal, anything that has to do with the sharing of the particulars of one's sexuality makes a person vulnerable. It is difficult enough to communicate about intimate sexual issues when we feel confident about them. But it becomes almost impossible to share our sexual failures. All our lives, we have been taught not to show and not to share anything sexual. This teaching is clearly part of the natural modesty that develops around age four or five. Thus, it is completely understandable that there is a hesitancy to talk about sexual problems. Yet this hesitancy must be overcome if the counselor is going to be able to help.

Revealing One's Value System

What is shared sexually reveals much about us beyond the sexual data. It tells the kind of persons we are, the values we believe in and live by, and our secret, inner world. Whenever deep sexual secrets, feelings, responses, or activities are shared, we let someone else into our inner world in a way that happens in few other situations in life. This becomes threatening and sometimes causes defensiveness and anxiety.

7

DEALING WITH PAST HURTS

Childhood Sexual Abuse

One major consequence of sexual discussion is that it may bring past hurts to the forefront. The pain of past sexual abuse is the most obvious example of this for both women and men. Estimates vary as to the percentage of women that were sexually abused as children. But it is commonly accepted that many women have experienced abuse as children. For some, those memories have been so totally repressed that they cannot be reported. For others, the feelings about past abuse may be so vague that they have not faced them directly.

For those whose memories are so vivid that they haunt and plague them, reliving those instances will seem like dragging out a dead corpse, a reminder of pain. The individual wants to be rid of the memory and to avoid talking about it. So it is frightening to speak openly because it means digging up the ugly past. Inevitably, the very difficulty that is the current dilemma in the adult sexual relationship is identical to the pain the child experienced. To be able to get relief from the current difficulty requires undoing those past hurts, yet the discomfort that comes with sharing those hurts will obviously nudge people toward resistance. The counselor must gently yet persistently encourage the person to explore the abuse so that he or she can experience grief-release and reduce the impact on the present sexual life.

Negative Body Image

A negative body image may be another source of past hurt that contributes to one's difficulty in talking about sex. A person may have struggled with a physical handicap, obesity, or accidental or congenital deformity. Or the individual's body may be attractive by all external standards, but because of having been labeled or teased as a young child, he or she has a negative body image, even though others do not agree. As the sexual history is exposed, some of those old hurts in regard to the body will also be revealed.

Past Sexual Experience

Past adult sexual experience may be painful to share because it was hurtful to the individual's self-worth, conscience, or image. Becoming pregnant outside of marriage is a major hurt for women, whether they suffered the embarrassment of having "had to" get married, the guilt of adoption, or the trauma of abortion. There may also be guilt from premarital sexual activity or self-depreciation because of long-term sexual dysfunction.

Low Self-Esteem

Low self-esteem contributes to difficulty in sharing personal sexual information because one's general self-esteem is greatly influenced by sexual self-esteem. Sexual self-esteem may have been hurt by cultural and societal input, by myths that are believed, by past experiences, and by lack of knowledge. Self-worth is determined in part by one's self-perception as a sexual being. Self-esteem, both general and sexual, influences how freely sexual details can be shared.

Uncomfortable Emotions and Arousal

Besides stirring up emotions of intense hurt, anger, and fear, explicit conversation about sex may even cause sexual arousal for both the sharer and the helper. When sensing arousal in the client, note this observation in the clinical data that is being gathered. Although the connection between the information shared and the observed arousal should be explored, the counselor works to avoid intentional stimulation. It may be necessary to focus on other details of the interview in order to distract from the arousal.

Couples coming for help with sexual struggles need permission to talk explicitly about their sexual lives. Giving permission is a role Christian counselors regularly must play because they are viewed as both professional and Christian authorities. This permission-giving happens first by an attitude that communicates and encourages the acceptableness of talking about one's sexual life. Permission may also need to be communicated very directly by reminding the counselee that sexual issues are important, so important that they can be talked about in detail.

The counselee also needs to hear that God intended for men and women to have sexual fulfillment in marriage. The only way for some of them to gain this satisfaction is to share their anxieties and difficulties. In order to build a positive, sexual self-esteem and establish new sexual patterns, the old must be clearly understood. It is vital that the counselor not be troubled by a counselee's tears or by the unusualness of a report.

The person seeking help may be testing to see if it is safe to share these private details, these secrets. It may not have been safe in the past. As a child, the counselee may have been met with stony silence, disapproval, or a loud, verbal reaction; as an adolescent, there may have been condemnation; and as an adult, sharing may have led to strife.

Sex is hard to talk about. Thus, it is essential for therapists to be comfortable and competent in talking about sex to create an atmosphere of ease for the client. Counselors must recognize and accept that they are in the permission-granting role.

CHAPTER TWO

THE THERAPIST: ARE YOU COMFORTABLE WITH YOUR SEXUALITY?

THERAPISTS' COMFORT with their own sexuality greatly determines their effectiveness as sexual counselors. You may have been reared in a home where sexuality was never dealt with, where it was abused, where it was seen as the woman's burden and the man's delight, where it was the source of most humor, or, most beneficially, where it was viewed as a natural fulfilling part of the marriage relationship. Whatever your background is, it will have shaped your current view of sexuality.

Naturally, as you have grown and had both personal and educational experiences outside your family of origin, your perspective on sexuality has been shaped, reshaped, and added to. Who you are today is a conglomeration of your *sexual development, sexual identity, sexual attitudes, sexual feelings, sexual experiences, sexual knowledge, belief system, value system, marital status, and professional skills*. This chapter takes a brief look at each of these facets of the therapist's sexual self-concept.

SEXUAL DEVELOPMENT

Sexual development is influenced by a number of significant events and patterns that are present during childhood and the teen-age years.[1] First, the type of affection that is expressed in the home during these years makes a powerful difference. It affects bonding during the very early months of life. Then, as the child grows older, it continues to shape how that child feels about his or her body, how comfortable he or she is with physical intimacy, and even the level of need for that intimacy.

During the toddler years, comfort with one's genitals develops. If a child perceives his or her genitals as a normal, natural bodily part—a part that brings greater physical pleasure than some other parts—a positive sense of the genitals will result. But, if the child sees them as dirty—as an area that should not be touched, handled, or talked about—he or she might have a tendency to view sex or anything connected with sex as the "dirty area" of life.

Between the ages of four and seven, curiosity takes different forms. Sometimes there will be natural questioning by the young child, not only about how the body works, but also about how babies are born, how the seed gets inside a "mommy's tummy," how the baby gets out—all the natural questions of a young child. If your parents' responses were calm and factual, they will have left a different impression than reprimands, silence, or embarrassment. Curiosity might also have taken on the form of exploratory play. It is quite natural for the five- or six-year-old to play doctor. How far the game was taken, and how it was handled when discovered, will have had a major impact on your developing sexuality and sense of sexualness and will have left its mark in adulthood.

Another object of curiosity is nudity. Various families handle this differently. If bodies are secret, never to be shared, the curiosity tends to be increased to such an extent that furtive activity may be engaged in to discover what men and women's genitals look like. If overexposure took place in your home (that is, exposure that goes beyond the natural process of family living and is designed for titillation, either of the child or for the benefit of the adult), you might have developed an aversion to the nude body or developed some form of sexual addiction. All types of curiosity, which are natural to one's development, have influenced who you are today.

Masturbation is a sexual expression common to most early adolescent boys and many girls. Unfortunately, though, it often is the big, secret issue that haunts them. The teaching (or absence thereof) on this subject shapes attitudes, but does relatively little to change the activity. Our clinical findings are that the warnings against masturbation in this and most other generations have had virtually no impact on decreasing the masturbatory activity of youth. However, teaching negatively shapes attitudes about sexuality, because the admonitions against masturbation are often the first direct teachings about sex.

If you were warned not to "play with" or "abuse" yourself, or were just commanded "not to," you learned that it was wrong to respond to this urge in your body. If the warnings were not accompanied with a positive message about sexuality, you probably assumed the urges were a negative force in your body. The secretiveness, guilt, shame, and sense of not being able to control these sexual urges may have troubled you as a developing young teen-ager who most likely had no resource person with whom to consult or confide.

If the "don't" messages about masturbation were connected with religious teachings, this may have been the first time religious input was received about sexuality. Even though such teaching is not biblical or Christian, it is often given in that context, and thus, sends the message that it represents the church and what good Christians believe. As a result, you may have come to believe that, from the Christian perspective, sex is bad.

Fortunately, not all parental or church input regarding developing sexuality is negative. Your parents may have done a wonderful job of presenting you with a balanced, healthy, and biblically based sexual perspective.

If you attended a church youth group or summer camp while growing up, you may have been influenced there by teaching about physical intimacy: from handholding to passionate kissing to intercourse. This input will have partially shaped your current view of sexuality. What you believed and what you did about premarital sex is also an important thread in the fabric of your current sexuality.

If you were reared in a non-religious setting with no careful moral guidelines to follow, and later made a commitment to Christ, the shift from living without sexual guidelines to following the biblical way will have had a powerful impact. The struggle you had through those transitions, and even the present battles with that prechristian past, most certainly will influence how you deal with others who are experiencing the same dilemmas.

13

Two contrasting consequences are apparent for those counselors who have experienced intense sexual struggles. In one scenario, the counselors become caring, warm, and empathic to those going through similar struggles. They know how difficult it is, how intense the turmoil can be, and how impossible it seems at times to stick with one's commitments. In the other situation, therapists take an aggressive, militant stand against any "sexual sins" that they themselves may have experienced in the past. This often indicates that they continue to struggle with the sexual issues of their past, even while railing against them. It is vital that helpers scrutinize how their own previous experiences contribute to the handling of their clients.

If you are a victim of sexual abuse, much work must be done to process the pain and trauma of that experience in order to be an effective helper. Certainly, healed abusive experiences can serve as bridges of understanding to those who are struggling through the consequences of similar abuse. However, if you have not effectively dealt with your own emotional scars, you will tend either to avoid abuse issues with clients or to work out personal conflicts while in the process of trying to help others.

Therefore, whether it is the initial bonding of infancy, the curiosity of childhood, or the decision-making of adolescence, the sexual development of your childhood and adolescence remains a continuing, lifelong force, even as you become a competent sexual helper.

SEXUAL ATTITUDES

Because the attitudes of the sexual counselor will inevitably be communicated to the counselee, therapists must look carefully at these attitudes. Some attitudes help, and some hinder. Let's look at both.

Holding the view that sexual arousal is an innate physical response will make a positive difference in how you deal with people in a counseling setting. Both counselors and counselees need to be reminded that the natural response patterns of sexual arousal begin at birth and continue throughout life. It is also very important that sex not be perceived as *merely* a physical release, because it is so much more than that. It involves all of our being, heart, soul, mind, and strength.

A misleading perspective that is often expressed by helpers, whether they are physicians, pastors, or counselors, is that sex works if we just do what comes naturally. For example, many newly married or about-to-be-married couples are instructed just to "let nature take its course." This notion might be acceptable in simpler, more primitive settings—those without social, cultural, or moral limitations. However, our society is highly complicated, where the idea of "just letting nature take its course" works for some people but leaves others with unconsummated marriages or sexual frustrations. While the sexual response is considered to be a very *natural* response, it also must be viewed as a very *complicated* response that draws from every aspect of our beings and is in a continual state of growth, change, and struggle.

A vital attitude for the Christian sexual helper is the perception of an individual's right to sexual pleasure. The sexual response is not just an expression of a physical drive or simply for the purpose of procreation. Rather, it is a source of pleasure that bonds two people who are committed to each other in marriage. As previously mentioned, the counselor may need to grant permission to the client couple to partake in erotic pleasure. Many couples will have implicitly learned that "if it feels good it must be wrong." To counteract the antipleasure attitude, we suggest reading the Song of Solomon, and that it be taken literally rather than symbolically.

Variation and experimentation are key components to a sexually fulfilling married life. This is in contrast to the attitude that sex is a right-or-wrong set of techniques and skills, or recipes that lead from one step to another as if each couple's experiences can be prescribed and mechanically repeated time after time. Popular magazines often contain articles offering four steps to be a better lover, or sixteen ways to lead a better sex life. These points may be helpful, but they imply that the sexual experience can be perfected, as in baking a good chocolate cake. This message misses the point. The idea that sex is like a tennis serve—that one can "get it down" and learn to do it the same way every time—leads to a sexual life of boredom and disinterest.

In contrast, the most helpful attitude is one which sees each experience as a meeting together of two people in a particular moment in time. A sexual encounter brings the couple together—their past experiences, the happenings of that day, the feelings at the moment—as well as their worries, concerns, joys, excitement, desire, need for touch, and general attitude about sexuality. Each sexual episode becomes a unique event. The sexual experience remains distinctive and interesting throughout life when a couple is able to allow for variation that leads to nonviolating experimentation.

The concept of sexual mutuality between men and women is an attitude that is expressed in the Scriptures. Mutuality means the sexual experience must evolve reciprocally, or mutually, between two married people, allowing the sexual meshing and union to happen in the way God designed it. Mutuality is evident from the way our bodies function sexually, and from the emotions that are brought to the sexual experience. This experience is likely to be stifled by the attitude that men are sexual animals who make love to women, or that a certain pattern of response is expected. History has led many persons to hold this attitude, and to believe that men have the sexual drive and that women do not like sex and want to avoid it. This belief is very destructive.

Although men and women have mutual needs for sexuality, their needs are not identical on all issues. The most obvious difference is that men tend to be more physically or genitally oriented in their sexual experiences (more external), while women tend to be more emotional and relational (more internal). The penis and the vagina symbolize this beautifully. As a man becomes aroused, his feelings become more genitally focused, and as he has an orgasm, it is as if all the feelings become centered in one place. As a woman becomes aroused and moves toward orgasm, she becomes internally focused. The orgasm is experienced throughout her body. In addition, she usually has a greater need to feel cared for, listened to, and loved.

Both men and women have a strong, mutual need for the sexual experience, even though they express this need in different ways. A number of recent, popular surveys have discovered that women would prefer cuddling to sexual intercourse if given the choice. Our clinical sense is that when women receive all of the cuddling they need, the loving affection will naturally grow into a sexual desire—if their experience has not been aversive or their responsiveness has not been shut down.

The acceptance of individual differences without stereotyping sex roles is another attitude that is essential for an effective sexual helper. For example, while it is true that most men are more physically oriented and that most women are more emotionally and relationally oriented, we meet couples where the exact opposite is true. The man wants to talk, interact, relate, and share, and the woman just wants to be physical. These couples have the same conflicts, but in reverse of the typical situation. The counselor must enter each session with an open attitude, aspiring to discover what represents each individual's reality.

Stereotypes or clichés regarding all women or all men should be avoided. In recent years, there has been a tendency to simplify our understanding of men, women, and marriage which has caused problems for those who do not fit into the stereotypes. For instance, while it is true that most women do not like the clitoris stimulated directly, some women do. And while it is true that most men prefer very gentle genital stimulation, some men prefer it to be much more vigorous. As a result, all the therapist can do is discover what is true for each individual and help the couple live out this truth with each other.

The healthy sexual attitude of the therapist is characterized by openness to seeing all of the dimensions of the sexual experience. A counselor needs to recognize pleasure as a main ingredient of the sexual experience and to be open to the variety of experiences that a couple might enjoy, as long as both people are fulfilled and drawn to each other in the process. An attitude of acceptance rather than stereotyping communicates a safe atmosphere in which to divulge sexual secrets.

SEXUAL FEELINGS

The therapist's own feelings about sex are likely to become evident to the client in the sexual therapy process. If the topic of sex makes the therapist squirm, this discomfort or embarrassment will be communicated. A counselor's guilt or shame will most certainly come through, regardless of how he or she tries to keep it hidden. In order to be an effective helper, you need to work through feelings of embarrassment, discomfort, or guilt, and gain an inner acceptance of your sexuality.

In your personal life, one of the measures of sexual maturity is the capacity to receive sexual pleasure. If you always feel the need to be giving and cannot receive, you will tend to struggle with accepting your sexual self. It is also terribly important for you as the counselor to feel loved apart from sexual experience and fulfillment. A person who only feels love through sex is frequently a victim of sexual addictions (see chapter 15). If your sexual responses and interests are connected with anger (as is often the case for the abused person), those feelings most certainly will block the free and easy exchange that is so necessary to be helpful in sexual consultation. In summary, a healthy sense of sexual self-worth, unencumbered with excessive guilt, shame, embarrassment, anger, or stress are qualities necessary for an effective sexual therapist to possess.

SEXUAL EXPERIENCE

Sexual experiences from the past help form what you, the therapist, bring to the counseling setting. Whether you experimented sexually as an adolescent or a young adult with people of the same or the opposite sex, were discovered or not discovered, and were reacted to helpfully or destructively will determine your own attitude as you counsel. Any past traumatic sexual experience will have a forcible impact on you as a counselor. So, too, will your married sexual experience. Your counseling may be influenced negatively or positively by your struggles or lack of struggles. If your first sexual experience took place on the honeymoon and was followed by struggles over the next few years, that will affect you. If you had active premarital sexual experience with accompanying guilt feelings, those may be relived. If your sexual life has been wonderfully fulfilling since the first event, even that will make a difference in you as a counselor.

So much of what the therapist believes has been shaped by personal experience. For example, the woman who has never experienced pain during intercourse may be less likely to take this disorder seriously than the one who has had a time of dyspareunia. The man who has never experienced impotence will, in some ways, be less empathic to the difficulty than the one who has been concerned about gaining or maintaining an erection. A therapist who has never struggled with sexual addiction and has no sense of its grasp on an individual certainly can be helpful, but he or she may be less effective than someone who has struggled to overcome such an addiction. This is not to say you must have experienced every sexual problem in order to be a good therapist. Rather, your personal experiences in the areas you counsel add one more component that helps shape the way you give sexual guidance.

SEXUAL KNOWLEDGE

Basic sexual knowledge is obviously essential to functioning effectively as a sexual therapist. You need to have accurate knowledge of how the body works and responds, of the role sexuality plays in human relationships—especially in the marriage relationship—of sexual dysfunctions and how they develop, and of the biblical teaching of sexuality.

Knowledge becomes effective when it is integrated and applied to client situations. Thus, the most effective knowledge is gained by on-the-job training. Various aspects of knowledge are woven together into the therapy process. For example, early in our practice, a couple came to us for one session, complaining about the wife's lack of desire. They also attended our seminar. They experienced only slight improvement. We did not hear from them for about eight years. During those intervening years, we interviewed hundreds of couples, read hundreds of letters, and supervised many clinicians in their practices. Our technical knowledge had not grown extensively during those years, but experientially we had grown enormously.

During the first session when this couple returned, we identified the fact that the woman had been sexually abused. She acknowledged the abuse almost immediately and began a therapy process that, this second time, was life changing. What was the difference? It was that, over the years, we had seen so many patterns and had integrated so many tiny pieces of information that the abuse which we had once missed completely was now obvious just fifteen minutes into the therapy session. One might also suggest that the wife was now more ready to talk about the abuse; but the fact is that she did not mention the abuse until after we brought it up.

Our work over the years has shown us that as knowledge and experience combine in intelligent ways, effectiveness increases both in the assessment and the treatment process.

BELIEF SYSTEM

What a therapist believes, both theologically and sexually, will affect the counseling process. The theological beliefs that all people are God's creation, that sexuality is part of that creation, and that it is the natural response of being human will positively direct you as a sexual therapist. On the other hand, if there is lurking within you the old myth that sex is a consequence of sin, first evident when Adam and Eve ate of the fruit of the tree in the garden, this belief also will be communicated to those who have come to you for help.

The belief in God's gracious redemption through Jesus Christ extends forgiveness to those who have past, "sinful" lives. This belief is in contrast to the judgmental view of God that focuses on his wrath and loads on the guilt, even to those who have not made a Christian commitment. Clearly, the belief in God's ongoing mercy and forgiveness after people have committed their lives to him communicates a very different message than the belief that the true "unpardonable sin" is a sexual sin. If you believe that bodily pleasure borders on evil, this belief will be communicated to couples who are looking for sexual enjoyment.

Similarly, sexual beliefs influence the counseling process. The belief that sexual curiosity is natural and sexual responsiveness is innate will lead you to help people discover what is already inside themselves, rather than seek to find a skill from outside. The belief that the man is responsible for pleasing the woman and the woman is responsible for pleasing the man creates a very different therapy approach than the belief that each is responsible for himself or herself, and that each must communicate his or her needs so the partner does not have to guess.

If you believe that man is a more sexual being than a woman, then from our perspective, you have misunderstood a woman's total makeup. Women do not lack an innate sexuality, nor were they created with less sexuality than men. In actuality, they are more complicated and sexually intricate than men. They have a much greater capacity for an intense response, which makes them much more open to complications. In contrast, men seem to be more oriented toward the genital quality of sex than they are toward the sexuality of the total person.

Issues traditionally viewed as controversial, such as oral stimulation, will be confronted in therapy. The belief that married couples should not engage in many activities because they are inherently wrong will present a different attitude and response than the belief that God made our bodies to be enjoyed. The latter belief holds that all mutually enjoyable activity is open to a couple, as long as nobody is violated or physically hurt, and the activity draws a couple together and toward God.

The belief that an aroused person is not responsible for his or her own behavior, in contrast to the belief that each person is responsible regardless of his or her state of arousal, will clearly affect how you deal with many counseling situations, especially with male sexual aggression. What you, the therapist, believe will indirectly impact how you counsel, even if you are not being directly judgmental.

VALUE SYSTEM

It is generally accepted that there is no such thing as value-free counseling. Values are communicated by the questions we ask, the content of our reflections, the direction of our conversation, the topics we repeat, and the specific information we add to the conversation. Christians also have the dimension of being followers of a moral code that is taught in the Scriptures; this adds a distinct value perspective to the counseling.

Therapy is easy when one is dealing with people who share the same value system. However, when working with clients who do not share our values or have not communicated their values, it is our practice to explain our own value system so the counselees clearly understand our perspectives. In turn, we hope we can be open and receptive to help the counselees from their perspectives. If those perspectives violate us, however, the clients need to be informed and referred.

Even within the Christian community, there are many different interpretations. For example, some Christians claim that all homosexual action is sin, and some do not. Some Christians believe all premarital sexual activity is wrong, while others disagree. There are also those who say all masturbation is wrong, and many do not agree with that. Still others would argue that an activity such as oral sex clearly falls outside the realm of acceptable behavior for the Christian, while others would not. This list could go on and on. The point is that what you, the therapist, believe and the value system that you hold will be a part of how you counsel.

For example, if you believe that all homosexual activity is a sin—a forsaking of the natural passions as described in Romans 1—your counseling will guide the person in controlling homosexual behaviors, even if you strive to remain nonjudgmental. We should not try to be value free in our counseling. Instead, we should be very aware of the values we hold, and be willing to own them, while keeping clear boundaries between the values of the couples we counsel and our own.

Marital Status

It is helpful for the married counselor to have or at least to be working on a fulfilling sexual life. The sexual therapist who is dealing with major sexual stresses faces the difficulty of keeping the boundaries clear between the personal and professional. Obviously, we must be aware of our own sexual stresses and make sure we don't work them out with the counselees. Such counter-transference will inevitably interfere. This is not to say that a therapist must have a perfect sexual life in order to be helpful, but it should be one that is at least somewhat fulfilling and in the process of becoming healthier.

It is vitally important that single therapists be in touch with their sexual feelings, even as they make conscious, distinct decisions regarding their sexual behavior. This often becomes the main source of difficulty for the single adult, especially one who is striving to live the Christian life.

A system of professional and moral accountability serves the counselor's and counselee's best interests. Accountability is built-in when two therapists work together as a team. For a staff of therapists, counselors, or pastors, accountability may be an automatic consequence of weekly staff meetings or informal consultations. A trainee is obviously accountable to his or her supervisor.

The biggest dilemma occurs when an individual functions alone in a private practice or on a staff of one in a church or community service. In this situation, a system of accountability should be built into one's weekly or monthly schedule. Because the sexual realm is so powerful, we serve ourselves best by being in a position to share with colleagues and other professionals. This is true not because most therapists intend to get involved with their clients, but because temptations are inevitable to us as human sexual beings. Accepting human vulnerability is the first step to prevention of inappropriate behavior. As therapists, we must protect ourselves and our clients from sexual mishappenings. At no time or for no reason can we excuse ourselves for acting out our sexual impulses with clients. In *all* situations, the client is the victim and we are responsible. Sexual therapists must have a defined plan of both professional and spiritual accountability in order to prevent legal and personal devastation.

Professional Skills

Basic therapeutic skills are essential in order to function as a sexual therapist, whether you are a psychiatrist, medical doctor, licensed clinical social worker, marriage and family counselor, pastor, nurse, or psychologist. Regardless of one's professional credentials and background, the sexual therapist should be well practiced in effective therapeutic interaction.

From our perspective, what psychologist Carl Rogers presented in *On Becoming a Person* as the therapeutic triad is absolutely essential. First, the therapist needs to have practiced the skills of *accurate empathy*, i.e., the capacity to "get with" a person in terms of the content, the emotion, the meaning, and the direction of what is being said. Second, *unconditional positive regard*, the communication of nonjudgmental warmth and acceptance, is necessary for the therapist. The third component of the therapeutic triad is *self-congruence* or *genuineness*, the capacity to always be genuine in what is expressed. This does not mean that everything a person thinks is expressed, but rather that everything that is expressed is a genuine representation of oneself.

We see these basic skills as being crucial in all effective counseling or therapy. Because of this necessity, we have come to believe that a person should not begin counseling by being a sexual therapist, but rather by first practicing as a general therapist or counselor, and then as a sexual therapist.

There are several books we recommend as minimal reading requirements for every sexual counselor:

Human Sexual Response, W. H. Masters and V. E. Johnson (Boston: Little, Brown, 1966)

Human Sexual Inadequacy, W. H. Masters and V. E. Johnson (Boston: Little, Brown, 1970)

The New Sex Therapy, H. S. Kaplan (New York: Brunner/Mazel, 1974)

Disorders of Sexual Desire, H. S. Kaplan (New York: Brunner/Mazel, 1979)

The Evaluation of Sexual Disorders, H. S. Kaplan (New York: Brunner/Mazel, 1983)

Sex for Christians, Lewis B. Smedes (Grand Rapids, Mich.: Eerdmans, 1976)

The Gift of Sex, A Christian Guide to Sexual Fulfillment, Clifford and Joyce Penner (Waco, Tex.: Word Books, 1981)

A Gift For All Ages, Clifford and Joyce Penner (Waco, Tex.: Word Books, 1986)

These eight books should be minimal preparatory reading for the Christian sexual therapist. These are foundational.

Graduate-level classes at universities or seminaries can serve as the foundation of gaining the skills needed. Seminars and training also are offered by W. H. Masters and V. E. Johnson in St. Louis, Missouri, Helen Singer Kaplan of Columbia University, Alan and Donna Brauer of Palo Alto, California, and Lonnie Barbach of Berkeley, California. Various other groups of therapists can also be helpful. It is best to do the reading and have some contact with clients who are dealing with sexual problems before you attend these seminars, unless they are given over an extended period of time and provide opportunity for supervised work.

The final preparation is supervised practice. This means experience that is supervised by a competent, recognized, and experienced sex therapist. Supervision should cover actual cases and should occur on a regular basis throughout the therapy. Tape recordings, or at least detailed notes, are the best way to facilitate active, direct supervision.

In summary, the sexual counselor should begin with basic therapeutic skills. Preparation should include minimal reading, classroom and seminar training, and supervision on an ongoing basis. Professional certification is available from the American Association of Sex Education Counselors and Therapists (AASECT). At this time, most states do not require sexual therapists to be licensed.

This chapter began by asking the therapist, "Are you comfortable with your sexuality?" Many facets that flow together to make an effective therapist have been reviewed in an effort to guide the therapist in answering that question. Now, having covered the material, we ask again, "Are you comfortable with your sexuality?" If you find areas of weakness or some major gaps, perhaps you need individual therapy or sexual therapy yourself. Perhaps you need to struggle with your belief and value systems to be clear about your family and church past in relation to what the Bible teaches. Or you may need to focus more on training. Whatever your situation, our challenge to you is to strive to be the most effective helper that you can be for those who are sexually troubled.

CHAPTER THREE

THE CHRISTIAN COMPONENT
— IT SETS YOU APART

WHAT IS THE DIFFERENCE between a responsible sexual therapist and a responsible *Christian* sexual therapist? Technically, there is none. The same skills are used, for instance, for treating premature ejaculation or vaginismus by both Christian and non-Christian therapists. Despite the similarities, though, the Christian counselor is distinct from the non-Christian counselor in two ways.

The first distinction is a practical one. Many clients come to the Christian counselor with their personal sexual lives intricately intertwined with their backgrounds of religious training. The Christian therapist should be especially skilled to help these clients sort through these interweavings of sexuality and religious training. The word *religious* is intentionally used here, because most of the time, when sexual freedom within marriage is inhibited for what seem to be "Christian" or "biblical" reasons, the barrier is actually caused by rigidity and religiosity rather than by specific biblical teaching. The Christian counselor is more likely to be trusted to understand both the individual's and the biblical perspectives in helping to sort out the wrong ideas, than is the nonbelieving sexual therapist.

The second and greater distinction between Christian and non-Christian therapists relates to their presuppositions about sexuality. The Scriptures present a high view of the human sexual dimension. In that sense, sex is similar to a family jewel or heirloom. However, in society today, sexuality is often treated more like a piece of junk jewelry, something given to a child at age fourteen to be worn to school and later thrown into the bottom of the bike bag.

The Bible speaks about sexuality in a highly prized way. It designates sex for marriage because it is in this context of commitment that the qualities of a highly held view of sexuality can be fulfilled. The Bible portrays sex as a symbol of the relationship between God and his people. It puts sex in the context of the deepest commitment that one human can make to another: a lifelong commitment to honor and cherish, and to be faithful, " 'til death do us part." When Christian counselors have integrated this high view of sex and sexuality as a precious gift from the Creator, it clearly sets them apart.

In the book of Genesis, the Bible tells how Adam and Eve were "naked and unashamed," experiencing a free, open relationship that had no barriers. Their relationship was not based on power, intimidation, social myths, or cultural control. Later, Scripture refers to Christ as the "last" or new Adam, and teaches that believers are in Christ's image (1 Cor. 15:45–50). This makes sex without shame a viable potential for the Christian. Unfortunately, the church has let social culture dictate many negative distortions about sexuality. When we as Christian couples can rid ourselves of these limitations and live lives of freedom and openness with each other, then we, of all people, ought to be the most sexually free and fulfilled.

The biblical understanding of sexuality is addressed in our previous books, *The Gift of Sex*, and *A Gift for All Ages* (see Bibliography). This biblically based view should be central to the Christian counselor's attitude in dealing with the sexual dilemma. Therefore, it is important to review the following principles which are clearly presented throughout the Scriptures. These principles form the foundation for our understanding of sexuality.

OUR SEXUALITY AS A PART OF THE CREATION ORDER

Men and women are not only sexual beings by birth, but also by creation, according to God's plan and design. The Bible is not an instruction book for sexual functioning, but it does give a clear picture of how highly God values humans as sexual beings and the sexual relationship in marriage. Because of this, we can affirm the physical body, including its sexuality, as being conceived in the mind of God. We are his creations, male and female, sinless before the Fall. Our maleness and femaleness are part of his perfect plan.

Another reason to affirm our sexuality is that it reflects God. Maleness and femaleness is in the image of God, as stated in Genesis 1:26 and 27:

> Then God said, "Let us make man in our image, in our likeness, and let them rule over the fish of the sea and the birds of the air, over the livestock, over all the earth, and over all the creatures that move along the ground."
>
> So God created man in his own image, in the image of God he created him; male and female he created them.

God created us with a particular model or design which is described as the "image of God." (See also Genesis 5:1–2 and Genesis 9:6.)

What does being created male and female in the image of God mean? The animals were created male and female. They have sexuality and physical bodies which they use to procreate. Yet they were not created in the image of God. How is mankind's sexuality different? As beings in the image of God, we have the desire and capacity to be in relationship with each other and with God; animals do not. Human beings can think, communicate with God and man, act self-consciously, and respond and interact at a relationship level.

When Kristine, our youngest child, was six years old, she seemed to have an answer for anything in the world. One time when our dog, Biff, ran off during a thunderstorm and had not returned by the next day, Joyce was beginning to explain that perhaps Biff had been lost and we would never see him again. Confidently Kristine said, "Well, I'm sure he's okay. He's probably just off mating. If I were mating, I wouldn't want Julene and Greg (her older brother and sister) to be around watching." Obviously at this age, she had not differentiated between the human dimension that is private, conscious of self, and made in the image of God, and the lack of this dimension in animals. We doubted that Biff was "off mating" since he had been neutered. Fortunately, though, he did return the next day.

The Genesis account of creation gives a basis for affirming sexuality and begins the biblical teaching that sexual intercourse in marriage is blessed by God and is for enjoyment. Many people grow up believing that sexual union is the result of man's fall into sin. Masters and Johnson, founders of the sexual counseling field, even refer to this misconception of the Adam and Eve story as though it were fact.

On the contrary, the first biblical reference to the sexual union is a teaching from God that occurs before Adam and Eve disobeyed God and fell into sin and shame. Genesis 2:24 reads, "For this reason a man will leave his father and mother and be united to his wife, and they will become one flesh." Becoming "one flesh" refers to sexual intercourse, which was part of God's perfect plan and design for us—not the result of our disobedient, sinful, human nature. Sexual union was without sin and shame in this blissful state. The relationship between man and woman was completely open: "The man and his wife were both naked, and they felt no shame" (Gen. 2:25). In the same way, Adam and Eve had a completely open relationship with God; they walked and talked with him. Sin interrupted this openness.

Sex is sin only when it is misused, when we break God's commands. God gave us rules to live by—not to punish or restrict—but rather for our good. God is a loving father who wants the best for us; he knows our humanness, and he knows the power of evil. His commandments and directions for Christian living take all of this knowledge into account. When we violate those commandments, we sin. Most often, sexual violations of biblical guidelines occur when we only look at the feelings of the moment. Fortunately, even when we have sinned, we can be forgiven.

So the underlying message is: *Sex and sexuality are of God.* Sex becomes sin *only* when we disobey God's guidelines for its practice.

Not only is our sexuality part of God's perfect plan and design, it also is confirmed in Scripture by the use of the sexual relationship between husband and wife to symbolize how God would choose to relate to us (Gen. 3:7–22). Disobedience interrupted the openness between God and man, and between man and woman. Genesis 3:7 says, "Then the eyes of both of them were opened, and they realized they were naked. . . ." They became ashamed and self-conscious with each other, whereas before they had been innocent and unashamed. They no longer had the perfect relationship that was in the image of God. It was lost as the result of sin.

Adam and Eve also became self-conscious in front of God, covering their genitals in shame. God accommodated them by providing permanent coverings for their genitals, thereby giving the impression that openness with genitals is symbolic of openness with God. Sin—disobeying God—brought about shame, sexual inhibition, and a break in both the sexual openness of marriage and the relationship with God.

The Hebrew word "to know" (Gen. 4:1, KJV) refers to sexual intercourse, and is the same word that is used in reference to knowing God. It is also a word for the genitals. Thus, the sexual union symbolizes the relationship between God and his people.

The concept of the sexual union being an example of the way God wants to relate to his people is further developed throughout the Old Testament. Israel is sometimes referred to as God's bride (Isa. 49:18 and Jer. 16:9), and the word "adultery" is used to describe Israel's sin of worshipping other gods (Jer. 7:9 and 23:10; Ezek. 23:37; and Isa. 57:3).

A romantic, sensual description of God's love for unfaithful Jerusalem is found in Ezekiel 16:8–19. The passage refers to bathing her, putting ointments on her, and clothing her; and yet she becomes an adulteress who takes strangers instead of her husband. In spite of this, God's grace is generous to his bride, Israel: "Yet I will remember the covenant I made with you. . . . and you will know that I am Lord" (Ezek. 16:60–62).

The entire book of Hosea is an account of God's steadfast love and mercy in his relationship with Israel. The sexual relationship symbolizes God's longing for a relationship with his people in Isaiah 62:5:

> As a young man marries a maiden,
>   so will your sons marry you;
> as a bridegroom rejoices over his bride,
>   so will your God rejoice over you.

This sexual symbolism continues in the New Testament, where the church (the body of believers) is described as Christ's bride. This teaching is found most explicitly in Ephesians 5:21–25: "Submit to one another out of reverence for Christ. Wives, submit to your husbands. . . . Husbands, love your wives, just as Christ loved the church and gave himself up for her. . . ." The passage interweaves the sexual relationship of husband and wife with the relationship of Christ and the church. In Ephesians 5:31, Paul summarizes this connection by quoting Genesis 2:24, the first reference to a sexual union in the Scriptures:

> For this reason a man will leave his father and mother and be united with his wife, and the two will become one flesh. This is a profound mystery—but I am talking about Christ and the church.

In the New Testament, the word "mystery" always refers to something that is partially revealed, or is in the process of being revealed and will become clear as we move into the Final Age.

The sexual relationship between a husband and wife is also used in the Book of the Revelation as the symbol of the relationship between Christ and the church, when the church is described as Christ's bride, coming for the wedding supper (Rev. 19:7–9). Again, the full meaning of this symbolism is a mystery.

While most people do not think about or experience the symbolism of Christ and the church during lovemaking, it is our belief that in this mystical union of two bodies, body and spirit have the potential to merge into one. In this intense fusion of body, emotion, and spirit with another, we experience a glimpse of the relationship that God would like to have with us—the total giving of ourselves to him. This elevates the sexual relationship to the level of a sacrament, leaving no room for recreational sex in the life of a Christian.

Principles from the Old Testament

The Old Testament portrays human beings in a way that is central to our view of sexuality. The Hebrews always viewed the human person as an integrated whole, not as a person divided into various parts. On the other hand, the Greeks saw the physical body as something to put down and the human spirit as important to be elevated. Their dyadic, gnostic view did not have high regard for the total person.

The Old Testament's description of the human sexual experience, "they will become one flesh" (Gen. 2:24), means more than physical union. This refers to the mystical union that encompasses the emotional, physical, and spiritual dimensions. Husband and wife join *all* of who they are with each other. This is truly the biblical view of sexual union!

Lovemaking cannot be simply a physical experience for the Christian couple. In order to have a fulfilling relationship, the total person— intellect, body, spirit, and will—must be shared with one's partner. When we truly understand Scripture, we recognize that the physical and sexual realms are integrated parts of the person. The sexual part of ourselves cannot be isolated. In generations past, there was little understanding that the integrated, whole person included the sexual dimension.

As Grandmother informed us during one visit in her convalescent home, Adam and Eve did not need sexual teaching, and she and her husband had done fine without it; so we should stop teaching about sex. "I disagree with what you do, but love you anyway," she told us. Well, we love Grandma, too. But as therapists, we realize how important it is to continue teaching the "whole-person dimension" of sex in order to help bring greater personal fulfillment and integration, especially to the Christian world.

A contrasting lesson from the Old Testament is that sexuality is more than a beautiful sacrament that symbolizes our relationship with God. Sexuality also involves earthy passion and earthly goals. This is illustrated by the lives of Old Testament men and women who are named in the "Hall of Faith" in Hebrews 11. Abraham, the father of our inheritance, visited his wife's handmaiden, Hagar, who then became pregnant (Gen. 16:4). Isaac lied about his relationship to Rebekah in order to save his own life, and then was found fondling her in public (Gen. 26:7–8). Jacob (Israel) produced four of the twelve sons of Israel by sleeping with his wives' maids (Gen. 30:7–12). David, who by faith conquered kingdoms, was attracted to the beautiful body of Bathsheba, the wife of Uriah, and became sexually involved with her. He then committed murder to cover up his sin. Even Rahab the harlot, who helped the Israelites conquer Jericho, was honored for her faith—"By faith the prostitute Rahab, because she welcomed the spies, was not killed with those who were disobedient" (Heb. 11:31). In fact, Rahab is listed in the genealogy of Jesus Christ in Matthew 1:5.

So the lesson for today is this: Human beings are accepted by God as beings with a sexual nature. He recognizes that the human sexual dimension is a very powerful element—a forceful drive. Sometimes it drives us to sin, as in the cases of some of the biblical men and women of faith. God does not condone disobedience to his standards in the expression of our sexuality; but neither does he condemn us for being intensely sexual persons. When we disobey his rules, we violate him as well as ourselves and those close to us. And we suffer the consequence of our sin. Nevertheless, his grace is available, even for sexual transgressions. We can be forgiven and continue to be used by God, even as were the men and women of faith, like David and Rahab.

How do the Old Testament rules inform us today? As we study the Old Testament to help form the basis for our decision-making in regard to right and wrong sexual behavior, we must be careful to study the laws within their context and purpose. Among other things, the Old Testament law was structured in terms of property rights, sanitation, and behavior "in the camp."

First, consider the issue of property rights. The woman, especially in the early Old Testament period, was part of the net worth of her father. While choice and love certainly were factors, when a man took a wife, this marriage was an exchange of property. The tenth commandment given to Moses said, "You shall not covet your neighbor's house. You shall not covet your neighbor's wife, or his manservant or maidservant, his ox or donkey, or anything that belongs to your neighbor" (Exod. 20:17). The commandment not to "covet" was for all of a man's possessions, including his wife.

The Old Testament rules against fornication had to do with the ruining of someone's property. During some periods of Hebrew history, the blood-stained sheet was necessary proof on the wedding night for the husband to be certain he had received a fair deal and his wife had not been "previously used." The rules were different for men—there was a dual system. No rules in the Old Testament stated that the man must be a virgin at marriage, but once married, he was not to commit adultery.

Many Old Testament rules about sanitation rights and rituals pertain to bodily excretions and what became known as acceptable behavior in the camp. This camp area was around the tabernacle the children of Israel used for worship. Most of the rules focused on protecting the tabernacle from unclean things such as certain kinds of animals, parts of animals, people with sicknesses, and all forms of bodily excretions (caused by diseases or natural bodily functions, such as menstruation, nocturnal emissions, defecation, afterbirth, and other things described in detail in the Pentateuch). These rules for living must be understood in the context of that biblical teaching that defined social and religious ritual.

PRINCIPLES FROM THE NEW TESTAMENT

The New Testament teaches that the barriers between men and women have been broken down because of Christ's death and resurrection. This teaching is a radical departure from the Old Testament culture; now, men and women no longer are to live by different sexual standards. Rather, the New Testament clearly teaches mutuality. This is not to suggest that men and women are sexually identical, nor that they play the same roles. But that because of Christ, men and women stand equally before God. This is symbolized in the sexual relationship. Gone are the days of male domination or control in the sexual realm. Christ has broken down these barriers.

Through Christ, we have the potential to reestablish the original design of creation—to be totally open and free with each other. This includes having an equal value, ability, and position before God: "There is neither Jew nor Greek, slave nor free, male nor female, for you are all one in Christ Jesus" (Gal. 3:28).

Ephesians 2:13–22, an extremely important passage regarding this teaching, tells how Christ broke down the human barriers and made us one household of God.

It might be said that as we become new creatures in Christ, we open up the possibility for a new kind of relationship within marriage. This is the beginning of a restoration of the experience of oneness that was lost in the Garden of Eden. In the same way that Christ has restored the possibility of a relationship with God, he opens the door to new and deeper relationships with each another.

The New Testament teaches that men and women have equal rights to sexual pleasure and release. Physically, emotionally, and spiritually, a woman needs sexual pleasure and release as much as a man does. Pelvic pressure builds up in a woman, just as scrotal pressure builds in a man. Emotionally, the bond of connection and affirmation is probably more important for women than for men. Spiritually, the biblical message clearly communicates the same sexual needs and expectation for women as it does for men.

Both men and women have the right to expect sexual pleasure and fulfillment. Husband and wife are told in Scripture to give themselves to each other. This is a mutual command, not one only for wives. It is not a command we can use to demand sex of each other; the command is not given in terms of the person's desire for sex. Rather, it is a response to each other's needs:

The husband should fulfill his marital duty to his wife, and likewise the wife to her husband. The wife's body does not belong to her alone but also to her husband. In the same way, the husband's body does not belong to him alone but also to his wife. Do not deprive each other except by mutual consent and for a time, so that you may devote yourselves to prayer. Then come together again so that Satan will not tempt you because of your lack of self-control.

(1 Cor. 7:3–5)

Each New Testament passage that addresses the husband-wife sexual relationship either begins or ends with a command for mutuality, including Ephesians 5. Not only are husbands and wives equal in God's sight, but they also have mutual rights and responsibilities.

The concept of love between husband and wife is an expected part of the marriage relationship according to New Testament teaching. Love becomes the guiding principle for sexual behavior in marriage. The husband-wife relationship is to depict the kind of love Christ lavishes on the church.

Husbands, love your wives, just as Christ loved the church and gave himself up for her. . . . husbands ought to love their own wives as their own bodies. He who loves his wife loves himself.

(Eph. 5:25, 28)

While there are many restrictions regarding extramarital sexual involvement, within marriage, love is the only rule; there are no "do's and don'ts," no obvious limitations or instructions on "how" to enjoy sex within marriage. The Song of Solomon is the only biblical example.

The writer to the Hebrews said, "Marriage should be honored by all, and the marriage bed kept pure. . . ." (Heb. 13:4). Translated into today's language, this passage might read, "In this troubled world, it is terribly important that we have a very high view of marriage. And by the way, sex within marriage is not dirty." What goes on in the sexual relationship as an outgrowth of the marital covenant is indeed honorable, wholesome, and healthy. From Genesis 2:24 throughout all of Scripture, the sexual union is referred to as "becoming one flesh." Dr. Louis H. Evans, Jr. has a wonderful comment on this succinctly expressed teaching on sexuality from the New Testament:

The one flesh in marriage is not just a physical phenomenon, but a uniting of the totality of two personalities. In marriage, we are one flesh spiritually by vow, economically by sharing, logistically by adjusting time and agreeing on the disbursement of all life's resources, experientially by trudging through the dark valleys and standing victoriously on the peaks of success, and sexually by the bonding of our bodies. In [intercourse], which is the expression created uniquely for marriage, the male and female fibers intertwine in complementation, creating a living fabric that cannot be undone without serious damage to the living fibers. When that happens, they are left scarred and therefore lacking in suppleness, circulation, sensitivity or strength. Scar tissue is not good tissue. Let [intercourse] be undefiled and untainted, undefiled and beautiful as God designed it.[1]

Because there are many different uses and meanings of the word "flesh" in the New Testament, it is vitally important that sexual helpers be careful and diligent in understanding Scripture. The previous paragraph described one positive use of the word "flesh." Now consider an example where the word "flesh" is almost synonymous with sin or evil:

> But I say, live by the Spirit, and you will not carry out the desire of the flesh. For the flesh sets its desire against the Spirit, and the Spirit against the flesh; for these are in opposition to one another, so that you may not do the things that you please. But if you are led by the Spirit, you are not under the Law. Now the deeds of the flesh are evident. . . .
>
> (Gal. 5:16–19, NASB)

The writer of Galations then records that well-known list that begins with immorality (Gal. 5:19–21). Verses 22 and 23 follow with the fruits of the Spirit. Verse 24 (NASB) then says, "Now those who belong to Christ Jesus have crucified the flesh with its passions and desires." This use of the word "flesh" is understood to depict man's sinful nature, which is organized against God to pursue its earthly wishes rather than those that are spiritually worthwhile.

Desiring a healthy, enthusiastic, and fulfilling sexual life within marriage clearly does not mean following the lusts of the flesh. Rather, this comes under the category of sharing our undefiled desires with the one to whom we have made a covenant for life. The mission of the Christian sexual helper is to help others distinguish the difference between lust-driven expressions of sexuality and the God-given gift of sexuality. This can be achieved if sexuality is allowed to grow within the context of a loving marriage, one in which the desire is to find fulfillment and joy that builds each other up and glorifies God.

Sexual Pleasure—A Biblical Expectation

Finally, sexual pleasure within marriage is biblically encouraged and expected. Husband and wife are always to be available to fulfill each other's sexual needs—not only at the time of the month when impregnation can occur. In this respect God created human beings to be different from the animal kingdom—animals only have sexual drives at the time of conception. To "be fruitful and multiply" is but one purpose of the sexual relationship between a husband and wife. The Bible also endorses the concept of sexual pleasure.

Earlier, we suggested having couples read the Song of Solomon to each other out loud. This book is a beautiful and erotic poem of a husband and wife totally enjoying each other's bodies. The following excerpts are from the *New American Standard Bible:*

> On my bed night after night I sought him
> Whom my soul loves. (3:1)
>
> My beloved is dazzling and ruddy . . .
> His head is like gold. . . .
> His eyes are like doves. . . .
> His lips are lilies,
> Dripping with liquid myrrh. . . .
> His legs are pillars of alabaster
> Set on pedestals of pure gold. . . .
> And he is wholly desirable. . . .(5:10–16)
>
> How beautiful are your feet in sandals. . . .
> The curves of your hips are like jewels. . . .
> Your belly is like a heap of wheat
> Fenced about with lilies.
> Your two breasts are like two fawns. . . .

> Your stature is like a palm tree. . . .
> I said, "I will climb the palm tree,
> I will take hold of its fruit stalks."
> Oh, may your breasts be like clusters of the vine. . . .
>
> Come, my beloved, let us go out into the country. . . . (7:1–11)

This husband and wife certainly viewed each other's bodies as a source of great pleasure to enjoy. Nothing seems to be restricted! Another romantic passage is found in Proverbs 5:18–19 (NASB):

> Let your fountain be blessed,
> And rejoice in the wife of your youth.
> As a loving hind and a graceful doe,
> Let her breasts satisfy you at all times;
> Be exhilarated always with her love.

Our bodies are each other's to enjoy in marriage. If we hold back for "religious" reasons, we fool ourselves, because there is no biblical basis to do so. We are not consistent with an understanding of what the Bible has to say if we take an antisexual or antipleasure view of sex in marriage.

Based on the Scriptures' high view of sex within marriage, the Christian therapist has a very positive message to bring to the Christian world, a world that is often in deep conflict about the acceptability of enthusiastic sexuality. To effectively transmit this freeing aspect of the gospel, though, our own attitudes must be clear. The world views Christian sexuality as constrictive. But the Scriptures teach a new freedom that can bring greater joy, greater release, and greater fulfillment as we help couples learn to enjoy each other ecstatically.

CHAPTER FOUR

THE MARRIAGE: SEX PROVIDES THE LUBRICATION, NOT THE FUEL

HOW IMPORTANT IS SEX in a marriage? A simple answer is that, when marriage is compared with an automobile, sex is to the marriage what oil is to the combustion engine. At least a little oil is necessary to keep the engine running—without sex, one's marriage engine will eventually break down.

When the sexual dimension is flowing naturally and each spouse is fulfilled, sex is vital but encompasses only a small percentage of the relationship. The more sexual problems there are, the larger sex looms. By the time most couples seek help for their sexual dilemmas, those problems seem to engulf at least 80 percent of the relationship and may be the only issue one or both spouses can think or talk about. The sexual problems have grown so large they have become the primary focus.

Even though the sexual dimension needs to be taken very seriously, it must be kept in proper perspective. Sex is not everything! The oil level of the car might be just fine, but without fuel and a full complement of working parts, the car just sits there. So what is the fuel in a marriage?

Intimacy! Everything that makes a marriage run smoothly falls under the category of intimacy: communication, interests, activities, finances, spiritual connection, parenting, household management, social life, and of course, sex. Intimacy, in the context of a lifelong commitment, sets the marriage apart from all other relationships. A marriage without intimacy is like a car that is resting up on blocks in the back yard. It is a car, but it no longer serves the function for which it was designed. A marriage without intimacy is technically still a marriage, but it does not fulfill its original purpose.

When a couple is struggling sexually, the sexual problem is either primary or secondary, depending on whether it is the main dilemma or one more symptom of a troubled relationship. If the sexual difficulty is secondary to a troubled relationship, even when marital problems are corrected, the sexual problems still need to be worked on.

For example, Ana and Haig sought our help several years ago for what they defined as "Haig's sexual problem"—impotence. After the initial interview, it was clear that even though Haig had "sown his wild oats" in the early years of their marriage, he was now a faithful husband. It was also clear that as Ana's star had risen in the corporate world, she had allowed all of her natural dominating and controlling behavior to come into her marriage. As she had become more aggressive, he had become more passive.

Before any work on the sexual problem could begin, they had to focus on changing their pattern of interaction. And even after their marriage improved, Haig continued to avoid sex for fear of impotency. At this point, sexual therapy was initiated. Thus, it clearly had been necessary to deal with the relationship problem first; but the sexual problem persisted after the conflict was resolved. The marriage needed both the fuel of a working, intimate relationship and the oil of a satisfying sexual relationship.

Although sexual therapy may be necessary to lubricate a marriage, at least minimal levels of communication, emotional openness, trust, respect, and the couple's open enjoyment of each other are necessary to fuel the marriage.

COMMUNICATION

If open communication is barely possible, sexual therapy will be extremely difficult. Couples who are unable or unwilling to share their activities, thoughts, or feelings will find it virtually impossible to break through the sexual barriers without the help of effective communication. Some may never have learned how to share openly. Their homes may have been functional rather than communicative homes. They may have chosen a partner who also does not communicate, or they may have continually sabotaged their intimacy by lack of ability or desire to communicate. Or they may have thwarted communication by their passive-aggressive style.

When inability to communicate is apparent, a strong attempt should be made to break through the communication barriers with "systems-oriented" marital therapy and communication exercises before attempting—or as a part of—the sexual therapy process.

EMOTIONAL OPENNESS

Vulnerability and self-disclosure are absolutely essential for sexual functioning. There is little possibility of sexual openness without the capacity to be able to share one's dreams and hopes, fears, insecurities, inadequacies, strengths, and weaknesses. Emotional nakedness is a prerequisite for physical nakedness, a fact that is distorted in current culture. Very often, couples begin a relationship with sexual intimacy—that is, with sexual nakedness—without being emotionally and personally vulnerable. The sexual revolution focused on being naked with each other; but physical nakedness brings very shallow fulfillment. True sexuality blossoms only when it is preceded by the communication, openness, and trust that grows out of a genuinely intimate relationship.

On the other hand, a marriage can suffer from destructive openness. We are referring to the unbridled anger and venom that sometimes develops either because of what each individual brought into the marriage or because of what has happened between the two in the marriage. The shallow anger that is in response to the irritations of daily living is relatively quickly resolved. In contrast, the anger that springs from deep pain or long-term frustration within the relationship requires more intense work. Some never get beyond that anger.

Don and Virginia had been in marital counseling for a year and a half when they came to us for sexual therapy. Don believed that resolving their sexual problems would help them avoid the stress in their marriage. After attempting to explore that hypothesis, we quickly discovered that the amount of distrust and anger between them made it impossible to resolve their sexual issues. The anger—even rage—and rejection between them was completely debilitating. Twenty-five years of deeply scarred hurts virtually blocked all possibility of working on the sexual issues until there was some resolution of their bitterness.

Sexual intimacy is impossible when a relationship has evolved to the point where much of the communication is penetratingly harsh and cutting. The starting focus must be on resolution of those emotional issues in order to bring the couple to the point of positive emotional openness and trust.

TRUST

Trust between the husband and wife is a natural prerequisite to sexual intimacy and is a consequence of effective communication and emotional openness. This is not merely the basic trust that one's husband or wife is sexually faithful—that is an obvious and necessary level of trust. The trust that is essential to effective sexual interaction involves believing that each spouse has the other's best interests at heart.

Trust at this level deals with safety. Feeling safe with another person makes it easier to be open with that person. Being naked with someone, whether physically or emotionally, demands that sense of confidence which says the other person will not take advantage of us if we are exposed. This kind of trust requires a safe history that allows the person to say, "I can be fully myself with this person without being hurt in response. In fact, the more fully I am myself, the closer we become and the more fulfilled I feel." We grow toward this level of trust as we allow sexual intimacy to evolve.

RESPECT

When the woman says, "But I just don't respect him," it is extremely difficult for the counselor to initiate positive momentum in the sexual relationship. It is also necessary for the man to respect his wife, but it seems even more important for the woman to respect her husband. Respect is that sense of "looking up to" or holding the other person in high esteem and considering that person worthy. It might be lacking for either spouse because of work or eating habits, drinking habits, parenting responses, one's background, or a great variety of other reasons.

Sometimes lack of respect is reported merely as a distraction for dealing with some deep anger. Most often, the complaint of not feeling respect is very real. When couples seek sexual therapy, it's a regular occurrence for one of the spouses to mention lack of respect as a barrier. Often we will begin the process of sexual therapy by dealing with this issue. We may use the assigned sexual experiences to understand the loss of respect and to build respect for each other.

OPEN ENJOYMENT OF EACH OTHER

Open enjoyment of each other is an essential ingredient to a fulfilling sexual life. We believe it must be minimally present in order to begin the sexual therapy process. If two people can not stand each other—if one is so turned off by the other that the dislike borders on repulsion or revulsion—the sexual therapy is not likely to progress. Just as the child who feels like a source of delight to the parent will blossom, so the sexual relationship in marriage can come to fulfillment when the enjoyment of each other is present. That sense of joyfulness in finding each other precious and of delighting in each other becomes a major resource for helping the couple through the difficult times in the sexual therapy process. When this sense of delight is not present and the couple is only staying together out of obligation, or because "God wants them to," working on the sexual aspects of the relationship is most difficult.

Although these qualities of effective communication, emotional openness, trust, respect, and open enjoyment are discussed as prerequisites to beginning the sexual therapy process, there are times when they are not present or are only minimally present, but we begin sexual therapy anyway. In such cases, it is made clear to the client couple that sexual therapy is the vehicle for working on these other aspects. Frequently these marital issues will distract from sexual therapy, but such interruptions should be considered as a method of using the sexual realm to discover and address these relationship qualities, not as resistance or defeat.

Sex must be understood in the context of the marriage. The sexual therapist carefully evaluates whether a couple's sexual dilemmas grow out of some other marital issue, and then whether those marital issues need to be dealt with first. When both a marital and a sexual problem are present, the therapist needs to determine the order of focus which the client couple labels as the problem. Ultimately, clinical judgment that grows out of experience will be your best guide. In our practice over the years, we have made a number of mistakes when we started working on the sexual therapy issues because the couple insisted on it, even though the relationship was not strong or stable enough for that to be effective. As time has given us more experience, our clinical judgment has improved, and such mistakes are less likely.

CHAPTER FIVE

THE BODY: SEXUAL ANATOMY AND THE PHYSICAL RESPONSE

EDUCATION ABOUT OUR BODIES does not need to be a boring anatomy and physiology lecture. When we teach seminars for married couples, we spend almost two of the ten hours talking about our bodies and how they work. After the seminar, many people report that the insight they gained from this presentation made a radical difference in understanding their own situations. To be effective as a sexual therapist, you need to have a thorough understanding of the body and how it works. Sex is much more than the coming together of various bodily parts. However, even when the feelings and spirit are in the right place, unless the parts come together correctly, sex is not going to work.

The starting point, therefore, is a thorough understanding of the body parts connected with our sexuality—the anatomy—and a thorough grasp of how those parts work—the physiology. Society has not become better educated about the sexual process, despite the sexual revolution. So this chapter will provide the needed information about how the body works. Not only does the sexual therapist need to have a grasp of how the body functions, but the clients do as well. In *The Gift of Sex*, we have written about the bodily aspect of sex, including guidelines for self-exams and mutual exams. Please refer to chapters 5 through 8 in that book as a resource for the couples with whom you are working.

All sexual anatomy is present at birth, confirming again that we have been created as sexual beings. Involuntary sexual responses are present almost from the moment a baby draws its first breath. A little boy has his first erection within minutes, and a little girl lubricates vaginally within hours after birth. Thus, not only is the anatomy complete at birth, but physiological responses are present as well. Obviously these responses do not have the same emotion or meaning that we associate with them in adolescence or adulthood.

Hormones influence the development of our sexual organs and feelings as adolescents and adults. These hormones begin to be secreted about three years before any observable bodily changes appear. Therefore, a seven-, eight-, or nine-year-old may experience some emotional fluctuation or sensitivity triggered by these bursts of hormones.

In the woman, the sex hormones are estrogen and progesterone. When these hormones are first secreted, they are very irregular and remain so until the girl has been menstruating a year or more. Eventually, the hormones should develop rhythmic monthly patterns which continue, except when the woman is pregnant or breast-feeding, until she reaches menopause.

In menopause, the changes that result from the decrease in hormonal levels may affect sexual functioning. Those changes are mainly the thinning of the vaginal walls and a decrease in vaginal lubrication. Both are best handled by using a lubricant and by the continued exercising of the PC (pupococcygeal) or Kegel muscle. If a woman of menopausal age complains of new or increased dyspareunia (pain during intercourse), a medical examination to confirm the source of these changes would certainly be indicated.

Testosterone is the male sex hormone, which increases in production when males are at the onset of puberty. Testosterone reaches its peak levels of production in the man's twenties and then dwindles as he ages. At least five changes occur as the result of the man's aging process and the decrease in testosterone levels:

45

1. There is a decrease in the frequency of urgent physical sexual desire.
2. It may take longer to get an erection and may require more direct, firm stimulation. A young man is likely to come to the lovemaking scene already aroused with an erection. As men age, this becomes less likely, with the erection and arousal usually occurring during the love play.
3. An older man may not feel the need to ejaculate with every sexual experience.
4. The force of the ejaculation lessens with age. When a man ejaculates in his twenties, it is usually with a spurt, whereas as men age, it moves more toward being a dribble.
5. The erections may not be as firm as they were in youth.

Just as the sex hormones influence the development of our sexual organs and affect our sexual functioning, they also enhance our sexual drive. This drive gives us energy not only for sexual arousal but also for getting things done in life. It is the reason adolescents are encouraged to keep very active and busy, while couples are encouraged to relax enough to have some time and energy left for sexual arousal.

Arousal is an automatic, involuntary, pleasure-seeking response in our bodies that is controlled by the relaxed or passive branch of our involuntary or autonomic nervous system—the parasympathetic branch. Some of us are more aware of the feelings of arousal than others; but all normal, healthy adult bodies experience arousal on a continual basis. A woman lubricates vaginally every eighty to ninety minutes while she sleeps, just as a man gets an erection every eighty to ninety minutes while he sleeps. Throughout a day, arousal may occur for various reasons, ranging from a full bladder or an erotic thought to a sexual touch or full sexual activity.

Sexual arousal may lead to a full sexual response if positive sexual stimulation is pursued. Sexual response is controlled by the active branch of the autonomic nervous system—the sympathetic branch. When we discuss the sexual response a little later in this chapter, we will detail how each of these systems works. For now, it is sufficient to say that while the response of orgasm follows arousal, the two are under opposite nervous systems' control.

Both men and women can experience sexual arousal without experiencing an orgasmic response. Also, it is possible, though less likely, for both men and women to experience orgasm without experiencing arousal.

For example, some men ejaculate without an erection or the usual sensations of arousal. While this is not the norm, it is important to understand that arousal and orgasm are two separate responses. This is what Helen Singer Kaplan, in her book, *The New Sex Therapy*, refers to as the "diphasic" physiological understanding of our sexual response.

Our sexual organs and their functioning during the sexual experience—our sexual anatomy and sexual physiology—are part of an awesome and beautiful system. Physiologically, we as men and women have all been set in motion to respond in a similar way. The intricate details of this sexual response have been measured by Masters and Johnson. Without their work, we would still be in the dark ages regarding our understanding of the sexual response. Much of what we share in this chapter grows directly out of the findings in their landmark research.

For descriptive purposes, Masters and Johnson have categorized their measurements of the sexual response into four phases. (See Figure 5–1.) The excitement and plateau phases comprise the arousal or parasympathetic dominant stage of the sexual experience, while the orgasmic phase is the sympathetic dominant stage. In the refractory period (also called the resolution phase) all the parts return at various rates to their prestimulated states.

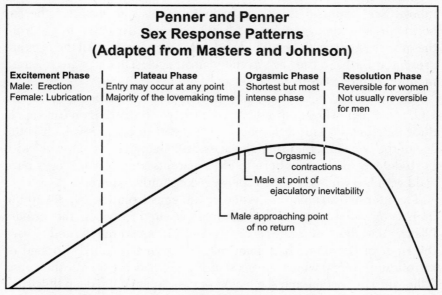

Penner and Penner
Sex Response Patterns
(Adapted from Masters and Johnson)

Excitement Phase	**Plateau Phase**	**Orgasmic Phase**	**Resolution Phase**
Male: Erection	Entry may occur at any point	Shortest but most	Reversible for women
Female: Lubrication	Majority of the lovemaking time	intense phase	Not usually reversible for men

Orgasmic contractions

Male at point of ejaculatory inevitability

Male approaching point of no return

Fig. 5–1
Sex Response Patterns

Whether the partners are married or unmarried, these responses in the body may occur due to sexual intercourse, manual or oral stimulation, self-stimulation, necking, deep kissing, petting or love play, or fantasies or visual input. Sexual intercourse is not necessary for a full sexual release, nor does sexual intercourse guarantee a full sexual release. This is vital information, especially as we teach the differentiation of sexual feelings and sexual behavior as the basis for making sexual decisions and accepting responsibility for sexual behavior.

THE SEXUAL ANATOMY

First, we will present the male and female genitalia in their pre-aroused state to give a better understanding of the changes that take place during arousal and release.

The Female Anatomy

The woman's primary sex organs are the ovaries, two almond-shaped organs located on either side of the uterus, below and behind the uterine tubes. (See Figure 5–2.) Their main function is to produce the sex hormones and the ova, or eggs, for reproduction. Release of eggs from the ovaries begins in puberty and ends after menopause. All the eggs are present at birth, so they age as the woman ages. The eggs are released monthly as they mature.

In contrast, the man continually produces sperm throughout his life. Unlike women, whose reproductive capacity is limited, men can reproduce indefinitely. This difference may suggest one reason why it is the age of the woman rather than the age of the man that is connected with birth defects in children born to older parents; the woman's eggs have aged with her while the man's sperm is constantly renewed.

The uterine (fallopian) tubes carry the eggs from the ovaries to the uterus, or womb, a pear-shaped organ located between the urinary bladder and the rectum. (See Figure 5–3.) It is naturally flexed toward the front of the body. A woman may have what is called a tipped or retroflexed uterus, which means that it is flipped back, with the cervix falling into the vagina, and she may experience pain upon deep thrusting. Also possible, though less frequent, would be an anteflexed uterus, which has moved too far forward and which would be likely to cause

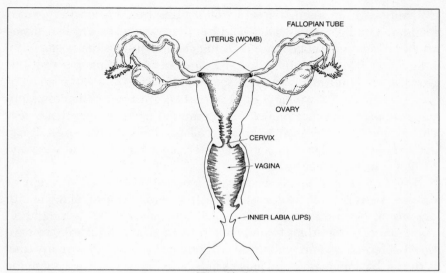

Fig. 5–2
Internal Female Genitalia (front view)

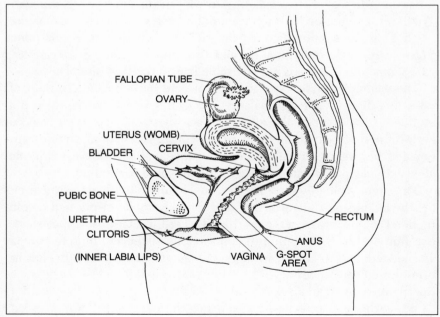

Fig. 5–3
Unaroused Internal Female Genitalia (side view)

difficulty with impregnation and would place pressure on the urinary bladder. The ligaments which hold the uterus in place are like strong rubber bands and can be injured during childbirth. This injury can make intercourse deeply painful. Obviously, a medical examination would be necessary to confirm any of these sources of pain.

The vagina is the woman's most important organ for sexual functioning. It is an organ of accommodation, a muscular passageway that is very changeable in size. It can be totally collapsed when unaroused, it can accommodate any size penis during intercourse, and it can also expand to allow birth of a baby.

The vagina is a clean passageway when it is free of infection or disease. In its natural, healthy state it is free of disease-producing microorganisms, but it does contain some friendly bacteria that help fight off infection. It is important to understand that in the genital area we have three different systems with three different conditions. The urinary tract is sterile, having no microorganisms in it. The vagina is clean, containing some friendly microorganisms. The anus, part of the gastrointestinal system, is highly contaminated. This is the reason it is always essential for women to learn when toileting to wipe from the front to the back. This is also the reason it is important to be freshly washed for sexual play, so there is no contamination from the anus to the vagina or penis. Because of anal contamination and the added threat of transmitting AIDS, anal intercourse is not advisable from a medical perspective.

The vagina maintains its own pH, or acid-base, balance to fight off infection. Because of this balance, douching is not normally recommended. Nutrition can also affect this acid-base balance. High-sugar or high-refined-carbohydrate diets, or the consumption of antibiotics, carbonated beverages, or caffeine can negatively affect the acid-base balance and may participate in bringing about vaginal irritation.

The vagina is highly sensitive to sexual stimulation. Regularly exercising the PC muscle enhances that sensitivity. For a description of recommended PC exercises, see page 149. To get the PC muscle into shape, two hundred to three hundred contractions of the PC muscle per day are needed, and to keep it in shape at least twenty-five to fifty contractions per day are necessary. The other way to maintain the sensitivity of the vagina is by regular sexual activity.

When the woman is in a relaxed state, lubrication will automatically occur, usually within the first twenty to thirty seconds after sexual stimulation begins. The vagina secretes lubrication like beads of perspiration along the wall of the vagina, a system obviously designed to make the entry of the penis into the vagina a smooth and comfortable activity.

While in the past, lubrication has always been seen as a sign of readiness for entry, it is clear now that it is only the sign of *physical* readiness. Only the woman can determine when she is *emotionally* ready for entry. The involuntary response of lubrication is controlled by the parasympathetic nervous system, that is, the relaxed branch of our involuntary nervous system. It is not something that someone can will to stop or start. Therefore, any kind of performance pressure or anxiety is likely to hinder the process of lubrication. When a couple is starting off their sexual life together, we always recommend that they use an artificial lubricant. Also, as mentioned earlier, lubrication does lessen after menopause, so this, too, would be a time for the use of an artificial lubricant.

Many different materials can be used to provide artificial lubrication. There is the old water-based standby, K-Y jelly. If the couple is not using a rubber barrier method of birth control, petroleum-based products like Allercreme and Albolene are very helpful. Natural oils are also often used. And when nothing else is available, saliva works well.

In recent years, there has been much ado about a spot or area in the upper interior of the vagina just beyond the PC muscle. This area has been called the G-spot, or Graffenburg spot, and has been found to be highly responsive to stimulation in certain women. These women report a deep orgasm that occurs when this area of the vagina is stimulated. For some of these women, there is a release of fluid connected with an orgasm brought about by G-spot-area stimulation. This is called a "flooding response" or female ejaculation.

Referring to Figure 5–4, which shows the front view of the external female genitalia, and beginning from the outside, note the outer lips, or the labia majora and the inner lips, or the labia minora. The top of these inner lips form the hood over the clitoris, which is a most unique bit of human anatomy. Its function is to receive and transmit sexual stimuli; no other part of the human body, male or female, has this function. Its existence certainly confirms that women have been created for sexual pleasure, not merely for procreation.

The structure of the clitoris has been compared to that of the penis. The hood—the upper juncture of the inner lips—is analogous to the foreskin of the penis as it covers the erectile tissue. The head, or glans, of the clitoris can be compared with the head of the penis. The little shaft of the clitoris which goes up under the hood could also be compared

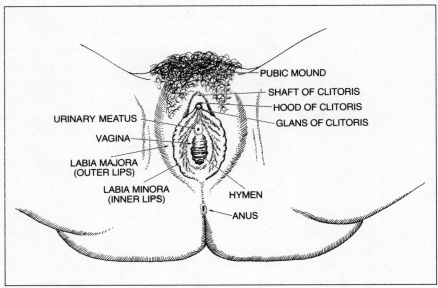

Fig. 5–4
External Female Genitalia (front view)

with the shaft of the penis. On the bottom end of the labia minora and majora is the perineum, which is the muscular floor between the vagina and the anus.

The breasts also play an important role in sexual stimulation. They are made up of the same structure and tissue in both the male and the female. Before puberty, the breasts are the same and have the same potential in both sexes. The female hormones cause the further development of breasts in girls. If men were given female hormones, they could also develop breasts which could produce milk.

It is important to note that the size of a woman's breasts has nothing to do with sexuality, sensuality, responsiveness, or sexual enjoyment. Because our culture has made larger beasts more sexual, some men may gain more pleasure from larger breasts, but a small-breasted woman and a large-breasted woman have equal potential for sexual intensity. Breast size certainly can make a difference in how a woman feels about herself, but large breasts do not bring any greater physical enjoyment than small breasts.

The breasts, especially the nipples, are a very important part of sex play and responsiveness for most women and some men. The woman's breasts are also a strong sexual stimulus for most men.

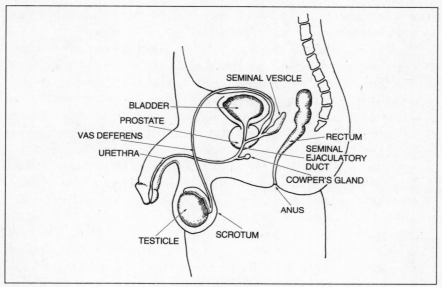

Fig. 5–5
Unaroused Internal Male Genitalia (side view)

The Male Anatomy

Just as the ovaries are the primary reproductive and sex organ for the woman, so are the testes, or testicles, for the man. The testicles are two small glands or balls held by the scrotum. (See Figure 5–5.) They function with the rest of the body in two ways. First, they produce the male hormone, testosterone, which is secreted into the body through the blood stream. Second, they also produce the sperm and a portion of the seminal fluid that carries the sperm. This seminal fluid and sperm are transmitted to the penis via the vas deferens, which travels up past the bladder through the prostate gland and then on down to the base of the penis and out the end of the penis.

A word about a vasectomy is appropriate here. As the term suggests, a vasectomy is the severing of the vas, or vas deferens, so that the sperm and seminal fluid from the testes can no longer be excreted during sexual arousal and release. Instead, the sperm and seminal fluid produced by the testicles are absorbed into the body, and their production decreases.

Sometimes men are concerned that a vasectomy will diminish their masculinity; but this need not be a fear. After a vasectomy, the testicles continue to produce testosterone, which is secreted into the blood stream. Seminal fluid continues to be reproduced by the seminal vesicles, so that a man will continue to ejaculate after a vasectomy.

The prostate gland is the donut-shaped gland around the y-shaped juncture where the outlet from the bladder (the urinary system) meets the vas deferens (the reproductive system). The prostate is an extremely sensitive body part that can easily give men trouble as they age. Whenever male clients talk about urinary urgency or a dull pain that is experienced in the lower abdomen, it is important that they be urged to have a medical exam for prostatitis by either their general-practice physician, an internist, or a urologist. Medications can often be prescribed which quickly reduce the difficulty and bring the man back to a healthy state.

Now the penis is a truly wonderful part of the human anatomy. (See Figure 5–6.) Unfortunately, it has often been used aggressively in the process of inflicting pain or inappropriately in the process of sexual abuse. The penis has a highly negative connotation for many women because it can potentially be used as a weapon by men. However, in the context of a warm and loving relationship, the penis is a delightful part of the body that is used in sexual activity. It is made up of erectile tissue with many venus sinuses (spaces) which rush full of blood under sexual stimulation. This rushing of blood brings about the man's erection, which is comparable to the woman's vaginal lubrication. It is controlled by the relaxed branch of the parasympathetic nervous system.

If the man is anxious, his sympathetic nervous system kicks in and interrupts or interferes with the erection. If the man is relaxed, turned on, and in good physical health, an erection is inevitable. There are times that men think of the penis as their "willful member." That is, it sometimes responds when it is not supposed to, and conversely, it sometimes does not respond when it is supposed to. This view of the penis generally develops in adolescence when a boy may be embarrassed by erections at inappropriate or embarrassing times. Ejaculations occurring during necking or petting, as well as during sleep, may also have brought adolescent embarrassment. It is reassuring to men to be informed that their concerns about the penis's willfulness are not unique to them. When we talk about this in our seminars, we usually get a welcoming laugh and many nods from the men in the audience.

In addition, many men are preoccupied with the size of their penises. While occasionally a man may worry that his penis is too big and might hurt a woman, most of the time the man is concerned that his penis is too small. Usually this stems from comparisons made in locker rooms, or stories and jokes heard about men with giant penises and how much pleasure they bring a woman.

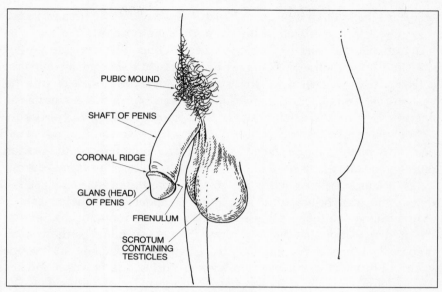

Fig. 5–6
Circumcised External Male Genitalia (side view)

In fact, the average length of the erect penis is about six inches, with a range of four and a half inches to eight inches. Often, however, men make the comparisons when the penis is flaccid. The differences from man to man in comparing flaccid penises are much greater. There is even fluctuation from time to time in each man's own penis size. The perspective of looking down on the penis from above tends to make the penis look smaller than if it were viewed from another angle, which tends to distort comparisons even further.

With regard to the whole idea that somehow the man with the larger penis is going to bring greater pleasure to the woman, we need to point out two facts: First of all, as already discussed, the vagina is an organ of accommodation, so it adjusts to various sizes. That is, it adjusts in both circumference and length. The vagina extends in length as the woman's arousal intensifies, and it adapts itself for the penis. Second, it should be noted that the outer third (one and a half to two inches) of the vagina is the erotic area; hence, great length is not necessary as long as the man has a firm enough erection to enter.

In all of our clinical experience, we have never encountered a male whose penis was not adequate for effective sexual intercourse. The only circumstance in which the penis may seem like it is not wide enough is when the woman's vagina, controlled by the PC muscle, has been overstretched as a result of childbirth and has not been reconditioned with exercise. In this case, the penis is flopping around inside rather than maintaining firm contact with the vaginal walls. However, this would have more to do with the woman's need to get her PC muscle in shape, or in the extreme circumstance, her need for corrective surgery, than it would pertain to the man's penis size.

Sometimes there is concern on the part of the woman that the man's penis may be too large. If the concern is about circumference, the woman must understand that as she learns to relax the muscles in her vagina, she can clearly accommodate a penis of any size, because the vagina is designed to expand enough to bear a baby. If the concern is about length, then she needs to understand that the vagina itself expands to make room for the penis as the uterus pulls up and out of the way. Sexual arousal helps the woman prepare the vagina for the entrance of the penis by this expansion as well as by the lubrication that comes seconds after sexual arousal begins. The fears, about a large penis, that some women carry forward from childhood may be incorporated into the anxieties that she experiences in the fear of penetration. These would need to be dealt with as serious but irrational anxieties. Often the facts presented in this chapter are enough to help a woman move past those anxieties.

THE FOUR PHASES OF THE SEXUAL RESPONSE CYCLE

The Excitement Phase—Arousal

The excitement phase is the first stage of the physical sexual response cycle as defined by Masters and Johnson. It may occur involuntarily without any stimulation when one is relaxed or asleep. We explained earlier how the body responds in a regular way with erections for the man and vaginal lubrication for the woman, especially during sleep. During active sexual activity, the excitement phase is often preceded by sexual desire or interest. Even that desire may bring out the very first signs of arousal. Hugging, kissing, bodily touching, or genital contact are activities that provide the stimulation which brings about the physical changes that occur during the excitement phase. For both the man and the woman, these changes are due to vasocongestion (blood and fluid rushing into the sexual organs).

Female Excitement Phase. The clitoris is most important for the woman during the excitement phase. It becomes engorged in a somewhat similar manner to the penis in that it increases in size two or three times its prestimulated length as its venus spaces rush full of blood and fluid. Although it is the most important receptor of sexual stimulation, it is vital to understand that most women prefer stimulation around the clitoris rather than directly on the glans (head).

It is also important to help women understand the pain/pleasure principle that operates most vividly with regard to the clitoris. Unstimulated and unaroused women experience little clitoral pleasure. As the woman's arousal moves to a point where there is intense pleasure, the clitoris becomes so sensitive that she can readily experience clitoral pain, especially if the stimulation is too directly on the head, too intense, or of too long duration. Many men believe that because the clitoris is the source of such great pleasure, the more and the harder they stimulate it, the better it is for the woman; yet most women report that a lighter, teasing touch is usually what satisfies the most. The intensity of the pain that can be experienced with too direct clitoral stimulation may make women on guard and stop their eagerness to pursue arousal. Both men and women need to accept the reality that the woman is the best authority on her own body, especially her own clitoris. She needs to accept the responsibility for guiding a man in regard to the clitoral touch. There is no way a man can automatically know what is going to be the most pleasurable.

In the excitement phase, the labia minora (inner lips) become engorged and extend outward, while the labia majora spread flat as if the genital area is opening up to receive the penis. As the arousal builds, the woman's genitals take on a slight funnel shape in preparation for penile entry.

Internally, the uterus begins to pull up and away from the vagina. This obviously then pulls the cervix out of the way so that the penis will not strike against it during thrusting. This preparation does not occur when the woman has a tipped uterus, however. The cervix does not get out of the way of the penis in this case; so it can be thrust against, causing a sharp, stabbing pain during deep thrusting.

The vagina lubricates within twenty seconds of any form of stimulation. This lubrication physically prepares the woman for entry. The inner two-thirds of the vagina lengthen and distend, allowing greater room for the penis during intercourse.

The breasts also change during the initial excitement phase. Their most obvious response is that of nipple erection, as well as general engorgement which causes a slight increase in breast size. The areola, the area around the nipple, usually darkens and becomes slightly engorged, especially as the woman moves toward the plateau phase.

Male Excitement Phase. The penis in the man is similar to the clitoris in the woman in that it is the receiver and transmitter of sexual sensations. The penile response of erection is parallel to vaginal lubrication in the woman in that it is the involuntary response that is necessary to pursue intercourse. This response occurs throughout the day and night, and can be brought about by sexual thoughts, indirect stimulation through general caressing, or direct stimulation on the penis itself. Whereas the woman's response is internal and less apparent, the man's response or lack of it is obvious. Because of this, the man often feels more pressure to respond. Therefore, some men may be highly anxious about responding, especially when they have experienced some difficulty with arousal or loss of erection.

The penis is a highly sensitive responder. It can quickly become erect with positive physical and emotional stimulation. This erection can easily be interrupted by some negative or nonsexual stimulation such as the telephone, a loud noise outside the door, a negative thought, a special concern, a harsh word, or a critical comment.

Erections can be lost and regained when relaxation and freedom exist to allow that response. During extended love play, this is likely to be the case; yet erections can also be maintained for extended periods of time without ejaculation. The latter is most likely to occur when the stimulation is varied and the intensity of the experience flows in waves. It is not uncommon for the erection to diminish slightly and then to be regained.

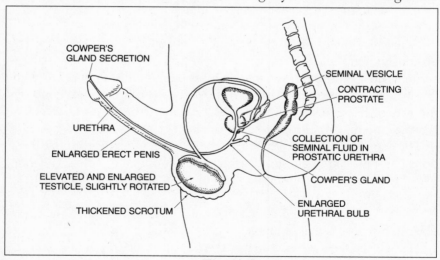

Fig. 5-7
Aroused Male Genitalia (side view)

In addition to the penis becoming erect as it rushes full of blood and fluid due to sexual arousal, the scrotum thickens and elevates partially. During the excitement phase, there may also be a general bodily response of the sexual flush in the upper third of the body (this is also true for women). Nipple erection occurs in about 60 percent of men. During this initial phase, there are no significant changes that occur internally.

The Plateau Phase

A simple way of understanding the plateau phase is to think of it as everything that occurs between the initial arousal, which happens in the first seconds or minutes, and the orgasm. The plateau phase could be a few minutes long—or hours long. It all depends on how each individual responds and what the couple desires. During extended love play, whether it is a prelude to intercourse or simply a fully clothed enjoyment of the intense response of two people with each other, the couple will be in the plateau phase. There will be arousal, but they will not yet have reached orgasm.

If there are sexual problems, they usually affect the plateau phase. Either the response is too quick, moving from excitement to orgasm without enough time between the two, or too slow, taking too long to get to the point of orgasm. The changes that occur during the plateau phase are due to the buildup of tension and increased congestion in the genitals. When a long, extended period of love play is allowed, this buildup of intensity will usually be experienced in waves of heightened arousal and then letdown. As long as there is the freedom to ride these waves, the intensity will build to the point of automatically triggering an orgasm.

The plateau phase is the phase that changes sex into lovemaking and goal-oriented, orgasm-directed activity into extended pleasure.

Male Plateau Phase. Externally, the penis may become slightly more engorged and deeper in color, while the glans or head of the penis increases in diameter. During the plateau phase, the scrotum also thickens and elevates more. (See Figure 5–7.) It should be noted that fluid containing sperm may seep from the penis during the plateau phase without ejaculation. In light of this, it is clear that the withdrawal method of birth control—the intentional withdrawal of the penis from the vagina before ejaculation—is not a reliable method. Adolescents most often attempt to use this method, and the statistics clearly indicate how ineffective it is.

Internally during this phase, the testes enlarge 50 to 100 percent. The right testicle rises and rotates a quarter turn. Near the end of the plateau

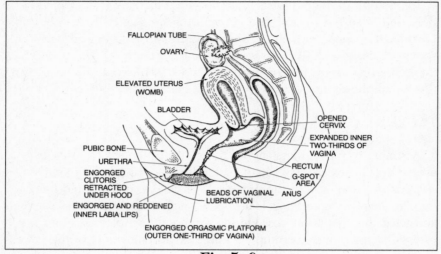

Fig. 5–8
Aroused Internal Female Genitalia (side view)

phase, some warning signs appear for the man that let him know that he is approaching the point of no return. All men are aware that as they get near the point of orgasm, they sense something in their bodies which tells them that they are about to ejaculate.

Three main changes take place at this point: As the scrotal sack thickens and pulls toward the body, the left testicle also rises and rotates about a quarter turn so it rests directly against the perineal wall. There are contractions in the prostate gland as the seminal fluid begins to gather in that area and travel to the base of the penis. The sphincter from the bladder shuts off so that no seminal fluid will be forced by retrograde ejaculation into the bladder, nor will any urine be expelled during the orgasm. Although a man is not aware of these specific changes, these physical events function as a warning that he is about to ejaculate.

It should be noted that once this process is in motion, the ejaculation is inevitable. The man is approaching the point of no return and is moving toward ejaculatory inevitability. If a man struggles with premature ejaculation, he clearly must gain control prior to these physical events, rather than attempt to stop the ejaculation once these warning signs have been sensed.

Female Plateau Phase. As the sexual experience progresses, more and more is happening internally for the woman and less and less is occurring externally. This symbolizes women's more experiential, internal report of the sexual experience, in contrast to men's more external, performance-oriented approach. In the woman, there are some slight changes externally in the labia minora. They increase in size and brighten somewhat in color a minute or two before orgasm.

The Bartholin gland secretes one to three drops of a substance designed to enhance the possibility of pregnancy by affecting the pH balance of the vagina. At the same time, the clitoral glans retracts under the clitoral hood, almost as a protection because of its heightened sensitivity under such intense stimulation and arousal.

Internally, significant changes must occur for the woman before she is ready for her orgasmic response. (See Figure 5–8.) The uterus, which began to elevate during the excitement phase, elevates even more. The inner two-thirds of the vagina expands or balloons outward to form the area that is known as the seminal pool. This is the nonerotic section of the vagina where contact with the penis neither is necessary for arousal nor provides much stimulation. The outer third of the vagina (one and a half to two inches) becomes intensely engorged as it forms the orgasmic platform. Some women are aware of a pleasurable vaginal grasping response as the arousal continues through the plateau phase.

Male and Female Transition from Plateau to Orgasm

Several of the specific changes that happen for both men and women during the transition from plateau to orgasm usually go relatively unnoticed. There is the involuntary extension of the foot called the carpopedal spasm. Both the heart rate and the blood pressure increase. Involuntary pelvic thrusting occurs as arousal moves near the point of orgasm, and general muscular tension takes place with almost spastic-like contractions.

Some more obvious changes also occur. The skin flushes in the chest, neck, and face areas—almost a blushing effect due to the widespread vasocongestion. Facial grimaces are common because of the involuntary contracting of the facial muscles, as well as grasping or moaning responses that may be due in part to hyperventilation (heavy breathing), which is virtually inevitable and necessary for both men and women to reach the orgasmic phase. Women who have difficulty allowing an orgasmic response usually have difficulty allowing these intense grasping, grimacing, and breathing responses because they are thought of as unladylike. It should also be noted that for both men and women the transition from the plateau phase to the orgasmic phase marks a shift from parasympathetic dominance to sympathetic dominance, a switch which helps nudge the individual toward the orgasmic response.

The Orgasmic Phase

The orgasmic response is the shortest and most intense of the four phases. It is a reflex response that lasts only a few seconds. We cannot choose to respond with an orgasm like we can choose to bend our elbow, but we can control or inhibit the response from happening by stopping the natural, involuntary responses in our bodies. Or we can enhance the possibility of an orgasmic response by becoming active and going after genital stimulation—by penile thrusting for the man and by clitoral or vaginal stimulation for the woman.

As the intensity builds in the body, the tension increases to the point where the orgasmic reflex is set off. Our autonomic, or involuntary, nervous system has switched control from the relaxed, receptive branch, to the active, fight-or-flight branch, as already explained. Hence, the more active a person is, the more the body is encouraged to respond orgasmically (which is usually what the woman needs), and the quieter and more passive a person is, the more the response is slowed down (which is usually what the man needs). In communicating about the sexual response, it is very important for the therapist to clearly relay that an orgasm is a reflex. A person actively receiving the right amount and duration of stimulation will be orgasmic.

Female Orgasmic Response. All significant activity for women takes place internally. It is for this reason that so much confusion has occurred regarding their orgasmic response. Women regularly report that they are not sure whether or not they have had an orgasm. Men do not report such doubt; they know if they have or have not.

Because the clitoris is completely retracted during the orgasmic phase, some women prefer very direct clitoral stimulation right at the point of orgasm. Internally, there are two centers of response for the woman. The uterus experiences contractions similar to those of the early stages of labor. This is why an orgasm may be ruled out if a woman is threatening to lose a pregnancy. When first experienced, these contractions may be felt as slightly painful; but as the woman learns to connect those contractions as part of her intense pleasure, they usually become highly enjoyable during the orgasm. The cervix of the uterus opens slightly at the end of the orgasm so as to be ready to receive the sperm.

The outer third of the vagina—the orgasmic platform—experiences contractions that are eight-tenths of a second apart, with three to five contractions in a mild orgasm and eight to twelve contractions in a more intense orgasm. These are the contractions of the PC muscle which surrounds both the vagina, forming the orgasmic platform, and the rectal sphincter, where contractions are also experienced.

Male Orgasmic Response. The man's orgasm is experienced in two stages. In the first stage, the internal genitalia respond a few seconds before ejaculation, as explained in the earlier description of the plateau phase. Like the contractions of the orgasmic platform in the woman, the man's contractions of the seminal duct system, including the prostate, occur at intervals of eight-tenths of a second. Contractions also occur in the rectal sphincter as well as in the urinary bladder. These contractions move the ejaculate to the base of the penis, preparing it for stage two.

During stage two, the actual seminal fluid, including the sperm, is expelled. Having reached the point of ejaculatory inevitability, there is nothing that can stop the response at this juncture; it is, indeed, inevitable. The length of time between those initial contractions and the expulsion is the length of time it takes the sperm to travel through the system of the penis. The contractions at the base of the penis are also at intervals of eight-tenths of a second. For the average healthy male, a standard ejaculation contains 3.5 to 5 cubic centimeters of ejaculate and 175 to 500 million spermatozoa.

The man's total-body responses are similar to those experienced by the woman. They include increased heart rate and elevated blood pressure, intense breathing, facial contractions with gasping responses, and foot spasms.

Male/Female Orgasmic Differences

There are a number of specific ways men and women vary in their bodily responses during the orgasmic phase. Women seem to differ from one another more than men in their total external expression of their orgasms, whereas men seem to share a more standard reaction. Some women are extremely quiet and internal, whereas other women are much more rambunctious.

Women have the potential to respond indefinitely with multiple or sequential orgasms. Not all women desire this nor feel the need for more than one response, but they are designed with that potential. Perhaps a word should be said here about the difference between a multiple and sequential orgasm. By a multiple orgasm we mean an orgasm where a woman reaches the orgasmic level and then seems to ride that wave in what Brauer and Brauer have referred to as an "extended sexual orgasm."[1]

63

The woman who responds with a sequential orgasm has a slight refractory period and then responds again with another orgasm.

Women have a physiologically unlimited potential for orgasms; they are limited only by their stamina and their desire. In contrast, men, except for a very small percentage, need a refractory period of at least twenty minutes—and usually several hours—before they can regain arousal, erection, and ejaculation. As a man ages, the refractory period generally increases. It also seems that the more frequently a man ejaculates, the longer it takes until he is able to ejaculate again.

The woman's orgasm can be interrupted at any point, whereas the man's cannot. Once the man has reached the point of ejaculatory inevitability, nothing can be done to stop it; the reflex is in motion. Because of this irreversibility, women have often been taught that they should not arouse a man, because once a man becomes aroused he is no longer responsible for his own actions. This distorted teaching leads adolescents to conclude that it is a girl's responsibility to set the limits on the boy for controlling their sexual activity. The fact is men *can* control themselves and are responsible to control their behavior, even as women are.

For men, control must happen at an earlier phase. Even if a man is about to ejaculate, he can still control where he does that; it does not have to happen inside a woman's vagina. Men should never be taught that their arousals excuse them from being responsible for their own actions.

If the sexual experience is the first one in a long time, a woman will tend to be slower in her response and will experience less freedom in her release, while a man will tend to be quicker in his arousal and release and experience more buildup and intensity. We believe this tendency to go in opposite directions is one more indication of the reality that we were created to be together and to experience sexual release on a regular basis.

While women experience more difficulty with and pressure to have an orgasm, most of the time, men do not struggle with the orgasmic response, but rather struggle with controlling the timing of the orgasm. Men's pressure to perform comes earlier in the sexual experience because their difficulty is usually either with getting or keeping an erection or with maintaining control of the ejaculation.

The Resolution Phase

During this final phase of the sexual response, the body reverses itself through the plateau and excitement changes to its prior, unstimulated state. Both the man and woman experience the sensation of tension loss due to the release of engorgement and the diminishing of vasocongestion. In the male, the most obvious sign of resolution is the gradual and sometimes immediate lessening of the erection. The full, firm erection will be gone immediately, but it may take some time for the penis to return to its prestimulated state.

Some men experience heightened sensitivity bordering on pain on the glans of the penis during resolution. When that is the case, the man may withdraw and pull away from his wife, leaving her feeling somewhat rejected. It is important that the man inform his wife of this sensitivity, and that the couple finds a way to continue the holding and affirmation without penile contact.

It is not uncommon for men to feel very relaxed and fall asleep quickly after an orgasm. This will often frustrate the woman who is coming down off her arousal more slowly and is looking for a time of intimacy through conversation and touch. Again, it is vital that the therapist recognize the great variation from one person to another. We must not impose a stereotype on a man or a woman that does not reflect the person's own individual desires. Each individual is the best authority on what he or she needs during the entire sexual experience, including the resolution phase.

The woman's arousal can be maintained or regained without complete loss of the vasocongestion. If stimulation is not continued after a woman has an orgasm, her body returns to its prestimulated, uncongested, relaxed state within a few moments. This is especially true if she has experienced a satisfying orgasm. If the woman has been aroused but not experienced release, she may feel the tension or the engorgement for an extended period of time after the sexual experience. When there has been no orgasmic release, or only partial release through a mild orgasm, the arousal dissipates slowly, often taking several hours. This can be a frustrating experience for the woman, sometimes eliciting involuntary crying, which then provides the release for her.

From the physiological perspective, we understand this crying as the body's way of bringing back parasympathetic nervous system dominance, which helps the woman relax. Unfortunately, crying may be taken by the husband as a rejection or criticism of him; as a result, he may turn away, deprecating and blaming himself or feeling anger toward his wife. The resolution phase can be a time of affection and intimacy, whether or not the woman has experienced an orgasm—and especially when she has not. When a couple realizes this, their resolution time can be a warm and affirming experience, in spite of the lack of fulfillment.

Externally for the woman, the clitoris returns to its normal position in five to ten seconds and to its normal size in five to ten minutes after an orgasm. It takes about this amount of time for the labia minora and majora to return to their normal size, position, and color. Internally, when there has been an orgasm, the uterus drops back into its anteflexed position relatively quickly. When there has not been an orgasm, it may take longer and may cause lower back pain. The vaginal wall collapses within five to eight minutes, while the congestion in the outer third of the vagina disappears in seconds.

In the resolution phase, the couple has the opportunity to experientially confirm their intimacy regardless of the physical fulfillment that has been experienced. Some couples like to fall asleep together, whereas others like to be very active after a fulfilling sexual experience. One couple liked to get up and jog after a sexual experience. This would certainly not be our preference; but they found it a fulfilling expression of their experience together. As the therapist, you will be able to sense the intimacy level that is achievable for each couple by what you hear from them about the resolution phase. It is vitally important that you respond carefully to each couple's uniqueness in all four phases rather than approaching them with preprogrammed expectations.

CHAPTER SIX

WHAT IS SEXUAL THERAPY?

SEXUAL THERAPY IS THE SYSTEMATIC APPROACH used to deal with unsatisfactory sexual experiences. A couple experiencing dissatisfaction is retrained to communicate and behave with each other in a way that reduces demand, enhances pleasure, and facilitates the natural physiological sexual response.

According to Helen Singer Kaplan, "Sex therapy differs from other forms of treatment for sexual dysfunctions in two respects: first, its goals are essentially limited to the relief of the patient's sexual symptoms and second, it departs from traditional techniques by employing a combination of prescribed sexual experiences and psychotherapy."[1]

All sexual therapy, when it is practiced effectively and responsibly, is quite similar. It is primarily behavioral therapy consisting of sensate focus (touching) exercises, communication exercises, and teaching exercises. The couple is taught about the human body and how it works, about the sexual experience, and about each other. Their successful completion of the assigned behavioral prescriptions determines the success of the sexual therapy process. These assignments are completed while the couple is alone and relaxed together. The more difficult it is for a couple to interact, the more precise the therapist needs to be in assigning the behavioral prescriptions. Masters and Johnson give the following insights regarding these behavioral prescriptions:

1. They *alter* a previously destructive sexual system. The secure ambience created by sex therapy provides the couple with an opportunity to *learn* to make love in freer and more enjoyable ways;

2. The resolution of sexual conflict is facilitated when the couple engages in previously avoided sexual experiences;

3. The tasks evoke the emergence of previously unconscious intrapsychic and dyadic conflicts which then become available for psychotherapeutic intervention and resolution.[2]

The sexual exercises that couples experience with each other stir up underlying psychodynamics and barriers, and lead naturally into the psychotherapy process. Thus, the two facets of the therapy process—sexual exercises and psychotherapy—interact together. The more complex the case, the more psychotherapy is required. If administered during the assessment process, the *Minnesota Multiphasic Personality Inventory (MMPI-2)* often helps predict underlying dynamics, personality problems, and marital conflicts that are likely to surface.

When deeper issues arise that require more time to resolve, the couple should be reassured that this is not a negative setback. Sexual therapy prescriptions require a capacity for intimacy and stability. A couple cannot hide underlying problematic issues and continue through the demanding interaction process. These issues are like toxic wastes that have been buried and now "bubble up" to the surface. If left underground, they pollute the system. It is better that they surface and be detoxified.

In our practice, we treat the couple, rather than the individual. Most of the time, both spouses have participated in the inadequate or destructive sexual interaction. But occasionally, we will work with one spouse more than the other. If one spouse brought dysfunction to the marriage, the other spouse may not have engaged in the pathology to perpetuate a disturbed system. Even in this case, most often both need to complete the shared experiences. The joint interaction is necessary for improvement in sexual functioning by breaking old habits and thereby bringing relief of the sexual distress.

Regardless of differences in treatment style, the goals of sexual therapy are to distract from anxiety, remove demand, and eliminate negative or failure experiences and feelings. In addition to alleviating the negative symptoms, we also aspire to help the couple build new patterns of sexual relating, both verbally and physically; to build trust; to develop the capacity for emotional and sexual intimacy; and to acquire positive sexual attitudes.

The above goals are best met by: 1) becoming knowledgeable about one's own body and each other's bodies, and how they function, 2) developing an awareness of and taking responsibility for one's own needs and feelings, 3) learning to focus on sensations of pleasure without the demand to respond to or to please one's spouse, 4) opening effective communication within and about the sexual experience, and 5) recognizing that sex is not limited to intercourse and orgasm, but includes total enjoyment of each other's bodies, minds, and spirits.

In conclusion, sexual therapy is not an additive like the acquiring of a new skill. Instead, it aims to release an innate ability. Sexual therapy may include some development of effective techniques; but primarily, it is a process in which capacity for sexual responsiveness and enjoyment is enhanced as knowledge and self-awareness are gained, trust and intimacy are built, conflicts and barriers are broken down, and attitudes are enlightened.

These positive sexual attitudes are hopefully instilled during the sexual therapy process: 1) sex is good and of God, 2) sexual curiosity is natural, 3) sexual responsiveness is innate, 4) decisions about sexual behavior can be made and followed because we are responsible before God and each other for all of our sexual behaviors, and 5) mutuality is the biblical guideline for sexual functioning in marriage.

CHAPTER SEVEN

WHY SEXUAL THERAPY?

GOD DESIGNED US AS SEXUAL BEINGS. The sexual response is controlled by one's involuntary nervous system; it begins at birth and continues throughout life. Then what is it that hinders the sexual process from flowing naturally for some couples or individuals? Why doesn't the sexual relationship just happen? Why is sex therapy even necessary?

In this chapter, we will examine the causes of sexual dysfunction from three different perspectives. First, we will look at the sexual developmental tasks that must be mastered from infancy to adulthood, particularly focusing on the dilemma that results when developmental mastery has not been accomplished. The second and third perspectives are the educational and emotional causes of sexual dysfunction.

DEVELOPMENTAL CAUSES

Although sexual response is automatically functioning throughout life, our sexuality is not only an automatic, physical response. Even though it is an integral, personal part of our total beings, it is externally influenced. Sexual feelings, responses, and behaviors seem to be very easily conditioned in either a positive or negative direction. They are subject to social and cultural conditioning that begins at birth and continues throughout life.

The stages of sexual development are charted in Table 7–1, and described in detail below.

Stages of Sexual Development

Stage	Critical Learning	Impact on Sexual Adjustment
Infancy	Bonding	Capacity for Intimacy
Toddlerhood	Touching, Naming, and Controlling of Genitals	Positive Acceptance of Genitals (User Friendly)
Preschool	Question-Asking	Open Communication Regarding Sexuality
School Age	Exploration	Sexual Awareness
Preadolescence	Erotic Feelings and Bumbling Discovery	Self-Acceptance and Competence in Relating to Opposite Sex
Adolescence	Decision-Making	Taking Responsibility for Own Sexuality

Table 7–1

Infancy

During infancy, from birth to age one, children learn about themselves as sexual persons from their primary caretakers, usually their parents. This learning occurs through the type of touch and holding the infant is given. When a close, warm, secure, and trusting bond is formed, children master the ability to form close relationships, including the physical relationship. Thus, capacity for sexual intimacy is developed both physically and emotionally at an early age.

Not mastering this early sexual developmental task of bonding interferes with the desire for and the ability to have sexual intimacy. The adult who was adopted after the first year of life, or was reared in an institution, or was brought up by an anxious, distant, or self-centered mother (who herself was unable to radiate warmth through her touch) may not feel the need for physical intimacy.

If bonding did not take place, sexual closeness may even be frightening. A male with this background may experience sexual drive, but will masturbate rather than have sexual desire for his wife. Or a man who did not get his intimate-touch needs met during infancy may express his desire for his wife inappropriately. His desire may be shown in an anxious, childlike manner that repulses his wife. A woman who missed bonding may not even be aware that she has any sexual needs. Infants who have not experienced the comfort of being touched and held closely learn to survive without that intimacy.

Toddlerhood

Toddlerhood is a genital-centered stage of development. From one to three years of age, it is natural for children to touch the genitals and learn that this feels good. This is the time when children learn to control elimination and to talk about and name the body parts. The cultural and social conditioning that takes place during this stage will determine whether a child accepts the genitals as a natural, beautiful part of God's creation or whether he or she views the genitals, and thus sexuality, as untouchable, unmentionable, and dirty.

Touching the genitals is natural for every toddler. Just as a child pokes a finger in his or her ear, nose, or "belly button," the little boy will play with his penis and the little girl will rub over her clitoris and between her labia. Both will discover the good feelings. That is how God created human beings. The rubbing or fondling, much like sucking a thumb or holding a "blankie," is soothing for the toddler. It is not usually erotic.

How toilet training is handled will affect the way children view their genitals specifically, and their sexuality in general. Body-waste elimination and sexual functioning are both connected with the genitals. If control is learned with a positive sense of mastery rather than a punitive rigidity or lax insecurity, children will gain a sense of accomplishment. If children are given an accurate understanding of "germ theory," they will learn to view their genitals as clean, rather than dirty.

The fact is, the urinary and reproductive systems (which are housed in the genitals) are clean; no disease-producing microorganisms are present. The urinary systems in both men and women and the reproductive system in men are not only clean, they are sterile. The vagina is a clean passageway. Although bacteria are present, they are part of normal flora that actually help fight infections. So the genitals are not dirty, unless they have become contaminated from the rectum during wiping. The rectum is highly contaminated with disease-producing microorganisms, thus requiring the washing of hands after toileting. This differentiation— between the clean genitals and the dirty rectum—is important for children to acquire during the toilet training process of toddlerhood.

How the parents refer to and name the genitals communicates vividly their view of sexuality. Parents are terribly proud when toddlers can say, "eyes," "ears," "elbow," or "wrist," but then often revert to names such as "wa-wa" and "doo-doo" when referring to the genitals and the process of elimination. Avoiding the accurate names for the genitals and their functions teaches children that these parts are difficult to talk about. In contrast, parents communicate to children an acceptance of sexuality when they call a penis a penis and a vagina a vagina.

When the hand is taken away and given a slap or a "no-no," the toddler playing with his or her genitals will think of them as untouchable, something to be afraid of, like the hot stove. A sense of disgust, rigidity, or "yuckiness" communicated about elimination can teach the toddler that sex is dirty (hence, "dirty" jokes). Similarly, the toddler may learn that the genitals are unmentionables, as well as untouchables, when real names are not given for them. This refusal to verbalize sexual words may lead to later difficulty in talking about sex with one's spouse. In contrast, when elimination is guided with praise and the genitals are named with pride, parents give their children a gift. The children then accept their genitals as a friendly part of themselves, just as some computer software is considered "User-Friendly."

Thus, when toddler sexual development was mastered, the adult later enters the marriage relationship with an integrated acceptance of his or her genitals. When this developmental task was not accomplished, the adult is likely to sense that the genitals are untouchable and unmentionable, and not a part of the body to be freely shared with his or her spouse.

Preschool

A preschooler's sexual curiosity is manifested in question-asking. How these sexual questions are handled at this age will set the tone for adulthood comfort regarding discussions of sexuality. If positive reinforcement was received for asking questions, and if open, factual sexual data were given with a matter-of-fact attitude, a person will be better able to communicate openly about sexuality. If sex simply was not talked about, the adult may have difficulty communicating openly about sexuality within marriage.

School Age

Curiosity continues into school age with the development of a sense of modesty, the indication of sexual awareness. During this age, nudity becomes an issue. Children begin to be shy about their bodies, first with nonfamily members and then rather inconsistently within the family. One time they will run around the house nude, and the next time they will cautiously cover themselves. This begins to occur around age four or five, usually sooner for girls than boys.

At the same time, children begin to be aware of sexual differences and may be stimulated by seeing a nude body, particularly the adult body of the opposite sex. A mother may notice her son staring at her. This is a signal to begin covering up and probably stop brother-sister baths. It is not that children should be kept from ever seeing parents' bodies nude, but rather that caution should be used not to elicit their sexual attentiveness or curiosity.

Both extremes, either overexposure or extreme modesty, inhibit the development of a healthy sexual awareness. Both produce difficulty in sharing one's body openly with a spouse or they may lead to inappropriate curiosity behaviors in adulthood, especially for men. Some men become voyeurs because they grew up with no exposure, whereas others become voyeurs because, unfortunately, they had an exposure to something addicting at this critical age of development. One man who struggled with peeping as an adult had happened to be walking home from school one day and innocently passed a home with two adolescent girls changing clothes by an open window. The scene was very arousing—and hooked him. So the principle is clear: If there were no violating experiences, if the privacy and need for modesty was respected, and if nudity was comfortable but not exploitive, an adult will most likely be comfortable being nude with his or her spouse and not having unhealthy sexual habits.

Exploratory play is almost inevitable for the school-age child. It may take the form of playing house, doctor, or "you show me yours and I'll show you mine." Exploratory play is a universal, innocent expression of sexual curiosity at this age. It signals to parents the need for specific sexual education and for teaching some matter-of-fact boundaries.

When there are no external limits, and sexual play continues repeatedly throughout the school age, sexual awareness is stimulated beyond the emotional developmental readiness of the child. Likewise, a parent's violent, traumatic reaction to the child who is found in exploratory play is devastating. Negative attention given to innocent curiosity leaves a child confused, because he or she connects sexuality with something seriously wrong. This makes natural sexual expression difficult in adulthood. Exploratory play—the checking out of each other's genitals—by children of the same age who have not been exposed to sexual experiences beyond their age level causes no harm. Boundaries are necessary, however. For example, children should be required to keep their underwear on and leave the doors open. Parents should be nearby and make their presence known. The lack of boundaries or a traumatic reaction to being found in exploratory play can cause incredible pain throughout life.

Preadolescence

Preadolescence brings awkwardness, bursts of energy, and emotional volatility. In our book *A Gift for All Ages*, we refer to this period as the "squirrelly years." Erotic feelings begin to tingle as the hormones spurt. This is the kiss-and-run stage. Bumbling and indirect interaction with persons of the opposite sex is natural. "Going steady" at this age has little romantic significance. If Jill and Jimmy are going steady, it means the following sequence of events probably took place: Jill called Karen to say she likes Jimmy; Karen called Bob to tell him that Jill likes Jimmy; Bob called Jimmy. It continued until Jill indirectly heard that Jimmy wanted to go steady. Her response to Jimmy got to him through at least two other friends.

Not all preadolescents are allowed this bumbling discovery of their sexuality. Some are pushed into adolescent dating patterns, even to the point of explicit male/female sexual activity. Others are restricted from the normal preadolescent interaction because they are socially shy, immature, overprotected by parents, or have health problems that inhibit their availability.

In the case of either extreme, self-acceptance and competence in relating to the opposite sex is not mastered. If a young person is pushed into sexual activity at this age, confusion is usually connected with the sexual relationships. If restricted from all boy-girl interaction, children will grow into adulthood still feeling inept when they relate physically with the opposite sex. This is more true for men than for women. The wives of inept men often refer to their husbands as "bumblers." On the other hand, inept women are more comfortable being taught by their husbands, and consequently, do not seem as inadequate.

Adolescence

Adolescence is the time to assume responsibility for sexual behaviors and develop patterns of responsible sexual wholesomeness. These decisions need to be consistent with Christian beliefs, family values, and commitment to the relationship. When the sexual activity engaged in is in conflict with the adolescent's inner beliefs and values, anxiety is triggered at the same time that pleasurable sexual feelings are aroused; thus, anxiety and sexual pleasure are paired. The resulting adrenaline-rush becomes addicting. When the adolescent becomes an adult and marries, there is no more fear of getting caught or fear of pregnancy; there is no more anxiety. Thus, there is also no pleasurable sexual arousal. The pleasurable response has developed a dependence on the "adrenaline hype."

Another difficulty can arise for the adolescents who shut down all sexual feelings so as not to violate their beliefs. Sexual feelings must be separated from sexual behaviors. God designed sexual feelings; sexual desire is good. Nevertheless, decisions must be made regarding the behaviors that occur in response to the desire. Adolescents can learn to redirect the sexual-drive energy into self-enhancing activities (e.g., sports, music, schoolwork, etc.). Learning to accept sexual feelings while making decisions that control sexual actions is the task of adolescence that, if successfully mastered, leads the adult to guilt-free, unrepressed sexual expression in marriage.

Hence, in order to pass through adolescence and move into a healthy single adulthood, adolescents must allow themselves to experience vital sexual feelings, while making clear decisions which limit their choices of sexual actions.

When the developmental task of each stage has been mastered, one should have an integrated sense of his or her sexuality and spirituality that will act as a guide for the tasks of adult relationships.

Not mastering one of the developmental tasks can leave a person with an inadequacy in the marital sexual relationship. Fortunately, developmental gaps can be filled; the later the stage of development, the easier the healing. For example, lack of bonding in infancy is much more difficult to replace than the lack of bumbling, heterosexual interactions during preadolescence. One of the functions of the sexual therapy process is to fill developmental gaps that have caused sexual dilemmas.

EDUCATIONAL CAUSES

In today's world, it is difficult to imagine that sexual ignorance can be a source of sexual dissatisfaction, or that it limits the full potential of sexual enjoyment for many couples. But it is true—sexual ignorance is extremely common.

When sexual inadequacies are due to a lack of knowledge rather than developmental lags or emotional issues, the task for correction is relatively simple and most rewarding. In this situation, self-help is the place to begin. Our book, *The Gift of Sex*, as well as *Intended for Pleasure* by Ed and Gaye Wheat and *The Act of Marriage* by Tim and Beverly LaHaye all contain beneficial information for the Christian couple. Couples who experienced the changes they desired in their sexual relationship as a direct result of attending our sexual-enhancement seminar, "Enjoying the Gift of Sex," were merely suffering from lack of knowledge.

In our practice, we find there are certain groups of sexually stressed people who benefit from education, either as a part of the sexual therapy process or without requiring sexual therapy. These are the physiologically uninformed, the experientially naive, the culturally misinformed, and the religiously inhibited.

The Physiologically Uninformed

The physiologically uninformed need information about how their bodies are made and how they function. On this subject, the physiological facts discussed in chapter 5 are most helpful.

For example, women who block out the feelings of sexual arousal believe they are unresponsive. However, when they learn that they are experiencing nipple erections and vaginal lubrication, which are indications of arousal, they finally are able to recognize and connect with their responsiveness.

Likewise, men who ejaculate prematurely can attune themselves to oncoming ejaculation by learning to recognize warning signs. Women can help when they learn that continual, vigorous penile stimulation without rest times will bring a man to ejaculation. So if a woman wants the arousal to last longer before ejaculation, she can stop and distract from the stimulation that brings the ejaculation. In addition, women must understand that, unlike a woman's orgasm, a man's ejaculation cannot be stopped once it has started. Control has to be enacted before the warning that the man is about to ejaculate. Although these facts may sound like common sense, they are not known by everyone.

Both husbands and wives need to be educated about the changes that take place in the woman's body during sexual activity. Stimulation and time are required for the reflex of orgasm to happen for her. It is common for both the man and the woman to rush from an erection for the man to entry, thrusting, and ejaculation, and then be dismayed that the woman is not responsive. Neither may know where the clitoris is, its erotic potential, or that nondirect stimulation is usually most delightful for the woman. In contrast to most men, a woman can respond indefinitely, so she may desire more stimulation even after an orgasm.

Lack of understanding of the involuntary nature of the sexual response causes erectile difficulty for many men. Erections can come and go with extended love play. Anxiety about maintaining an erection often interferes with the body's normal response. Erections are involuntary responses that occur every eighty to ninety minutes while men sleep, so every erection is not a precious commodity that must be used. In fact, most are never used, without resulting crises.

For their own orgasmic satisfaction, some women demand that their husbands keep their erections and intensity even after ejaculation. That demand is relieved by understanding that most men need a refractory period ranging from twenty minutes to several hours after ejaculation before they can be restimulated to another erection.

Women who inhibit their orgasmic responses are helped greatly by learning two facts. First, the orgasmic response is an active response, so women should be active and participate in going after what their bodies hunger for, rather than merely lying back and hoping it will happen. Second, the facial grimaces, gasping noises, and heavy breathing are involuntary, positive sexual responses. If women inhibit those responses because of discomfort with behavior that is overtly sexual, they will inhibit their orgasms as well.

There are questions that are unique to the virginal premarital couple as they prepare to consummate their marriage. For example, they might ask, "Is there a mess after the act of intercourse? If so, what do you do with it?" Anxiety is relieved by knowing that there will be secretions, which can be handled by having a box of tissues beside the bed, or a hand towel or wash cloth available for wiping. For women who are susceptible to cystitis, it is recommended that they urinate and rinse off their genitals after sexual intercourse.

Some men who are going into marriage as virgins are concerned that when they have an erection their penis points to one side or upward. They worry that this is abnormal and will make intercourse difficult. It is important to know that the penis can be aimed easily in any direction— men's penises vary greatly as to where they point when they are erect. A few women have been concerned that their nipples look ugly when they are aroused or get cold. They think this would be negative and disappointing to a husband. They are greatly relieved to discover that nipple erection is a positive sign of sexual arousal for all women and a "turn-on" for men.

General and specific anatomical and physiological knowledge brings freedom, new discovery, and intensity to the sexual experience.

The Experientially Naive

The experientially naive person has been raised in a social and emotional vacuum. This person's parents did not model affection and sexual express- siveness, and emotions were not easily conveyed within the family. Intensity was not acceptable. The spoken or unspoken goal of the home was to keep the environment even-tempered. Because of this milieu, the person has had minimal or no recognition of sexual stirrings. Without this sexual awareness, there was probably no exploratory play, self-stimulation, or bumbling, junior-high activities. Consequently, this adult may be totally ignorant about being a sexual person. Passionate kissing or touching does not come naturally. In marriage, this naiveness may cause awkwardness about knowing what to do and how to get the bodies together—nothing flows naturally. It is one cause of unconsummated marriages.

Education is vital for the experientially naive and should include both information about the process and facts of a sexual experience, as well as instructions for hands-on sexual encounters. Reading, attending a sexual-enhancement seminar such as our *Enjoying the Gift of Sex*, and being guided through the talking, touching, and teaching exercises of sexual therapy are all positive, life-changing events. In these settings, naive individuals are like empty sponges, ready to soak up anything that is offered to help them. Change is rapid.

The Culturally Misinformed

Despite years of well-publicized sexual facts, our sexually conflicted culture seems to perpetuate numerous erroneous beliefs that are destructive to couples' sexual functioning. Even though the misinformation places demands on both the husband and wife, men seem to propagate many of the myths. Girls are more likely to discover accurate sexual data because they tend to discuss sexuality in an intimate relationship with another girl; whereas, boys are more likely to pick up sexual misinformation because they learn from the "herd." Their learning comes from "cool guy talk" in the locker room, or on the sports field, or from work-place jokes. These stories exaggerate men's prowess, leaving the listener comparing himself, and trying to measure up to the apparent norm.

Common Myths about Masculinity and Femininity. Sometimes education is a matter of refuting prevailing sexual myths. We have addressed some of those myths below:

Myth 1: Some men's penises are not large enough to "satisfy" a woman. Dr. Barry McCarthy, author of *Male Sexual Awareness*, suggests that two out of three men think their penises are smaller than average.[1] The fact is, even though flaccid penis size varies greatly from one man to another, erect penises are pretty much the same. When erect, most penises measure about five to six inches from the symphysis pubis to the meatus. (See Figure 5–6.) Length is irrelevant to satisfying a woman, because the erotic area of the vagina is in the outer or lower one-and-one-half to two inches. This area is controlled by the PC muscle, which becomes engorged during sexual arousal, forming the orgasmic platform. So all a man needs to satisfy a woman is a one-and-a-half- to two-inch erect penis. There is little or no contact between the penis and the area beyond the PC muscle area, because the inner part of the vagina elongates and balloons out. The vagina is an organ of accommodation, and penis size has nothing to do with masculinity or sexual competence.

Myth 2: It is a man's duty to "turn on" a woman. The assumption is that when a woman has difficulty in being aroused or having an orgasm, that difficulty is the result of the man's sexual incompetence. It may be true that the couple does not engage in effective sexual stimulation for the woman, or has inadequate lovemaking patterns, or practices poor sexual techniques. But these problems reflect a *mutual* lack of knowledge. The woman has to become knowledgeable about herself and communicate this awareness to her husband. The man, in turn, needs to be willing to learn and participate effectively. But the project is a joint effort, not a demand on the man to "provide for" the woman.

Myth 3: It is the woman's duty to give the man sexual release. The false assumption behind this myth is that men need sexual release more than women. Thus, even if a woman does not experience arousal or release for herself, she still needs to satisfy him to keep him at home and happy. This demand ultimately leaves both husband and wife unfulfilled.

Myth 4: To be sexually aggressive is not ladylike. This myth can affect the sexual experience for both the husband and the wife. To blatantly admit desire by initiating sexual activity is not congruent with some women's sense of femininity. To these women, sexual aggressiveness is synonymous with maleness. Yet men desire the affirmation of being pursued by their wives. Therefore, women need to be given permission to be overtly sexual and to be taught how to initiate sexual activity.

The view that women are subtly rather than overtly sexual carries over into the actual sexual encounters and may be the basis for some anorgasmia. To be actively enjoying oneself during a sexual experience requires an acceptance of oneself as an overtly sexual person. However, many women are the passive receptacles of their husband's male aggressiveness. They accommodate rather than participate. They only apply one side of the teaching in 1 Corinthians 7, that our bodies are each other's to enjoy. These women believe and practice the idea that their bodies are their husband's to enjoy, but not that they are to actively take pleasure in their husband's bodies, as well. When confronted with this concept, the women say, "But that feels so selfish." The husbands want to scream, "Be selfish. Use me!"

Myth 5: Simultaneous orgasms or female orgasm during intercourse is the ultimate goal in a sexual experience. In fact, this belief can wreak havoc on the husband-wife relationship. The husband, his prowess at stake, believes he is inadequate because he is unable to make it happen. The wife feels like a failure because she cannot respond at the appropriate time. Both falsely believe they are falling short of sexual normalcy.

Sure, it can be fun to have mutual orgasms, and the woman may desire the sensation of orgasm with the penis in the vagina; but neither has anything to do with sexual competence. The fact is that the higher percentage of women do not have orgasms during intercourse. Only a very small percentage of couples report experiencing simultaneous orgasms. And even when it does occur, it is not reported as the ultimate in sexual bliss. In fact, many prefer to take turns in order to double their pleasure. They can enjoy each other's and their own.

Changes that Occur with Aging. Many people get into trouble sexually as they age because they have not been informed about the normal process of aging. Men and women also need to be taught the changes that occur with aging. For example, men's testosterone levels decrease with age and will produce some changes; but these changes do not have to negatively affect the sexual relationship. For women, changes are caused by the reduction of estrogen. Some of these changes are described below:

Change 1. Older men will not feel the sexual urgency they had when they were younger. Their desire will be more similar to women's desire for pleasure and closeness, and the arousal and release that will follow. They can continue to enjoy sex as often as every day; but they will not feel a desperate need for it every day or even every week. The more active they continue to be sexually, the greater the felt need.

Change 2. A man may need direct penile stimulation to become erect. In younger years, just words, thoughts, or the sight of his wife's nude body may have produced a response. Now that response comes as the result of sexual play. Some older men come to us complaining of loss of sexual desire. But when we gather the data, we discover that they have assumed arousal and desire to be synonymous rather than accepting the fact that desire precedes arousal. They expect to come to the sexual experience with an erection as they may have done when they were younger. When the initiative is not the direct response to an erection, they assume they are experiencing loss of desire.

Change 3. The man's erections may not be as firm as in earlier years. That does not mean a man is impotent or unable to perform sexually. Anxiety about the lessened degree of penile fullness may lead to impotence, but the change in penile fullness is the result of aging, and not a sign of impotence.

Change 4. With age, men may need longer and more intense stimulation to bring them to ejaculation. (This is usually a benefit to most women.) Older men also may not need to ejaculate with each sexual encounter. As long as they know this fact, it does not interfere with their pleasure.

Change 5. If their ovaries have not been removed, the primary changes in older women are the thinning of the vaginal walls and the lessening of vaginal lubrication. Both are taken care of by the use of a vaginal lubricant or the use of an estrogen-replacement cream. Neither is a sign of decreasing sexuality. They are only physical changes that result from menopause. The ovaries continue to produce androgen hormones even after natural menopause, and these hormones keep sexual desire alive. However, when surgical menopause (a complete hysterectomy) has taken place as a result of the removal of the ovaries, women may experience a lack of sexual desire. Sometimes small amounts of androgen may be given to aid the return of a woman's sexual drive.

It is a myth that the elderly are not sexual beings—a myth which, unfortunately, is generally accepted in our culture. For the elderly to have sexual desires is often seen by their children or by younger adults as disgusting. The fact is, we are all sexual beings from the moment of birth until death—that is the way God designed us. Elderly people do have sexual and sensual needs. Many times those needs are not being met, but this does not mean the elderly are void of feelings.

The oldest spouses we have counseled for sexual therapy were in their late eighties. They apologized for seeking help at their age. They had always had a fulfilling sexual relationship, but were struggling with some changes. A few sessions later they were happily on their way.[2]

Whether sexual myths are about masculinity, femininity, or aging, they need to be dispelled with accurate information that will free couples of all ages to function fully in their sexual lives.

The Religiously Inhibited

Sexual pleasure has been falsely connected with sin for the religiously inhibited, regardless of their religious orientation. When this connection has been made, the believer has had difficulty enjoying sexual feelings within the sanctified married relationship.

Rich Buhler hosts a popular Christian radio talk show in Los Angeles called "Talk from the Heart." One day when we were the substitute hosts, we chatted about this phenomenon at the opening of the show. Then, for four hours we received telephone calls from Christians who struggled with the dilemma of sexual pleasure and its connection with sin. Each problem had a different history, but the common denominator was the lack of sexual enjoyment in marriage. Some unmarried couples

83

had been sexually active and fulfilled before they became Christians. Then, their Christian mentors required that they no longer live together and that they abstain from sex. As newborn babes in Christ, they heard the message that sex was sin. Now they were married and their previous sinful, but enjoyable, sexual life seemed a far distant past.

Other people had lived promiscuous sexual lives, and then had become Christians, straightening up their lives, meeting and marrying Christians, and expecting sex to be wonderful. But they found they had no sexual desire. Still others had been raised in strict Christian homes with strong teachings against masturbation, with rigid premarital physical boundaries, without much affection between the mother and father, and with no teaching that sex was good and of God. Usually these people felt intense sexual desire during dating, but they felt nothing once married.

Teaching the Bible's pro-sexual message counteracts this association of sex and sin, and pairs religious beliefs with sexual pleasure. It encourages people to invite God into their sexual feelings and experiences. We encourage them to thank God every time they have a sexual thought or feeling. When they do a self-genital exam, they are to focus on the uniqueness of God's creative power. During their sexual experiences, they are to verbally recognize pleasure as a gift from God. Sometimes we bring their spiritual mentors into the therapy process to help teach them a healthy view of the integration of sexuality and spirituality.

In teaching the pro-sexual message, we attempt to show how the religious institution incorporates the cultural limitations of an era and couches them in religious dogma. These innately cultural restrictions are then used inappropriately by the church to put controls on lusty passion within marriage. This inhibition has been perpetuated by the failure of the church to differentiate between God-given, healthy sexual feelings and sexual misbehavior outside of marriage.

Some of the common questions we have received reflect the confusion about spirituality and sexuality:

One man asked, "Biblically speaking, is there any sex technique which is not acceptable? What about oral sex?"

One woman wrote, "My husband and I have fun using sexy words and slang language when we make love. It's exciting for us. Is there anything biblically wrong with this kind of sex play, if it's just between the two of us?"

We are also asked many questions about the rightness of birth control. One person said, "A real hindrance and problem for us is birth control.

We pray but cannot get clear in our minds whether to rely on God's supremacy, all-trustworthiness, etc., or to take responsibility, knowing that his plan for the human body has been set into motion to work as it does (i.e., when a sperm meets an egg, pregnancy results). God does not go against his plan of creation and the technical workings of the body; but on the other hand, if he is truly in control, does he keep a sperm from meeting an egg?" Another asks, "Is there a sensuous, biblical, and effective method of birth control?"

Masturbation is always a question of right and wrong, too. People ask, "What does the Bible say regarding masturbation?" and "What about masturbation in marriage?"

The Gift of Sex provides the information for answering these questions. When the Bible is silent on an issue, we use the Pauline principle that all things are lawful, but not all things are edifying, and one should not be enslaved by anything. We also raise the question of whether the behavior being considered will edify or distract from the couple's relationship with each other and their relationship with God. When the activity being questioned is within the bounds of scriptural teaching, we use biblical passages to give permission to freely enjoy each other as a married couple.

Education has a powerful impact on couples who have failed to engage in effective sexual behavior because one or both of them were physiologically uninformed, experientially naive, culturally misinformed, or religiously inhibited.

EMOTIONAL CAUSES

Emotional barriers and conflicts that are brought to the sexual relationship in marriage often are the source of sexual dysfunction. These emotional factors keep individuals from freely abandoning themselves to the sexual experience and thus interfere with the creatively designed sexual response cycle.

Unconscious Avoidance

Many of God's sexual beings have never allowed themselves the joy of delighting in each other's bodies as did the lovers described in the Song of Solomon. They unconsciously avoid the inevitability of passionate eroticism by keeping obsessed with the tasks of life, pulling away from effective stimulation, or stopping sexual arousal with mundane thoughts of household chores or business contracts.

Why would some individuals exert so much energy fighting what could come so naturally, and then work so hard to try to get the very result they are unconsciously avoiding?

Guilt, whether it is authentic or inauthentic, is one of the arousal stoppers. Authentic guilt occurs when individuals have engaged or are engaging in sexual behaviors that are in conflict with the marriage relationship and Christian values. These behaviors might be affairs, pornography, cross-dressing, voyeurism, or other illicit sexual behaviors. Because these behaviors have not been confessed, forgiven, and brought under control, the bondage of that sin is the source of avoidance of sexual eroticism with one's spouse.

Unfortunately, inauthentic guilt produces the same result. Even though no biblical principle or marriage commitment has been violated, the feelings of guilt are as powerful as if there had been violation. Possible sources of this internally created guilt are previous sexual abuse and rigid antisex teaching, either religious or moral. A woman who comes for therapy to learn to be orgasmic may stop the process because she feels uncomfortable with the results. One woman who had been sexually abused by her stepfather had her first orgasm after our third session. This was too rapid success for someone who would be frightened by the response. She did not have another orgasm for some time after that experience. She verbalized clearly that she did not like being that way even though she had come to therapy to be able to be orgasmic.

One young man who had never ejaculated would stop his wife when she started to intensely stimulate his penis. He had come to therapy to learn to be able to ejaculate with his wife. Many women will not allow the pleasurable process of sexual interaction. They will rush their husbands quickly to intercourse and ejaculation because the erotic sensations are associated with past abuse or past promiscuous relationships.

The most tenacious avoiders of any type of sexual interaction are daughters of alcoholic fathers or women from emotionally tumultuous homes. As young children, there were no firm boundaries to "bounce off of," so they internalized the need to be in control. These women need order and control in all dimensions of their lives, and sex is no exception. It simply causes more havoc, because the control affects their husbands. The adult daughter of an alcoholic typically resists sex with more vehemence than any other individual who lacks sexual desire. The confusion for the husband is great: once he can coerce his wife into sexual activity and when her bodily arousal finally kicks in, she becomes intensely aroused, and has an orgasm; but then she immediately shuts down, does not want to be close, and may even feel badly about what just happened.

The brick wall that may have taken a month of approaching and a half-hour of stimulation to carefully break down piece by piece can reconstruct itself within minutes. It is like a slapstick-comedy movie, with the scenes of the brick and mortar being laid running at high speed. The fear of being out of control is the mortar that holds the bricks together. The scenes of tediously chiseling the mortar away and removing the bricks one by one occur in slow motion, emphasizing the painstaking process.

Anger is another form of unconscious avoidance. In her book, *How to Make Love to the Same Person for the Rest of Your Life and Still Love It,* Dagmar O'Connor recommends that couples learn how to make anger, as well as love. She suggests having a ping-pong ball fight (throwing the balls at each other), a pillow fight in the nude, or other creative methods to release current anger with each another.[3]

But deeper anger is not that easily defused. Sometimes anger has been brought from the past and displaced on the spouse. Other times there is long-term marital tension. One of the hardest angers to undo is the resentment of having had to get married because of pregnancy. Often each spouse blames the other and neither feels he or she chose the other—or was chosen.

When deep, unresolved anger inhibits the sexual process, Dr. Neil Warren's book, *Make Anger Your Ally: Harnessing One of Your Most Powerful Emotions,*[4] is highly recommended for use with couples. This book presents a most helpful program for assessing anger and then making the emotions of anger work for a person, rather than using them against oneself and others.

Lack of self-worth and a poor body image may also keep one from intimacy with the opposite sex. These barriers may not only block sexual desire within marriage, they may actually keep someone from marrying. Women, particularly, who have not accepted themselves will sabotage the development of a marriageable relationship (e.g., by weight gain), even though they consciously want the intimacy of marriage more than anything. Others may marry, but then inhibit the sexual experience because they do not feel worthy of their husbands' attention or cannot believe that their husbands could be attracted to them.

Whether the source of unconscious avoidance is guilt, anger, fear of being out of control, or lack of self-worth, psychotherapeutic intervention should be combined with sexual experiences to resolve the inner conflicts. Pleasuring experiences will inevitably reveal the difficulty with the giving and/or receiving of pleasure and will help to accurately define the exact nature of the conflict.

Blocked Erotic Feelings (Conscious Avoidance)

Sometimes the blocking of eroticism may not be unconscious. It may be deliberate. The woman who came to us to learn to be orgasmic and *was* orgasmic following the third session, then decided she did not want that to happen again. She changed from an unconscious avoider to a deliberate limiter of potentially arousing activities.

Both men and women choose to block erotic feelings for a number of reasons. They may not want to kiss passionately or be stimulated genitally, but most often they are not sure why. They only know that it makes them uncomfortable. Other times, there is a clear belief that eroticism is wrong. One devout Christian man said that he could not imagine the Song of Solomon being in the Bible. Eroticism may be avoided because of fear of emotional or physical pain. Women who have pain during intercourse may refuse to engage in other stimulating activities for fear that those activities will lead to intercourse. At times, both men and women do not allow themselves the vulnerability of intense sexual arousal with their spouses for fear of not being handled tenderly after sharing such intensity.

A physical reason for some women to block intense arousal may be the sensation of having to urinate. A small percentage of women have a flooding response, or female ejaculation, when they are orgasmic. As these women become intensely aroused, the sensation that they are going to urinate if the stimulation is continued causes many of them to inhibit the orgasmic response. Dr. Kolodny of The Masters and Johnson Institute reported to us a number of years ago that the physician at the institute had catheterized women with this response so that their urinary bladders were empty. The women were then stimulated to an orgasmic response by their husbands. The fluid released was collected and examined. It was not urine in chemical composition or in appearance, even though it came from the urinary bladder.

Ladas, Whipple, and Perry discuss the phenomenon of female ejaculation in their book, *The G-Spot*.[5] Women with this sensation are encouraged to read this book and discuss with their husbands the possibility of a fluid release. Then they should protect the bed and "go for it" to see what happens. Many times the result is an intense orgasm.

Conscious blocking of sexual feelings is sometimes used as a way for Christian singles to control sexual behavior before marriage. Unfortunately, when the behavior is controlled by shutting out the feelings rather than through decision-making about behavior and control of external circumstances, the feelings do not automatically turn on again with the words, "I do."

Past Traumatic Experience

Although past traumatic experience may be the source of unconscious avoidance of eroticism, as discussed previously, the impact may manifest itself in other sexual difficulties. We will address some of those difficulties in this section.

Childhood sexual molestation is the most commonly discussed past traumatic experience that leaves a scar on the adult's sexual wholeness. When sexual feelings are stimulated in a child or adolescent by an older person, the child is left confused. Something that is designed to be pleasurable becomes associated with fear, guilt, and pain. If the violator is a family member, trust is betrayed and a sense of aloneness results.

Many times the abuse is not remembered, but there is a pattern that is typical of those who were abused as children. These children have a heightened awareness of sexuality which leads to active sexual expression—maybe even promiscuity—before marriage, and then shuts off as the person moves toward marriage, or shortly after marriage begins. Once sexuality is expected or demanded, there is no interest. There may be aversions or panic reactions to specific activities. A woman may not be able to allow her husband to touch her breasts or stimulate her genitals. Or she may be unable to look at or touch his genitals. The aversion is an indication of the abusive behavior that occurred in the past.

Witnessing explicit sexual activity during childhood can have the same effect as actually being sexually abused. This is one of the hazards of cable television and video use in homes with young children. Sexual awareness beyond developmental readiness is elicited and may be harmful.

Severe parental reaction to peer exploration or self-stimulation can also function as a past trauma. In the same way, when an older sibling acts out sexually and maybe even becomes pregnant, the turmoil in the home may serve as a traumatic event for the younger observer. Being determined that this will never happen to him or her, this younger child may repress sexual feelings and expressions.

Many parents do not realize that spankings on a bare bottom, especially after age eight or nine, will often arouse the involuntary response of erection in boys and vaginal lubrication in girls. The pairing of sexual arousal with the pain of the spanking causes conflict about sexuality, similar to abuse.

Traumatic events of adolescence and young adulthood are also part of the history of sexual dysfunction. Two of the most commonly reported events are premarital sex associated with force or guilt, and traumatic medical examinations. Date rape often is not clearly perceived by either party as rape. There may have been sex play and arousal that led to entry of the penis into the vagina. The female may have verbally resisted while her body gave mixed messages. One young woman reported that she and her date had been engaging in heavy petting when all of a sudden he shifted positions and pushed his penis into her vagina. She pushed him out just as fast as he had entered, yet ten years later, she was unable to consummate her marriage because of vaginismus (the involuntary closing of the muscle controlling the opening of the vagina).

Considering the other common traumatic event that often occurs during adolescence or young adulthood, we beg physicians: When you need to genitally examine or treat a young woman, use extreme caution and extraordinary sensitivity. Many hours and thousands of dollars are spent undoing the trauma of urinary catheterizations or gynecological examinations. We have heard many horror stories. One was of a thirteen-year-old girl (now twenty-six years old with an eight-year unconsummated marriage) who was catheterized by a male physician who laughed at and belittled her when she reacted with fear and started crying. Another was of a nineteen-year-old who had difficulty relaxing for a vaginal exam. The doctor, unable to insert the speculum in the vagina, forced it in so violently that tearing and bleeding resulted—which had to be treated three weeks later by another physician. Insensitive treatment by a physician under the clout of medical necessity can be as traumatizing as rape.

The Need for Guilt and Risk

Either past trauma or rigid antisex teaching can be the stimulus that conditions a person to need guilt or risk in order to become aroused. Masturbation that is associated with guilt and the risk of being caught is the most common source. For this reason, we caution parents not to teach against masturbation. Anti-masturbation teaching does not stop the activity; it only connects sexual pleasure with the "hooking" adrenaline rush that accompanies the anxiety of doing something wrong. Sexual response is easily conditioned in a positive or negative direction. Adrenaline hype adds so much intensity to our sexual response, that even if the adrenaline comes from doing wrong, it hooks us. Then, when sex is right and of God in marriage, we cannot enjoy it. We have become dependent on the adrenaline-guilt connection.

Sexual Anxiety

Anxiety is at the base of most sexual dysfunction, even though developmental lags, educational gaps, or other emotional factors are involved.

Sexual anxiety can occur because of fear of failure, demand for performance, fear of not pleasing one's spouse, or a combination of these factors. Sexual anxiety operates much like insomnia. The parasympathetic nervous system, the relaxed branch of the involuntary nervous system, must be dominant for the involuntary response of sexual arousal or sleep to occur. When a person is anxious, the sympathetic nervous system kicks in. This is the fight-or-flight mechanism which counters relaxation and getting "turned on." Thus, anxiety interrupts sexual arousal.

Women fear the failure of being able to become aroused, have an orgasm, respond in some way that their husbands desire, or produce a desired response in their husbands. Husbands' fears are similar. They fear they will be unable to get or keep an erection, or to hold off from ejaculating too quickly, or to stimulate their wives effectively.

The demand for performance is closely tied with the fear of failure. Such a demand may come from the spouse, or from oneself. It may be a demand from the man for the woman to be orgasmic, from the woman for the man to give her an orgasm, from the woman for the man to get and keep his erection or control his ejaculation, or from the man for the woman to get him erect. Or demand also may come from internal expectations that the person places on himself or herself. Even though the wife might not blame her husband for her orgasmic difficulty, he may believe he is not performing adequately if she is not orgasmic. As a result, the woman feels a need to be orgasmic so that her husband will feel good about himself. The situation turns into a vicious circle.

The need to please becomes tied up with fear of failure and demand for performance as it blocks the focus on the good feelings and inhibits sexual freedom and enjoyment. Consequently, the goal to please becomes counterproductive to actual pleasure. The person whose goal in the experience is to win approval by "doing well" usually feels like a failure because, ironically, trying to "do well" prevents "doing well."

We teach couples to switch from aspiring to please to focusing on pleasure, with each taking responsibility for his or her own sexuality. The couple can then freely enjoy and delight in each other's bodies—this indeed is most pleasurable. It is similar to the central concept of the gospel—when we lose ourselves, we find ourselves. When we give up trying to please and totally lose ourselves to each other, the result is pleasing.

Usually the sensate focus exercises of sexual therapy distract from sexual anxiety and retrain the couple to enjoy each other for the sake of pleasure. One couple had such an extreme combination of fear of failure, performance demand, and excessive need to please that even the nondemand experiences became demands. The wife had an incredible fear of not being aroused and not enjoying the sexual experience. In response, the husband put unbelievable pressure on himself to be a good lover so that she could respond. In addition, his technical analysis—his spectatoring—of each sexual move created a feeling of demand from him for her to respond. They both had a high need to please each other. So even before they started making love, they would be in spectator roles (i.e., watching rather than just participating in the experience).

This situation had to be worked with in daily therapy sessions in order to keep tight control on all factors that might trigger the anxiety. It was important that the wife not become orgasmic too quickly, because then she would feel the demand to analyze how it had happened, study the process, and try to repeat it. Whenever there is an attempt to re-create a positive sexual experience, demand ensues. Each experience must be allowed to evolve on its own. We had to try to teach the husband not to evaluate every move. For example, the wife reported that she was feeling some sexual tingling when doing some self-stimulation exercises we had assigned. The husband's first response was, "Why can't she do that with me?" That evaluative questioning had to be curtailed.

Being able to simply enjoy and love each other without feeling the need to please, demanding performance, or fearing failure is vital to the involuntary mechanisms of sexual responsiveness and the spiritual bonding of two bodies united in holy matrimony.

Destructive Relationship Patterns

The same couple described above as experiencing sexual anxiety could also be used as an example of destructive relationship patterns. Many categories of the causes of sexual problems overlap one another. For this couple, though, the negative pattern was purely sexual. Their other areas of intimacy and commitment were functioning healthily.

The most difficult sexual therapy cases have severe relationship problems mixed with the sexual dysfunction. Most often, intense individual psychotherapy is necessary for one or both of the spouses. Marital counseling may be important in addition to the joint sexual therapy sessions. Again, the *Minnesota Multiphasic Personality Inventory* helps direct this process.

One destructive relationship pattern appears at first to be an individual disorder, but is actually the couple's joint dilemma. When this pattern exists, one spouse comes with limited emotional capacity and may or may not be psychologically dysfunctional. The other is extremely bright, very able to verbalize emotions, very sensitive to being hurt, yet also is able to articulate blame and solution. Initially, the verbal one seems totally healthy. However, with time and skill, the destructiveness of both becomes evident.

Another pattern has the following components: the woman comes to the marriage with sexual immaturity or some sexual barrier (e.g., past abuse or an Adult Child of an Alcoholic [ACA] background); the husband comes feeling unsure of himself in relation to women. Perhaps he lacked adequate affirmation from his mother, had little or no junior-high-level interaction with girls, and/or had limited dating experience. Consequently, his wife's hesitancy about sex becomes the source of his anxiety about his masculinity. Her inhibitions—her inability to initiate sex or to be responsive sexually—give him deep feelings of inadequacy. These feelings in the husband are communicated to the wife as persistent sexual neediness.

As a result, she feels that all he can think of is sex. And he is convinced that she never wants anything to do with sex, even though there is usually a flickering desire that could be kindled with love and warm wooing, rather than with anxious demanding. The husband has usually read and encouraged his wife to read every book available on the subject of sex. He is usually the one who seeks our help; she may participate because of his demand. Usually she is so fed up with sex, she does not want to have anything to do with a sexual therapist.

The husband in this pattern needs to be helped to see his power in the situation and how his neediness thwarts the very response he so desires from his wife. Her barriers may or may not need to be worked on in therapy; they may become insignificant as the husband is able to disconnect his need for sexual release from his sense of self-worth and emotional stability. (See chapter 11.)

Still a third relationship problem occurs when one spouse is a second-choice mate. For example, the wife was engaged before and her fiancé was killed, or he broke the engagement. She is now married to her second choice, and the passion just is not available to her.

Other relationship issues are more superficial and more easily correctable. Effective communication may never have been practiced, so one spouse may have no idea what the other is thinking or feeling sexually. Power struggles with the need for control may also interfere. Or sabotaging patterns may have developed. For example, the husband always likes sex in the morning, but the wife is a night person, so does not want to be awakened in the morning.

Feeling rejected by one's spouse in other areas of intimacy or commitment may make sexual response difficult. If one spouse has violated the spoken or unspoken contract, sexual responsiveness to that spouse may be difficult or even undesired. All of these emotional hindrances, whether deeply problematic or superficially symptomatic, are significant reasons to seek sexual therapy.

CHAPTER EIGHT

ASSESSMENT

ASSESSMENT OF THE SEXUAL DISORDER is the first task of the sexual therapy process. *Precise* assessment is the key to effective sexual therapy! Imagine a mechanic attempting to repair your car without determining the exact mechanical difficulty causing the problem. Surgery for abdominal pain without a thorough diagnostic workup would be out of the question. Likewise, the counselor cannot treat the sexual complaints of a couple without a thorough knowledge of the history and nature of those complaints.

Accurate gathering of a distressed individual's or couple's personal sexual data requires both a *relaxed, qualified therapist and a well-defined assessment system.*

THE ASSESSOR

A relaxed, qualified therapist must manifest certain personal prerequisites in order to function as a sex therapist. (See chapter 2.) A brief review of these qualifications is helpful at this point.

First, the therapist must have an integrated, positive sense of his or her personal sexuality. It is important that married helpers experience a fulfilling, working sexual relationship with their own spouses. And it is vital that single counselors have full awareness of their own sexuality, accompanied by clear decisions regarding sexual actions. All sexual therapists need a planned system of accountability in order to handle their vulnerability for sexual transference. Finally, Christian sexual therapists need a biblical knowledge of sexual teachings and a confident, secure relationship with God.

What about professionalism? Effective therapeutic skills and specific preparation for sexual therapy were also discussed in chapter 2. We will now focus on the *therapeutic style* of the sexual therapist during the process of data gathering.

Picture this example—a couple we have never counseled sits in the waiting room, having been greeted by the receptionist and given several informational forms to complete. We have tended to necessary office details during our ten-minute break between clients, checked our date books for our new clients' names, Ted and Angela, and are ready to greet them. We open the door to the waiting room, about to introduce ourselves and shake hands, when Ted immediately stands up. He introduces himself and with a rapid, anxious voice begins asking questions and explaining how he has completed the forms. We respond calmly and warmly to his concern, and then firmly and professionally steer the conversation to the evaluation process.

Cliff explains that in our practice for the first session he usually meets with the wife and Joyce with the husband. (We have recently reversed this order.) Cliff then invites Angela into his office and likewise, Joyce invites Ted. Joyce motions Ted to a seat, but even before he sits down, he asks, "Do you mind if I pray?" By Ted's actions in the first few moments, it is clear that he is anxious and searching for a way to cope with the uncomfortable task of discussing his sex life.

At moments like this, therapeutic style is of critical importance. It is helpful to have a comfortable, pleasant, nonjudgmental, clinical, matter-of-fact attitude that communicates warmth, but allows safe distance. Being able to pray with Ted not only showed acceptance of his way of handling his anxiety, but also invited God's guidance into the situation. Professional warmth and clinical competence gently led him to share the specific details of his sexual difficulty and sexual interaction with his wife.

How is professional warmth and clinical competence communicated? Each professional has a unique personality, which contributes to his or her interviewing style. Yet some ingredients should be incorporated by all professionals to assist in gathering very private, emotionally loaded sexual content. For the most part, the subjective reports that are accumulated during the interviewing process become the basis for a diagnosis and treatment plan. Thus, it is critical to address and focus on the details that help develop the interviewer's style.

An experience of a number of years ago was most beneficial to improving our interviewing style. We presented a series entitled "Pure and Simple Sex" on a Los Angeles television station's nightly news program. As part of that ten-day series, we filmed sessions with several of our client couples. Seeing ourselves in action was very helpful feedback for improving our interviewing style. For example, attentiveness is a vital ingredient to therapeutic style—the client should experience the therapist's total involvement while sharing personal, sensitive data. Yet, upon seeing herself, Joyce discovered her attentiveness was accompanied by such a serious look on her face that it could have been mistaken for a frown. As a result, she has learned to relax her facial muscles with a more pleasant look while still communicating attentiveness. Cliff saw that he pointed his finger while communicating intensely, which made him come across as scolding. We learned from this experience that the use of a video camera (with appropriate permission from the client) can be a most beneficial learning experience.

We have already mentioned some of the important ingredients of a sexual interviewer's style—professional warmth, clinical competence, and attentiveness, as well as a pleasant, relaxed face with a smile, rather than a frown, and hand movements that are inviting rather than distancing.

Initially, general questions help us connect with counselees emotionally rather than intimidate them. Specific details do need to be gathered until after rapport is established. It is comfortable to chat a bit first, find out where the couple lives, where they are staying in town, or what they talked about on the way to the office. It's helpful to know how they heard about you and how they feel about being there for counseling. We mention that "talking about sex usually makes people anxious," so we find it helpful to dive right in. Usually our first general question is, "What brought you here?"

A matter-of-fact style is the most effective way to gather explicit details of a couple's sexual experience. Use direct terminology that is nontechnical, but avoid slang. In other words, ask about sexual intercourse, not coitus—but do not use "making it." Avoid euphemisms and prudish responses. Making sexual jokes, using street language, or laughing at a client's experience is never acceptable for the counselor, although being familiar with street language is helpful. When clients use slang, repeat back to them your understanding in clinical, nontechnical terms (see chapter 1). Laughing with a client about a humorous event can lighten tension and teach them that sex does not have to be deadly serious business. Laughter can help to ease the tension, especially during the first interview session.

A nonjudgmental approach may be the most difficult quality for the Christian sexual therapist. Some sexual behaviors we believe to be biblically wrong—the Bible is clear about adultery, homosexuality, and other misuses of sex outside of marriage. How do we keep from showing our biases and thereby slanting the accuracy of the data we receive? And how do we balance our responsibility as Christian authorities not to condone sexual misconduct while fulfilling our obligation as therapists to be nonjudgmental? This is an ongoing struggle! If we are empathic, warm, and understanding, clients may believe "the Penners think that what I'm doing is okay." On the other hand, if we communicate dissenting beliefs, we quickly shut doors to the sharing of information that is necessary to guide the couple in finding sexual fulfillment, as well as to help an individual come to grips with the specific sexual behavior. It is a Catch 22!

A suggestion may be helpful—counselors should commit themselves and each of their sessions to God, even as they fulfill their obligations as nonjudgmental therapists. Ask for God's wisdom, presence, and protection, knowing your intention is not to condone sin. Eventually, the therapeutic goals will be consistent with the spiritual goals for Christian clients. They will be at peace with themselves and with God, their behaviors will coincide with their beliefs, and they will function at the center of their beings where Christ abides. Through the counselor's empathy, genuineness, and nonjudgmental warmth, it is hoped that Christian clients, rather than the therapist, will be ready to address "right" and "wrong."

Teaching is also part of the interview style, particularly as counseling progresses. It probably will not take place in the initial interview. In our practice, we correct misinformation and apply specific information as it is requested or seems pertinent to the situation and when it can be imparted without passing judgment.

The sexual therapist must anticipate all issues that might be discussed; he or she should be unshockable. The sexual therapist can neither blush nor lead the client away from difficult but important data.

Eliciting a sexual history from anyone is a necessary invasion into a person's inner experience. Hence, absolute privacy and confidentiality must be assured. Each interviewee needs to be regarded with respect and concern. The client's comfort and welfare is of utmost importance.

The sexual therapeutic relationship, more than any other psychotherapeutic relationship, requires professionalism—a professionalism that portrays availability. A stiff, cold, distant style is as much of a deterrent to collecting accurate details as a disrespectful, nonchalant manner which may make light of a painful situation.

The Rogerian triad of empathy, genuineness, and warmth best exemplifies the therapeutic style we are describing (see chapter 2). These, we believe, are Christ-like qualities. The Christian therapist can exemplify the Philippian Scriptures, practicing the servant leadership that Christ has called us to live. Clients will feel the Christ-like care and acceptance of them as persons, rather than a condoning or condemning of them and their behaviors.

Professional availability; pleasant, Christ-like counseling; and a well-informed interviewing style will provide the environment for clients to disclose their inner beings and private sexual lives. The ultimate goal is that they find the fulfillment of their sexual union that God intended for them to enjoy.

THE ASSESSMENT SYSTEM

Sexual data-gathering requires an organized, systematic approach. The sexual interview needs to be more structured than the typical psychotherapeutic interview for a number of reasons.

First, many people never talk to anyone, not even their spouses, about their sexual feelings, fantasies, or behaviors. Without specific guidance from the interviewer, they do not know how to express what needs to be communicated.

Second, sexual data are loaded with emotion. Structure provides safety for those emotions for both client and therapist. Just as hyperactive children need firm boundaries, so also anxious clients need a sense of definition. When clients seem as if they are "bouncing off the walls," they need to sense that the interviewer is in command of the situation. The interviewer must maintain control of the interview.

On the one hand, "doors" must be opened to allow accurate data to be revealed. On the other hand, doors must be closed when rambling occurs or emotions are stirred that frighten the client. An initial interview that is too volatile may scare the client away from talking about a given area of pain. Therefore, an established format provides the structure to assist the therapist in maintaining control, and in opening and closing doors to self disclosure.

Similarly, the structure of using interview forms may help the therapist's emotions. Sexually explicit information has the potential to stir up incredible emotion in us as therapists. For example, imagine that a beautiful young woman sat directly across from us and shared the gory details and the overwhelming guilt of a saline abortion at age fourteen when she was in her sixth month of pregnancy. She had been naively rushed into the abortion by her mother. As she described the procedure, all of our convictions and feelings about abortion swelled up inside and choked us with their intensity. At that moment, having a structured form to guide the interview might be the harness necessary to bridle our emotions. The structure allows us to empathically reflect the pain that was shared, and put aside our own emotions. As a result, we can focus on the young woman's grief so that she experiences our care, yet senses our ability to move on with the interview.

Third, since sexual therapy is a behavioral retraining program, exact, detailed, and explicit data is necessary. A couple cannot be retrained in new ways of sexual behavior unless there is an accurate picture of their present behavior. Each sexual behavior needs to be defined: how they kiss and what it is like for each of them, when in the intercourse process entry occurs, who initiates entry, and how each would like that to change; and so on for all behaviors.

Structured assessment forms ensure that the therapist gathers *all* the vital information necessary to make professional judgments about the meaning of the data.

For example, when we began our practice as sexual therapists in the mid 1970s, we routinely asked clients about the history of their masturbatory practices. But we never asked them to describe *how* they stimulated themselves. That question became vital when we reached a roadblock with a couple who had an unconsummated marriage. The husband had masturbated to the point of ejaculation since he was twelve or thirteen years old. Since he had experienced an active masturbatory practice, we falsely assumed he could build on and transfer his ability to ejaculate into the process of consummating their marriage. However, we had missed important information—he masturbated by losing his erection and pushing his penis inside his body and rubbing it (making it almost like a clitoris), until he would ejaculate. Obviously, this procedure didn't work for intercourse with his wife. So he had to relearn arousal and release with a full, protruding penis before entry of the penis into the vagina was possible. This was an entirely different training process than we had assumed necessary.

Clearly, an interview structure is essential to obtain complete and accurate information pertinent to a couple's sexual problem. The results allow the counselor to design the behavioral-retraining sexual therapy process, so that the couple can fulfill their sexual goals.

OUR SYSTEM OF EVALUATION

Every text on sexual therapy will have assessment forms: Brauer and Brauer, Kaplan, Masters and Johnson, Pomeroy, and others. We want to share with you our system, both the process and the structure. There is nothing sacred or more right about ours. We simply suggest that you start with forms that you like—ours or other counselors', and adapt them to your style, clientele, and therapeutic needs. We continue to change and improve our assessment system forms as we work with them.

The Process

The actual process of evaluation begins with the initial telephone contact from the client. Although the client should not be engaged in the therapy process over the telephone, it is necessary to gather initial data in order to guide the client to the appropriate help. Questions could be asked, such as: "What is the specific problem you are experiencing sexually?" "What help have you tried thus far?" "Was that effective?" "What led you to us and why?" "If a current therapist is working with you, has he or she approved of our involvement?" "Would you work best with a team, a man, or a woman?"

Once we determine by telephone that sexual therapy is needed and that we are the most qualified and appropriate (financially and otherwise) to work with their dilemma, the evaluation process is scheduled.

The evaluation process begins at our offices. It is most efficient and effective to schedule a three-hour block of time for the initial assessment. The framework for this three-hour session is described below. When clients can afford a team and we judge it to be of benefit to them, we recommend that they start with both of us. But a team approach is not necessary, and most sexual therapists work individually. The process for both an individual counselor and a team approach is described below. The team approach will represent how we function as a male/female team. Our functioning is affected by our particular, individual uniqueness and educational backgrounds. Those specifics may need to be adapted to the comfort and skill of another team.

The Assessment Process Outline
The three-hour assessment might be broken down as follows:

First fifty-minute session:

INDIVIDUAL THERAPIST
Meet with wife.
Husband completes form and tests.

TEAM APPROACH
Male therapist meets with husband to assess "Background History" while female therapist meets with wife for the "Sexual Evaluation" (or vise versa).

Second fifty-minute session:

INDIVIDUAL THERAPIST
Meet with husband.
Wife completes forms and tests.

TEAM APPROACH
Male therapist meets with wife to assess "Background History" while female therapist meets with husband for the "Sexual Evaluation."

Third fifty-minute session:

Therapist or therapy team meets with husband and wife for feedback session. (Use "Sexual Therapy Feedback Session" form.)

The Structure

The forms that follow this section (beginning on page 106) provide structure for the evaluation process. The Physical History form can be given to the couple when they first arrive, to be completed while in the waiting room. If the couple is not finished before we begin the sessions, we ask them to complete them during the ten-minute breaks between sessions.

The Background History and the Sexual Evaluation forms are used to gather data from the clients. The Sexual Therapy Feedback form is used by the therapist(s) to summarize the data and make professional judgments as to the meaning of the information. The data and the interpretations are organized in a way that communicates an understanding of the clients' sexual dysfunction, their goals for the therapy process, and some direction for attaining those goals.

When the couple gives feedback that says, "Finally, someone understands our sexual problem and offers us some hope!" we feel we have accurately assessed the situation. But there are times when this has not happened by the end of the three-hour assessment process.

When that sense of understanding the problem is not present, more data gathering is necessary. We may refer to other professionals for essential data. A urological examination is always necessary when either impotence or retarded ejaculation is the complaint. If genital infections are present, a medical consultation would be in order. The woman who experiences vaginal dryness or pain during intercourse needs to be examined by a gynecologist, and perhaps a gynecologist/urologist who specializes in dyspareunia.

Medical assessment is also needed when the couple has not consummated their marriage. Hormonal studies may be warranted for a lack of sexual desire. When the sexual dysfunction is global rather than situational, careful medical attention is necessary. A routine physical examination is recommended for both partners if they have not had one in the past year or two. If either is receiving medical treatment, that treatment (especially medications) must be understood by the therapist. Contact should be established with the physician.

More psychodynamic assessment may be necessary. Many times we send the *Minnesota Multiphasic Personality Inventory* (MMPI) home to be completed by the couple and returned to us. Their responses are analyzed and reported back to us by a professional scorer and interpreter. Cliff shares this data with each spouse in individual psychotherapy sessions. Other assessment tools such as the Taylor-Johnson Temperament Analysis can also add insight. The goal is to have a complete picture of each spouse and of the couple—their relationship and their patterns of sexual behavior.

The results of the assessment process vary. These assessment results may be the solution to the problem, or the start of positive interaction, or produce no change at all. Occasionally, the assessment process itself brings the desired change. This has happened with relatively newly married couples when the understanding they acquired by explaining the details to us and having us "paint the picture for them," relieves their tension.

It is particularly difficult for a couple to leave the assessment process with more conflict stirred up than was present before the sessions. Fortunately, this only happens occasionally, typically when communication between the spouses is very poor. In these situations, the details of the sexual experience that are gathered from each spouse differ so greatly that it is difficult to believe they belong to each other. Because of the dichotomy of their stories, the feedback session must be handled gingerly. Each spouse needs to be presented with the way the other experiences the sexual relationship. Then, the differences should be tactfully clarified, and hopefully, common goals are defined.

The recommendations at the conclusion of the assessment process will vary with the data and interpretation of that data. For a couple with a healthy, working relationship and solid personalities, self-help may be recommended. In those cases, we write out a plan for the couple to follow, probably using *The Gift of Sex* and/or *A Gift for All Ages*. A follow-up session will be scheduled for six weeks later.

When one person brings some intense intrapersonal conflicts to the relationship, individual therapy will be recommended for that spouse either before or in conjunction with the couple's sexual therapy. A relationship may require marital counseling rather than sexual therapy; however, sometimes we pursue sexual therapy in spite of the interpersonal conflicts. We employ sexual therapy as a means to spotlight and work on the interpersonal issues.

Sexual therapy is recommended when the following problems exist:

1. A difference in sexual desire or inhibited desire for one or both spouses;
2. Frustration with any aspect of the sexual experience;
3. Anxiety about sexual performance or response;
4. Inability to respond in some way that is desired;
5. Blocked sexual feelings;
6. Inability to talk about sex;

7. Guilt or conflict about sex;
8. Pain or inability to have sexual intercourse; or
9. Any negative patterns of sexual functioning.

Sexual therapy can be pursued in two ways: either in an intensive session or on a weekly basis over time. In an *intensive* session, the couple is seen for one session every day for ten days to two weeks. This is recommended for two reasons:

1. Barriers are present that need to be broken down (blasted through). Weekly sessions would allow the defenses to keep the barriers intact.
2. Conditioning is essential to the retraining process. For example, most cases of premature ejaculation, orgasmic inhibition, and impotence respond with fewer sessions when treatment is conducted on an intensive rather than weekly sessions.

Weekly sexual therapy sessions are recommended for the following reasons:

1. For the above conditions (see numbers 1 and 2 above) when an intensive session is impossible from a practical sense;
2. The family system interferes with sexual functioning;
3. Relationship issues need to be dealt with concurrent to the sexual retraining;
4. The treatment of sexual desire problems that are major, not secondary to sexual dysfunction;
5. The therapist(s) anticipate that too-rapid success will thwart the retraining process;
6. Sexual abuse, rigid antisex teachings, or other deeper issues are known or thought to be the cause of the sexual difficulty.

It is helpful to leave the recommendations for treatment open-ended. For example, the therapists might say, "This strategy is our first choice, but another approach is also a very viable option. If you choose this approach, and it is not connecting for you, let us know and we will reconsider."

Even the most thorough assessment is dependent upon the accuracy of the clients' subjective reports. Therefore, ongoing observation for new or confirming data is necessary to the therapy process that follows. On the following pages are the four assessment forms used by the authors in sexual therapy. These may be duplicated for counselor use without obtaining permission from the author or publisher.

Initial Assessment
Form 1

Physical History
(To be completed by client)

Name: _____
Date: _____
Age: _____
Height: _____
Weight: _____

I. Health History (birth to present):

General Description	Illness and Treatments	Surgical Operations
Childhood:		
Adolescence:		
Adulthood:		

Were you a bed wetter? _____ If so, how was that handled?

  Until what age? _____

II. Current Health:

General Description	Illness and Treatments	Surgical Operations

Specific Difficulties (Circle any of the following that apply to you):

headaches	loss of appetite	sedatives usage
dizziness	bowel disturbances	depression
fainting spells	fatigue	anxiousness or fears
palpitations	insomnia	suicidal thoughts
stomach trouble	nightmares	alcoholism

Allergies:

Special Diet:

List any and all medications you are currently taking:

Substance Intake: If yes:

	yes	no	frequency	amount	type
Tobacco					
Alcohol					
Non-prescription drugs					
Other					

Other illnesses or difficulties within the family:

III. Mental Health:
Describe how you usually feel emotionally?

What mental health difficulties have been a struggle for you?

How have these been diagnosed and treated?

Are you currently being treated? ___ By whom?_____

IV. Medical Tests:

If you have been tested for any of the following, please list the results of those tests:
    Thyroid function___
    Hormonal levels___
    Diabetes___
    Cardiovascular Disease___
    Sexually Transmitted Disease___
    Other___

V. Reproductive and Sexual Health Status: Men

Age of first ejaculation?____Did this occur by: wet dream (nocturnal emission), self-stimulation (masturbation), or sexual play with another person? Circle the response that applies to you.

Describe any difficulty you had as a child with your:
    breasts___
    penis___
    testes___
    rectum___
    other reproductive or sexually related functions

Describe any difficulty you've had as an adult or have now with your:
    breasts___
    penis___
    testes___
    rectum___
    prostate___
    other___

List any genital infections and sexually transmitted diseases that you have had or currently have:

Genital Disease or STD	Dates of Infection	Treatments and Results

What form(s) of birth control have you and your wife used?

How did you respond? (Did you like it? Did it interfere? etc.)

VI. Reproductive and Sexual Health Status: Women

Menstrual History:
    Age of first period (menses) _____
    What preparation had you received?

What was your reaction to your first period?

Describe any menstrual difficulties:

Are you regular?
Do you have pain?
Do you experience mood or physical changes before your period (PMS)?
Describe:

Reproductive History:

	Age	Describe	Complications
Pregnancies:			
Deliveries:			
Miscarriages:			
Abortions:			
Infertility problems:			

Describe any difficulty you had as a child with your:
    breasts____
    genitals____
    vagina____
    urethra or bladder____
    rectum____
    uterus or cervix____
    other____
Describe any difficulty you have had or now have as an adult with any of the above areas of your body_____

Do you have frequent vaginal or urinary infections?____ If so, what kind?

    Treatment?

List any genital infections and sexually transmitted diseases (STD) you have had or currently have:

Genital Disease or STD	Dates of Infection	Treatments and Results

What form(s) of birth control have you and your husband used?

    How did you respond (Did you like it? Did it interfere? etc.)?

Initial Assessment
Form 2

Background History
(To be used by the therapist)

Name: _____
Date: _____

Family History:
Describe your family of origin.

Who lived in the household? Describe each person:

Relationship with your mother? Her attitude toward you?

Relationship with your father? His attitude toward you?

Relationship with each of your siblings?

Parents' relationship with each other?

What was your impression of your household?

How were you punished as a child?

Sexual Development:
    Parents' attitudes toward sex_____

    Education about sex:
    When?

    What?

    By whom?

Sexual Experimentation:
    Exploratory Play?   When?   Reaction?

    Peer input: sex play?   dirty jokes?

    pornography?   other?

    Masturbation:
    History of:

    Technique (How?):

Feelings and teachings about?

Homosexual play and/or fantasies:

Sexual Abuse :
How was nudity handled in your home?

As a child, were you ever exposed to an adolescent's or adult's body in a way that made you feel uncomfortable?

Were you ever touched on your breasts or genitals by an adolescent or adult?

Were sexual or uncomfortable feelings ever stirred up in you in relation to an older person?

At what age did you first witness an explicit sexual scene in each of the following?

On Television?　　Movies?　　Magazines?　　Other?

Dating History :
First date or romance?

Others?

Spouse?

Age of first sexual intercourse? _____
Describe the circumstances:

Your reaction:

Marital History :
First Marriage: Date?   How long?

If terminated, why?

Other marriages:

Current marriage: Date?   How long?

Areas of compatibility:

Areas of tension:

Children:

Describe the atmosphere in your household:

Religious History:
Home influence:

Church experience and influence:

Personal faith and beliefs:

Personal Data:
What fearful or distressing experiences have you never shared?

How would you describe:
Yourself?

Your spouse?

Initial Assessment
Form 3

Sexual Evaluation
(To be used by the therapist)

Name: _____

Date: _____

Get acquainted:
Referring party:
What particular sexual difficulty are you experiencing?

How is it affecting:
  You?

  Your spouse?

When and how did the problem first develop?

What have you done about it (other counseling, reading, self-help, etc.)?

Which one of you initiated your coming?

Details of Sexual Experience :
  Frequency:

  Desire:

  Initiation: (Who? How? When? Where? How would you like it
  to be different?)

Pleasuring and stimulation: What actually happens?
   Kissing:

   Total body caressing:

   Breasts:

   Genitals: (Response to being touched; response to your spouse's genitals)

   Entry: (Who determines? When does it occur? How does it feel?)

   Arousal: (What stimulates it? Any problems? etc.)
      For him:

      For her:

   Orgasm (when):
      For him:

      For her:

What sexual activities cause conflict between the two of you?

117

What are your feelings following intercourse?

What happens after intercourse?

How would you like your sexual life to be? (What are your goals?)

What difference would those changes make:
   For you as a person?

   For your relationship as a couple?

Initial Assessment
Form 4

Sexual Assessment Feedback
(To be used by the therapist)

Name _____
Date _____

An Overall Picture of the Sexual Problem:
Paint a verbal picture of the sexual problem:

Describe what each spouse brought to the marriage that contributes to the current sexual problem:

Describe how the problem developed between husband and wife:

Describe how the marital relationship has kept the problem going (how each feeds the dilemma):

Identify the patterns of sexual dysfunction:

Clarify differences in the data as each spouse has reported it:

Goals for Therapy:
　　Reflect back to the couple their sexual therapy goals:
　　Husband's:

　　Wife's:

　　Compare their personal goals with the therapeutic goals:

Therapy Plan :
　　Recommendations for treatment:
　　Possibilities include:
　　　　Individual therapy
　　　　Marital counseling
　　　　Intensive sex therapy
　　　　Weekly sex therapy
　　　　Self-help

　　Define the recommended treatment process:

　　Format for Sex Therapy =
　　Weekly sessions: one fifty-minute session per week
　　Intensive: one fifty-minute session every day for ten days
　　to two weeks
　　Experiences are assigned for:
　　　　Teaching
　　　　Touching
　　　　Talking

These experiences require three, two- to three-hour blocks of time for the couple between counseling sessions. Intercourse is not allowed during the therapy process until it is prescribed. The completed experiences are discussed at the following session.

CHAPTER NINE

SEXUAL THERAPY

THE SEXUAL THERAPY PROCESS is informed by the results of the assessment. The data were gathered and interpreted, the goals were defined, and the treatment plan was recommended. Now the retraining-therapy process begins.

THE PROCESS

Initially, the sexual therapy process is the same, despite the problem. The specific treatment format becomes individualized to the disorders and the desired goals as the process progresses. Prescribed sexual experiences and psychotherapy are the ingredients common to all sexual therapy. The sessions may be conducted by one therapist, male or female, or by co-therapists. The co-therapy team may include a medically trained professional and a psychologically prepared professional. Or both therapists may be educated in either field. The team may be a male-female team or a same-gender team.

The therapy plan may be designed for a limited period of time, such as our ten-day to two-week intensive therapy, which we refer to simply as an "intensive." In this period of time, the couple meets with the therapist or team every day for one session. Not all sexual therapy is conducted in such a time-limited approach, however. The counselors may see the couple one to three times a week for a limited or unlimited length of time.

Sometimes it is recommended that a couple leave home during the treatment assignments. Other times, the distractions of the home are removed for a limited time, or designated times are set aside each week for the couple to be able to complete the assignments without distraction. Individual therapy, couple therapy, group therapy for individuals, and couples groups are all possibilities, although the most common approach is couple therapy.

During the retraining therapy process, the therapist is actively in control, and the guidelines are clearly defined. (Refer to the Guidelines for Sexual Therapy, page 132.) Limitations regarding sexual activities are an important part of the learning process. These need to be clearly adhered to in order to build trust. Intercourse or attempts at intercourse are usually ruled out. This restriction typically brings relief from demand rather than disappointment. Specific teaching, talking, and touching experiences are assigned (see pages 132–175). These exercises follow a graduated process of learning. The couple starts as if they are embarking on their sexual relationship for the first time.

In contrast to traditional psychotherapy, it is the specific behavioral assignments—the teaching, talking, and touching exercises—that the therapist prescribes and the couple completes alone together which are the key to producing the necessary change. These exercises are listed on pages 127–131 in the order typically assigned. This list is the Sexual Therapy Plan which is used by the therapist to log the experiences assigned and to write the comments the clients report in response to each exercise they have completed.

During the first session after the initial assessment, the therapists explain the guidelines (page 132) to the couple. The Principles for

Bodily Pleasure (pages 133–134) and the Communication Format (page 135) are introduced. Then the specific assignments are given. The therapist should enter the names of each spouse where appropriate on each form. The assignments the couples are given to complete during the first twenty-four-hour period of the intensive therapy, or the first week of a weekly session program, are:

1. Read aloud together and discuss the Guidelines for Sexual Therapy, the Underlying Principles for Bodily Pleasuring, and the Communication Format.
2. Individually complete A Sexual Assessment (pages 136–138), and then share with each other using the directions of the Communication Format.
3. Read aloud together, discuss, and then follow the typed instructions for the Foot and Hand Caress (page 139).
4. Read aloud together, discuss, and then follow the typed instructions for the Body Awareness-Mirror assignment (page 140).

All hindrances to proceeding with the exercises are hopefully avoided by deciding every behavioral detail during the sessions with the therapist. Specific periods of time are selected for these assignments to be completed. For example, the first exercise might be assigned for 1 P.M. on Monday, the second for 4 P.M., the third for 7 P.M. and the fourth for 9 A.M. on Tuesday. One spouse is assigned responsibility for choosing the setting, creating a pleasant atmosphere, and initiating the event. The other spouse is the first active participant in the event; that is, the first one to pleasure, to share, or to teach. The responsibility is reversed for each assignment, so that the couple takes turns being the initiator versus the first active participant.

The couple is encouraged to allow two to three hours for each assignment. This means they should start the exercise two to three hours before they will need to stop for eating, sleeping, or any other commitment. Once they have *allowed* the time, then they are to ignore it. We recommend they have no watch or clock within sight. The purpose is not to fill the two to three hours, but rather to listen and respond from within, without feeling rushed or time oriented.

The touching exercises—the sensate focus exercises or bodily caresses—allow the couple to learn to enjoy each other's bodies for their own pleasure when touching, and to soak in the pleasure when being touched. All demands are removed. Any anxious or negative feelings are to be expressed, the anxiety-provoking behavior stopped, and new distracting activities are to be initiated. Thus, new patterns of physical relating are being established as they each are developing an awareness of their own sensations and taking responsibility to pursue their desires and communicate their needs, but not at the expense of the other.

The teaching exercises guide the couple to learn about their own and each other's bodies (Self-exams, Assignment 11; Body Awareness, Assignment 4; Clinical Genital Exam, Assignment 15; and Vaginal Exam, Assignment 16). In the Nondemand Teaching Exercise, they also guide and verbally teach each other about the type of touch they most enjoy.

The communication exercises serve to both open communication concerning their sexual experience, as well as teach each other about their sexual experience (Defining Your Sexual Experience, Assignment 18) and about their sexual responses (Graphing Your Sexual Response, Assignment 13).

The later, more creative assignments, such as the Pleasuring, "No Hands," and Creative Pleasuring assignments help them realize the fun and enjoyment of each other's bodies, minds, and spirits without a goal-oriented focus of intercourse or orgasm.

At the second session and all subsequent sessions, the couple shares the details of and their reactions to what happened in the assigned experiences. Emotional barriers that block further progress in the sexual therapy process are likely to surface. The first difficulty may arise in reaction to the Body Awareness-Mirror assignment. When resistance to doing an assignment is expressed, it is important to address those fears and concerns. Sometimes the experience is modified to make it less threatening. Sometimes the experience is delayed. And sometimes the assignment is not as difficult as the client anticipates.

Other times the therapy process of dealing with the resistance resolves the issue of concern. Safety may need to be assured. Psychotherapy is enacted to deal with the barriers, and the behavioral assignments are adjusted to adapt to the barriers. It is the ability to assess the need for and make necessary creative adjustments which will produce a sexual therapist who is highly successful in dealing with tough barriers. The determination to find a way, along with the use of the detailed, structured directions are the keys to a happy outcome. At *all* times, the couple is encouraged to communicate their feelings with each other and the therapist(s).

At the end of the second session, the assignments are given and time periods selected for the next twenty-four hours or the next week. And that is how the process proceeds. Although alterations are made for each couple, the assignments are usually given in the following sequence:

First Session—Guidelines for Sexual Therapy, Underlying Principles for Bodily Pleasuring, and the Communication Format (Communication Exercise)

> A Sexual Assessment (Communication)
> Foot and Hand Caress (Teaching)
> Body Awareness-Mirror (Teaching)

Second Session—Facial Caress (Touching Experience)

> My Sexual Development (Communication)
> Back Caress (Touching)

Third Session—Sharing Myself (Communication)

> Total Body: Excluding Breasts and Genitals (Touching—Therapist must emphasize respect of the boundaries)
> Female Self-Exam and PC Muscle Exercise are usually combined (Teaching)
> Male Self-Exam (Teaching)

Fourth Session—Graphing Your Sexual Response (Teaching)

> Total Body including breast and genitals, generally—not for stimulation (Touching)
> Clinical Genital Exam and Vaginal Exam are usually combined, but not when the client has vaginismus (Touching)

Fifth Session—Nondemand Teaching (Touching/Teaching)

> Defining Your Sexual Experience (Communication)
> Kissing Exercise (Touching/Teaching)

Sixth Session—You and Me (Communication)

> Creative Pleasuring (Touching/Fun)
> Simulating Arousal Response (Teaching), this is especially important for anorgasmic women and for men with difficulty ejaculating

Seventh Session—Total Body, with breast and genital stimulation (Touching)

> Sharing Love (Communication)
> Reading Assignments (Teaching)

Eighth Session—Pleasuring, No Hands—Using the Penis as a Paint Brush (Touching)

Ninth Session—Total Body Pleasuring with Mutual Manual Stimulation
(Touching)
   Principles Learned Applicable to Ongoing Life Together (Teaching)
Tenth Session—Total Body Pleasuring, Entry by Invitation (Touching)
   Application of Learning to Home Life—Making a Plan (Communication)

Assignments are often repeated, so the plan does not always go exactly as outlined here. Additional exercises are also created in the therapy process to address unique barriers. And the exercises specific to certain problems are incorporated in the process. These exercises will be discussed in the following chapters.

The sexual therapy process is terminated when the symptoms are relieved and the goals have been realized. An evaluation session with the couple and the therapist(s) is suggested to assess the results of the process. In this session we review how each spouse saw the problem at the time of the initial interview, and compare that assessment with his or her current view of the sexual situation. Determine which of the couple's original goals have been actualized. Of the goals that have not been achieved, decide what needs to be done, if anything. Some goals may no longer seem important. Have the partners discuss the effects of the therapy, both positive and negative. Then address their questions and concerns. Have them consider where they see themselves now and where they would like to be.

After the evaluation session, any additional therapeutic goals are pursued. Then the termination and follow-up plan is determined.

THE SEXUAL THERAPY PLAN

The Sexual Therapy Plan which follows lists thirty-one assignments which are common to all sexual therapy. They are followed by specific assignments unique to a particular sexual dilemma, which will be addressed in later chapters.

Sexual Therapy Plan
(for the therapist's records)
© Copyright 1990
Penner & Penner

FOR: _____

Experiences	C = Communicating (Talking)
	P = Pleasuring (Touching)
	T = Teaching

Comments

1.   C: Guidelines for Sexual Therapy
       Underlying Principles
       for Bodily Pleasure,
       Communication Format

2.   C: A Sexual Assessment

3.   P: Foot and Hand Caress

4.   T: Body Awareness-Mirror
       (Postpone until later if
       nudity is difficult)

5.   P: Facial Caress

6.   C: My Sexual Development

7.   P: Back Caress

8.   T: Bathe/Shower Together
       (No written instructions)
       Instruct each couple according
       to their need for safety vs.
       freedom)

9. C: Sharing Myself

        _____
        _____
        _____
        _____

10. P: Total Body Pleasuring,
    Excluding Breasts
    and Genitals

11. T: Female and
    Male Self-Exam

12. T: PC Muscle Exercise

13. C: Graphing Your
    Sexual Response

14. P: Total Body Pleasuring,
    Including Breasts and
    Genitals, Without
    Purposeful Stimulation

15. T: Clinical Genital Exam

16. T: Vaginal Exam

17. T: Nondemand Teaching

18. C: Defining Your Sexual
    Experience

    _____
    _____
    _____
    _____

19. T: Kissing Exercise

    _____
    _____
    _____

20. C: You and Me

    _____
    _____
    _____

21. P: Creative Pleasuring

    _____
    _____
    _____

22. T: Simulating Arousal Responses

    _____
    _____
    _____

23. C: Assigned Readings
    and Discussion

    _____
    _____
    _____
    _____

24. P: Total Body Pleasuring,
    with Breast and
    Genital Stimulation

    _____
    _____
    _____
    _____
    _____

25. C: Sharing Love

    _____
    _____
    _____

26. P: Pleasuring Not Using
    Hands (Penis as a
    Paint Brush)

    _____
    _____
    _____
    _____
    _____

27. T: Shared Self-Stimulation
    (Optional)

    _____
    _____
    _____
    _____
    _____

28. P: Total Body and Mutual
     Manual Stimulation

29. C: Principles Learned
     Applicable to Ongoing
     Life Together

30. P: Total Body Pleasuring,
     Entry by Invitation

31. C: Application of Learning
     to Life: Making a Plan

For Women with Orgasmic or Trust Barriers:

1. Redefine Goal

2. Nondemand Pleasuring
     to Build Trust (from McCarthy
     and McCarthy)

3. Self-Stimulation Steps
     (Optional)

4. Simulating Arousal Responses
     During Pleasuring

5. Female Exaggerations
     (Parasympathetic Nervous
     System to Sympathetic
     Nervous System)

6. Verbalize "Spectatoring"

For Men with Premature Ejaculation:

1. Squeeze
   No entry, no ejaculation
   No entry, ejaculation
   Entry, quiet vagina
   Entry, quiet, thrust
   Entry and ejaculation
2. Stop/Start

For Vaginismus:

1. Dialators
2. PC Muscle Exercise
3. Journal/Log

For Impotence:

1. Naming Genitals
2. Patting and Affirming
   Genitals
3. Penis as a Paint Brush
4. Poking into Vagina
   in JND (just noticeable
   difference)
5. Verbalize "Spectatoring"
6. Distract and Affirm

For Retarded Ejaculation:
(Refer to detailed plan in chapter 13).

THE SEXUAL THERAPY ASSIGNMENTS

The balance of this chapter is comprised of thirty-one assignments the counselor can use in the sexual therapy process. Read these carefully so as to be familiar with the whole step-by-step plan.

Date:_____

Time:_____

Sexual Therapy Assignment 1A
Guidelines for Sexual Therapy

1. No sexual intercourse or attempts at intercourse should be made until it is decided upon as part of the experience. (If you should go ahead before recommended, please let us know so that we can adjust the therapy plan accordingly.)

2. You may repeat any previously assigned experience, but don't go ahead of what has been assigned.

3. Responsibility will be assigned to one spouse to initiate each experience. When you are assigned to initiate an experience, you will be responsible to set the atmosphere. Be creative with the setting. Try to vary the location and the accoutrements (candles, music, etc.). Select a setting different from that of your usual sexual experiences.

4. Allow one to three hours for each experience. Once the time period is available, turn clocks around and ignore the time. You may set an alarm for the maximum time you have available. There is no need to fill the time allowed.

5. Protect against interruptions by turning off the telephone and doorbell, locking all doors, and putting pets outside.

6. Even though there will be a need to push through barriers, there should be no negative experiences. Demands or anxieties should be verbalized the moment they are felt. It's better not to complete the exercise than to repeat past negative patterns and feelings.

7. The moment you feel anxiety, demand, or uncomfortable touch, verbalize your feelings, talk about them, and come at the experience again in another way.

8. The focus of all touching experiences will be pleasure. As long as it feels comfortable or it is not negative, the experience has been successful. As both pleasurer and receiver, your goal is to learn how to soak in the pleasure of the other person's body (refer to Underlying Principles for Bodily Pleasuring in Sexual Therapy Assignment 1B).

9. After each experience, talk about your reactions and feelings. Listen carefully and try to understand how your spouse feels without evaluating or judging his or her reaction. Each spouse's reactions are valid.

Date:_____

Time:_____

Sexual Therapy Assignment 1B
Underlying Principles for Bodily Pleasuring

1. **Concept of Mutuality:** 1 Corinthians 7:3–5 teaches that our bodies are each other's to enjoy. This mutuality works best when pleasuring is scheduled into our lives on a regular basis and when it is free from demand for arousal, release, or intercourse. The only expectation is that we give our bodies to each other for mutual pleasure. Pleasure cannot be demanded from each other, but rather is freely sought after.

2. **Sexual Arousal and Responsiveness:** These involuntary processes may occur when we are relaxed and soaking in sexual pleasure, but they cannot be the goal. When we *try* to get aroused or *try* to have an orgasm, our *trying* is likely to interfere with the natural bodily responses. That is why it is important to distract from any anxiety about responsiveness by verbalizing when we feel that demand. In all pleasuring exercises, *do not become concerned if there is or is not arousal.*

3. **Body Awareness/Sensate Focus:** *The purpose of the pleasuring exercises is body awareness.* They are not to be therapeutic massages, but rather sensuous touches that communicate warmth. Even though our bodies are designed for pleasure, many of us have not learned to enjoy the giving and receiving of bodily pleasure.

4. **Receiving and Pleasuring:** As both pleasurer and receiver, we must take responsibility for discovering, communicating, and going after our sexual feelings and needs, but not at the other's expense. Demand is reduced when we can count on each other to share from within, rather than expecting the other to produce a response in us. We *can* give our bodies to each other to enjoy, but *cannot* produce in each other the involuntary response of sexual arousal and release. Therefore, as

Receiver: Your only task is to soak in the pleasure and to redirect the pleasurer when the touch is not pleasing. Check with your spouse if at any time you become concerned that he or she is not enjoying himself or herself.

Pleasurer: Your task is to lovingly touch your spouse in a way that feels good to you, enjoying his or her body for your pleasure. Think of radiating warmth through your fingertips (or any other part of your body) and taking in the sensation of warmth and the pulsation of your spouse's body. You might imagine that you are a blind person discovering your spouse through touch.

133

Trust that your spouse will redirect you if what you are doing is negative to him or her. Express your concern if at any time you become anxious rather than enjoying your spouse's body. Caress SLOWLY. *Take time to mesh, relax, and discover* the kind of touch that feels best to both of you.

5. **Counteracting Interferences to Body Pleasure**:

   a. *Not taking enough time to mesh, feeling rushed:* Schedule one- to three-hour blocks of time free of distractions and interruptions. Follow all the preparatory steps for each experience.

   b. *Anxiety about sexual performance or fear of failure:* If *anything* in a sexual therapy assignment feels like a demand that you could fail, redefine it until there is no way you can fail. Talk with us.

   c. *Uncomfortableness with bodily pleasure:* If there is a belief that bodily pleasure is wrong, let's talk about that—include your spiritual mentor and the Bible. If you notice yourself pulling away from good feelings, consciously work on moving your body toward the source of touch that is producing those feelings. Talk about the conflict.

   d. *Barriers, aversions, or panic reactions:* When you come up against a brick wall, stop and talk about it and try approaching the experience differently. We work around the brick wall rather than blast through it. Sometimes, though, we encourage you to push against the brick wall to see if it might tumble.

   e. *Inability to let go and be out of control:* Reducing fears and self-consciousness requires building trust, feeling affirmed, and accepting the intensity of natural arousal responses.

Have Fun! Learn to laugh and cry together as you move through the process.

Date:_____

Time:_____

Sexual Therapy Assignment 1C
Communication Format

For all communication exercises, the goals are learning to actively listen and learning to share honestly and openly with no sense of judgment from each other. There are no right or wrong answers, only your responses. The communication forms are to stimulate your thinking individually and your communication with each other. Do not limit yourselves to the exact response requested.

Complete each communication form individually. Then share with each other using this format:

1. Partner #1 will share his or her response.

2. Partner #2 will not be thinking about his or her own response, but will be attempting to understand what Partner #1 is really thinking and feeling. He or she will provide feedback of what he or she has understood Partner #1 to mean.

3. Partner #1 will confirm, clarify, or expand what was fed back.

4. When both are clear that the message has been communicated and received accurately, reverse roles.

Date:_____

Time:_____

Sexual Therapy Assignment 2
A Sexual Assessment

Assess where you are sexually by completing the following form. Work privately. Do this as quickly as you can. Do not spend time deliberating over each response. Your most immediate, spontaneous response will be the most accurate answer you can give. Note that you are responding in terms of knowledge, feelings, attitudes, and behaviors.

1. Knowledge: (Complete each of the sentences as honestly as you can.)

   a. Physiological:
   When it is said that our sexual response is a natural bodily function, I understand that to mean _____

   _____

   b. Psychological:
   Every individual needs sexual fulfillment because _____

   _____

   _____

   c. Biblical:
   The Bible teaches that sexual pleasure within the marriage relationship is

   _____

   _____

2. Feelings: (Complete each of the sentences as honestly as you can.)
   When I become aware of my sexual feelings, I feel _____

   _____

   Ten years ago my feelings about sex were _____

   _____

   _____

   Now when I make love I feel _____

   _____

   _____

   The best feeling in a sexual experience is _____

   _____

   _____

Share your responses using the Communication Format.

3. Attitudes: (Check the column that is closest to your response to the statements below)

	Agree	Disagree	Uncertain
Sex is one of the most beautiful aspects of life	_____	_____	_____
It is more enjoyable to give than to receive	_____	_____	_____
Bodily pleasure is fleshly and not of God	_____	_____	_____
Sexual intercourse is primarily for physical release	_____	_____	_____
My religious beliefs have the greatest influence on our attitudes toward sexual behaviors	_____	_____	_____
Men and women have equal right to sexual pleasure	_____	_____	_____
There are sexual activities that I would consider wrong for a married couple to practice	_____	_____	_____
If you agree with the above, please list:	_____	_____	_____
To be satisfying, intercourse must lead to simultaneous orgasm	_____	_____	_____
Sexual fantasies are normal	_____	_____	_____
Masturbation (self-stimulation) is an acceptable means for sexual pleasuring and release	_____	_____	_____
The male should be the aggressor in sexual activity	_____	_____	_____
In general, women do not enjoy sex as much as men do	_____	_____	_____
Men should be allowed more freedom in sexual behavior than women	_____	_____	_____
The quality of a sexual relationship is more than just the physical release	_____	_____	_____

Comparing Your Attitudes:

a. Hold your papers side by side and compare your responses.

b. Briefly talk about each of your feelings behind your responses, especially the statements that one or both of you had strong feelings about. Notice where your responses agree and disagree with each other.

4. Behaviors:

Lovemaking is a good experience for me: Yes_____ No_____

We make love ___ time(s) a month. Woman initiates ____ percent of the time; man initiates ___ percent.

I would like to enhance the sexual fulfillment aspect of our marriage by working on the following areas: (check as many as desired)
_____frequency of intercourse
_____variety within the lovemaking experience
_____interest: for myself _____ for my partner _____
_____change in pattern of initiation
_____control of ejaculation for the man
_____orgasmic responsiveness for the woman
_____ease of gaining and keeping an erection for the man
_____reducing pain for the woman
_____general pleasuring of each other's body
_____freedom of sexual activity between my partner and me
_____other:

Comparing Your Responses:

1. Compare and discuss.

2. Determine individually and then together which is the most important area to work on together.

Date:_____
Time:_____

Sexual Therapy Assignment 3
Foot and Hand Caress

Step 1:   _____ will take responsibility to initiate this experience and set the atmosphere. Choose a location in which the receiver can be seated or reclined in a comfortable, upholstered, high-backed chair or couch. The pleasurer should be positioned to be able to comfortably caress the receiver's feet and hands.

Step 2:   Bathe or shower individually. Wear comfortable clothes or robes. You may bring a pan of warm, soapy water to soak each other's feet if you both desire.

Step 3:   _____ will be the first pleasurer, _____ will be the first receiver.

Step 4:   Read Underlying Principles for Bodily Pleasuring in assignment 1B. Read and discuss the current assignment.

Step 5:   *Receiver:* Get comfortable in the chair or couch selected. Lie back and close your eyes. Breathe in deeply and exhale slowly several times, letting your body sink into the chair or couch. Soak in the gift of your spouse's touch. If your feet should feel ticklish, this is a positive sign of intense responsiveness. To relieve the ticklishness and help you receive the sensuous touch, focus on the sensations of the skin contact. You may need to direct your spouse to touch more firmly and/or move to a different part of your foot.

Pleasurer: You may or may not use a lotion. If you do, warm it in your hands first. With or without lotion, start caressing your spouse's foot. Get to know his/her foot through touch. *Slowly* explore the toes, arch, top of foot, ankle, and even the lower leg. Always maintain contact with the body part being caressed and inform your spouse before you move to the next part. Caress one foot and then the other. In the same manner, caress one hand and then the other. Enjoy all surfaces and parts of each hand and lower arm. Inform your spouse when you are finished.

Step 6:   You may want to take a rest or break before you reverse roles and repeat Step 5. _____ will be the pleasurer. _____ will be the receiver.

Step 7:   Discuss this experience: What did you enjoy most? What was difficult? Write your reactions below or on the back of this paper.

Date:_____

Time:_____

Sexual Therapy Assignment 4
Body Awareness Exercise

Spouse #1: Stand in front of a full-length mirror in the nude. Describe your body as honestly as you can to your partner. Start with general feelings about your body as you see it. Then talk about each specific body part, starting with your hair and working down. Talk about how it feels and looks, ways you wish you were different, what you feel particularly good about.

Spouse #2: Only listen and observe. Listen both to the words and feelings of your partner as he or she talks. *Do not interrupt!* When your partner is finished, provide feedback to him or her what you have sensed and heard.

Spouse #1: Clarify or expand on what your partner has heard from you.

Spouse #2: Fill in any positive messages that you can give that will build up him or her.

Spouse #1: When you feel you have been understood accurately, reverse this procedure. You will now be the quiet observer and listener while your partner describes his or her body.

The first time:

       Spouse #1 = _____

       Spouse #2 = _____

The second time:

       Spouse #1 = _____

       Spouse #2 = _____

Date:_____
Time:_____

Sexual Therapy Assignment 5
Facial Caress

Step 1: _____ will take responsibility to initiate this experience and set the environment, making certain to provide comfort for both of you.

Step 2: Bathe or shower individually. Have hair clean, dry, and away from face. Man should be cleanly shaven.

Step 3: _____ will be the first pleasurer, and _____ will be the first receiver.

Step 4: Together, reread Underlying Principles for Bodily Pleasuring. Read and discuss the current assignment.

Step 5: *Receiver:* a) Position yourself comfortably on a bed or couch, with or without a pillow, with your head near the unobstructed edge of the bed or couch. b) Let yourself relax with eyes closed. Breathe in deeply and exhale slowly a few times, letting your body sink into the bed or couch.

Pleasurer: a) Sit in a comfortable chair, positioned so that you have easy access to your partner's face. b) You may or may not use a facial lotion or cream (Allercreme is great). Close your eyes and focus on the sensation of the touch as you explore your partner's face. Pleasure and explore as if you are a blind person getting to know your spouse through touch. Find eyebrows, eyes, all aspects of the nose, cheeks, forehead, chin, lips. Gently, sensuously, and lovingly enjoy the warmth of your partner's face. Inform your partner when you finish.

Step 6: You may want to take a rest or break before you reverse roles and repeat step 5. _____ will be the first pleasurer, and _____ will be the first receiver.

Step 7: Discuss the experience: What did you enjoy most? What was difficult? Write your reactions here.

Date:_____

Time:_____

Sexual Therapy Assignment 6
My Sexual Development

Write a brief memory of each of the following:

Type of affection in home:

Mother-Father interaction:

Parents to children:

Children to each other:

Genital discovery (first remembrance of your genitals or sexual awareness):

Names for genitals, urination, defecation:

Exploratory play (playing doctor, playing house, etc.):

Nudity in the home:

How sexual questions were handled:

Masturbation:

What were you taught?

What was your practice?

In adolescence:

Messages you got about your sexuality from

home:

peers:

Sexual Activity:
Extent:

Decision-Making Process (what decisions did you make about your sexual behavior?):

Briefly describe any traumatic sexual experience (in childhood, adolescence, or adulthood):

Describe any compulsive sexual habits that developed for you:

List positive sexual role models (men or women whom you believe influenced who you are today as a man or woman):

Date:_____

Time:_____

Sexual Therapy Assignment 7
Back Caress

Step 1: _____ will take responsibility to initiate this experience and set the atmosphere, making certain the temperature of the room is comfortable and there is privacy.

Step 2: Bathe or shower, individually. If possible, you will be nude for this experience. If nudity is too difficult, use the minimal covering to provide the safety needed.

Step 3: _____will be the first pleasurer; _____will be the first receiver.

Step 4: Together, reread the Underlying Principles for Bodily Pleasuring. Read and discuss the current assignment.

Step 5: *Receiver.* Get comfortable lying front down on the bed or location chosen. Focus on the enjoyment, relaxation, and gift of your spouse's touch.

Pleasurer. Position yourself so that you can comfortably enjoy your spouse's body. Start by putting your hands flat on his or her back and just feeling the pulsation and warmth of the other's skin. Move your hands over his/her back at a slow sensuous rhythm that comes from inside you. If you want to add lotion, inform your spouse and warm the lotion in your hands before you apply it to his or her back.

Step 6: You may want to take a rest or break before you reverse roles and repeat step 5. _____will be the pleasurer, and _____will be the receiver.

Step 7: Discuss the experience, each giving your feelings and reactions and what you learned about yourself. Write your reaction here or on the back.

Date:_____
Time:_____

Sexual Therapy Assignment 8
Bathe or Shower Together

Instructions to be supplied by therapist

Date:_____
Time:_____

Sexual Therapy Assignment 9
Sharing Myself

1. Usually I am the kind of person who

2. When things aren't going well I

3. I want to become the kind of person who

4. I like such things as

5. Ten years from now I

6. My best attribute is

7. My greatest weakness is

8. In conflict situations between people, I usually

9. I usually react to negative criticism by

10. I prefer to be with people who

11. Right now I'm feeling

12. I'm hoping that

13. If I could just

Date:_____

Time:_____

Sexual Therapy Assignment 10
Total Body Pleasuring Excluding Breasts and Genitals

Step 1: _____ will take responsibility to initiate this experience and set the atmosphere. The room temperature should be set so both of you will be comfortable without clothes and covers. Prepare a room that is softly lit and has a relaxed, uncluttered environment.

Step 2: Bathe or shower together. You may wash each other's nonsexual body parts.

Step 3: _____ will be the first pleasurer, and _____ will be the first receiver.

Step 4: Read the Underlying Principles for Bodily Pleasuring. Discuss the current instructions. As more of the body is included in the pleasuring, it is important to remember that sexual arousal is an involuntary response and not the goal or purpose of this experience. *Do not become concerned if there is or is not arousal: the purpose of this experience is body awareness.*

Step 5: *Receiver:* Lie on abdomen in a comfortable position.

Pleasurer: Place hands on the back of your spouse. With your eyes closed, focus on the sensations of your spouse's body: warmth, pulsation, vibrations, etc. Begin to move over his or her entire back with sensuous touch, radiating your warmth and care. Proceed in the same manner to neck, arms, and legs. Inform your spouse when you are ready for him or her to turn over.

Receiver: Turn onto your back.

Pleasurer: Sitting with your spouse's face in your lap (if it is more comfortable for you or your spouse, cover your genitals), proceed with a facial caress. Then continue down his or her neck, shoulders, arms, and hands. Move to the side of your spouse to enjoy his or her abdomen, legs and feet. Do not touch breasts or genitals.

Step 6: You may want to rest or take a break before you reverse roles and repeat Step 5: _____ will be the pleasurer; _____ will be the receiver.

Step 7: Discuss the experience. Were there uncomfortable movements? What anxieties or demands slipped through your minds? What was most relaxing? Most pleasurable? Write your reactions.

Date:_____
Time:_____

Sexual Therapy Assignment 11A
Female Self-Examination

Step 1: Have diagram of female external genitalia (see Figure 5–4). Have hand mirror and extension lamp or spotlight.

Step 2: Shower or bathe leisurely in order to relax.

Step 3: Assume comfortable position with legs spread apart, light focused on genitals, diagram within view, and hand mirror between legs so you can see genitals clearly. Look at how your outer labia come together. Then spread outer labia and identify the inner labia. Find the clitoris and note how the labia form a hood over the clitoris. See if you can feel the shaft of the clitoris, almost like a hidden, small penis up behind the tip of the clitoris. Touch the tip or glans of the clitoris and then the areas around and identify what kind of touch feels good and where.

Identify urinary meatus, vaginal opening, and any other points of interest. Think about what genital stimulation your partner has given you or you have given yourself in the past that has felt good, what you would like more of, what touching has been negative, and how stimulation of genitals might be enhanced. Thank God for his creation of each of these intricate parts. Thank him for any good feelings associated with your genitals. Pray for healing from any pain or scars connected with them.

This is a clinical learning experience, not for the purpose of arousal. However, if arousal should occur, it is okay.

Date:_____

Time:_____

Sexual Therapy Assignment 11B
Male Self-Examination

Step 1: Have diagram of male external genitalia (see Figure 5–6).

Step 2: Shower.

Step 3: In a private, well-lit room, with diagram of male genitals in view, identify all the specific parts of the penis and testes. Note the coronal ridge and the frenulum or "seam" on the backside of the penis. Think about the kind of touch and stimulation you have enjoyed, either when you have stimulated yourself or when your spouse has stimulated you. Imagine other kinds of touch and stimulation you might try. Think about how you might teach your spouse what you would enjoy, without placing demands on her.

Thank God for the specialness of the creation of your genitals and all the positive feelings they have given you. Pray for healing of any pain associated with them.

This is a clinical experience, not for the purpose of arousal. However, if arousal should occur, it is okay.

Date:_____
Time:_____

Sexual Therapy Assignment 12
Pubococcygeus (PC) Muscle Exercise (Kegel's)

Step 1: Identify the sensation of tightening and relaxing this muscle. While sitting on the toilet to urinate, spread your legs apart. Start urination. Then stop urination for three seconds. Repeat this several times before you are finished emptying your bladder. Some women have difficulty stopping urination. Those women need to work on tightening the PC muscle. Other women need to work on the voluntary relaxing of the PC muscle. If you can do both easily, you only need to tighten and relax the PC muscle twenty-five times per day to *keep* it in good condition. For those who need to improve the voluntary control of their PC muscle, proceed with the steps below.

Step 2: Do ten to twenty repetitions of this exercise one to four times per day: Gradually tighten the PC muscle tighter and tighter to the count of four. Then hold the muscle as tight as you can while you again count to four. Now gradually relax the muscle, letting go of the tension a little at a time as you count to four.

Step 3: Do ten to twenty repetitions of this exercise one to four times per day: Start to tighten your vagina by thinking of bringing your labia (lips) closer together, like closing an elevator door. Imagine that your vagina is an elevator. You start to tighten at the ground floor. Bring the muscles up from floor to floor, tightening and holding at each floor. Keep your breathing even and relaxed. Do not hold your breath. Go to the fifth floor. Then go down, relaxing the tension of the muscle, one floor at a time. When you get to the bottom, bear down as though you are opening the elevator door (the vagina) and letting something out.

Step 4: Do ten to twenty repetitions of this exercise one to four times per day: Rapidly tighten and relax the PC muscle at the opening of the vagina, in almost a flickering or fluttering type movement.

These exercises will improve vaginal sensation to sexual stimulation, enhance both the voluntary tightening and opening of the vagina, and will keep the vagina and its surrounding structures in better health for more years.

Date:_____
Time:_____

Sexual Therapy Assignment 13
Graphing Your Sexual Response

Step 1: _____, take the graph of the Sex Response Pattern for men (Fig. 9–1) and _____, take the graph of the Sex Response Pattern for women (Fig. 9–2). Read the details of what happens in the man's or woman's body during each of the phases of the sexual response. Circle any of the responses that you are aware of happening or assume are probably happening. Put a check by any of the responses that you believe are difficult for you or are not happening.

Step 2: Each partner should take a copy of an empty copy of Graphing Your Response. Draw one or more graph lines that represent how you respond or have responded through any form of stimulation. You may want to draw one line to represent response to self-stimulation and one to intercourse. Or your graph lines may represent how you respond today and how you've responded in the past.

Step 3: On the graph(s) you drew, each partner should note any points of difficulty that occur for you repeatedly. For example, if you ejaculate prematurely or if you inhibit your orgasmic response, note what is happening when that problem arises—what is happening inside of you and between the two of you.

Step 4: Share your graphs with each other. _____, share yours first. Go over all the details you circled or checked on the Sex Response Pattern and the graphs you drew and problem areas you described. _____, listen carefully. Reflect back what you understand so that _____ can clarify, in case he or she has miscommunicated or you have misunderstood. Add any details that you have observed that _____ may not have noticed about his or her response. Positive facts are particularly helpful.

Step 5: _____, share your graph and Sex Response Pattern with _____, using the same process described in Step 4.

Step 6: Talk about what you learned about each other that was new.

Sex Response Pattern
for Men

Excitement Phase	Plateau Phase	Orgasmic Phase	Resolution Phase
External Genitals: Penis becomes erect as it rushes full of blood Scrotum thickens and partially elevates	External Genitals: Penis engorges more and deepens in color Fluid containing sperm seeps from penis Scrotum thickens	External Genitals: Penis contracts expelling the seminal fluid	External Genitals: Penis becomes flaccid Scrotum thins and drops
Internal Genitalia: No significant change	Internal Genitalia: Testes enlarge Right testicle rises and rotates early *When approaching point of no return- Left testicle rises and rotates Prostate contracts Seminal vesical contracts	Internal Genitalia: Seminal duct system contracts	Internal Genitalia: Testes descend and return to normal size
Total Body: Nipples become erect in 60% of men	Total Body: Skin flushes on chest, neck and face Foot contracts downward (carpopedal spasm) Heart rate increases Blood pressure rises Pelvis thrusts Muscles tense	Total body: Rectal sphincter contracts Foot spasms continue Heart rate increases more Blood pressure rises more Breathing increases Facial muscles contract Gasping occurs	Total body: Relief of vasocongestion and engorgement Skin perspires Muscles relax
Characteristics: Arousal	Characteristics: Entry may occur at any time Ejaculatory control must be learned for extended love play	Characteristics: Shortest, but most intense phase Internal experience	Characteristics: Tension loss Not usually reversible (rest period required before more arousal)

Phases of the Sexual Response

Level of Sexual Arousal

Fig. 9–1

Adapted from Masters and Johnson Human Sexual Response Boston; Brown, Little & Co., 1966

Sex Response Pattern
for Women

Excitement Phase	Plateau Phase	Orgasmic Phase	Resolution Phase
External Genitals: Clitoris lengthens Outer lips spread flat Inner lips enlarge	External Genitals: Clitoris retracts under hood Inner lips turn bright red and enlarge (about 1min. before orgasmic response)	External Genitals: No noticeable change	External Genitals: Clitoris returns to normal size Inner and outer lips return to normal size and position
Internal Genitalia: Vagina lubricates (within 10–20 sec.) Uterus elevates	Internal Genitalia: Inner 2/3 of vagina expands Outer 1/3 of vagina thickens and contracts forming orgasmic platform Uterus elevates fully	Internal Genitalia: Outer 1/3 of vagina contracts 3 to 12 times Uterus contracts	Internal Genitalia: Cervix opens slightly and drops into seminal pool Uterus drops back toward front of pelvis Vagina collapses and thins
Total Body: Nipples become erect Breasts enlarge	Total Body: Skin flushes over abdomen, chest, etc. Foot contracts downward (carpopedal spasm) Heart rate increases Blood pressure rises Pelvis thrusts Muscles tense	Total body: Rectal sphincter contracts Foot spasms continue Heart rate increases more Blood pressure rises more Breathing increases Facial muscles contract Gasping occurs	Total body: Relief of vasocongestion and engorgement Skin perspires Muscles relax Breasts and nipples return to prestimulated appearance
Characteristics: Arousal	Characteristics: Entry may occur at any time Majority of love play	Characteristics: Shortest, but most intense phase Internal experience	Characteristics: Tension loss Reversible

Adapted from Masters and Johnson
Human Sexual Response
Boston; Brown, Little & Co.,
1966

Fig. 9–2

Level of Sexual Arousal

Phases of the Sexual Response

Graphing Your Response

Excitement Phase	Plateau Phase	Orgasmic Phase	Resolution Phase

Level of Sexual Arousal

Phases of the Sexual Response   Draw a graph(s) of your physical, sexual response pattern(s). © Copyright 1990 Penner & Penner

Date:_____
Time:_____

Sexual Therapy Assignment 14
Total Body Pleasuring Including Breasts and Genitals,
without Purposeful Stimulation

Step 1:   _____will take responsibility to initiate the experience and set the atmosphere with attention to temperature, privacy, and mood.

Step 2:   Bathe or shower together. You may wash each other's bodies, totally.

Step 3:   _____will be the first pleasurer;   _____ will be the first receiver.

Step 4:   Read the Underlying Principles for Bodily Pleasuring. Discuss the current instructions. Continue to remember that sexual arousal is an involuntary response and not the goal of this experience. *Do not become concerned if there is or is not arousal. The purpose of the experience is body awareness.*

Step 5:   *Receiver:* Lie on your abdomen in a comfortable position.

Pleasurer: Place your hands on the back of your spouse and proceed to pleasure, taking in the warmth and sensations of your spouse's back, buttocks, arms, and legs. Take time to enjoy each part as you have in previous pleasuring exercises. Inform your spouse when you are ready for him or her to turn over.

Receiver: Turn onto your back. Positively redirect your spouse if anything he or she does is negative or demanding.

Pleasurer: Sitting with your spouse's face in your lap (with your genitals covered), proceed with a facial caress. Then continue down his or her neck, shoulders, chest, arms, and hands. Do not focus on the breasts. Just include them as you have every other part of the body. Move to the side of your spouse (or between his or her legs) to pleasure his or her abdomen, genitals, legs, and feet. Include the genitals in general stroking, but with no specific stimulation. Inform your spouse when you are finished.

Step 6:   You may want to rest or take a break before you reverse roles and repeat Step 5. _____ will be the pleasurer; _____ will be the receiver.

Step 7:   Discuss the experience. Particularly attend to any demands that are arising and any enjoyment that is flowing. Write your reactions.

Date:_____
Time:_____

Sexual Therapy Assignment 15
Clinical Genital Examination

Step 1: Have diagrams of male genitalia and female external genitalia (see Figures 5–4 and 5–6). Have hand mirror and extension lamp or spotlight.

Step 2: Shower or bathe together; suds up each other's bodies and enjoy the pleasure and relaxation of touching each other in that process, not for the purpose of arousal.

Step 3: In a private, well-lit room, with diagram of male genitalia; _____ (husband) identify all the specific parts of the penis and testes. _____, (wife) join in the exploration by touching various parts as they are identified. Particularly note the coronal ridge and the frenulum or "seam" on the back side of the penis. After exploring the various parts of the genitals, talk about what kind of touch feels good, any stimulation of the genitals your partner has given you in the past that you would like more of and any stimulation or handling of the genitals that has been unpleasant for you. _____, (wife) talk about ways you enjoy pleasuring his genitals and/or feelings of discomfort you have with male genitals.

Step 4: Female assumes comfortable position with legs spread apart, light focusing on genitals, diagram within view, and hand mirror between legs so you can see genitals clearly. Look at how your outer labia come together. Then spread the outer labia and identify the inner labia. Find the clitoris and note how the labia form a hood over the clitoris. See if you can feel the shaft of the clitoris, almost like a hidden, small penis up behind the tip of the clitoris. Touch the tip or glans of the clitoris and then the areas around and talk with your husband about what kind of touch feels good and where. _____, (husband) join in exploration and touching as is comfortable.

Identify urinary meatus, vaginal opening, and any other points of interest. Talk about what genital stimulation your partner has given you in the past that has felt good, what you would like more of, what touching has been negative, and how stimulation of genitals might be enhanced. _____, (husband) talk about ways you enjoy pleasuring her genitals and/or feelings of discomfort you have with female genitalia.

Step 5: Talk about what this has felt like for each of you, what was comfortable or uncomfortable and what you learned about yourselves and each other.

This is a clinical, learning experience, not for the purpose of arousal. If arousal should occur, it is okay. But do not focus on it; ignore it or enjoy it without pursuing it.

Date:_____

Time:_____

Sexual Therapy Assignment 16
Vaginal Examination

Step 1: Shower or bathe together, enjoying each other's bodies as you do, but not for the purpose of arousal. Scrub finger nails with a brush.

Step 2: Lotion or oil each other's bodies.

Step 3: With closely trimmed nails, _____, (husband) gently insert finger in wife's vagina to the second knuckle. Then gently press on the wall of the vagina. If you think of the opening of the vagina as a clock, start at the twelve-o'clock position and then slowly move around the wall of the vagina, pressing or stroking at every hour. Try varying degrees of pressure and types of touch. The wife should provide feedback about what sensations she notes. Particularly be aware of any points of pain or pleasure.

After completing this exploration, female tightens PC muscle when male's finger is in vagina. Talk about how that feels to each of you. Now with the husband's finger in the vagina and the PC muscle tightened, insert your finger just beyond the inner ridge of the PC muscle. This is the G-spot area (refer to diagram of aroused internal female genitalia in Figure 5–4). Explore that area with various degrees of pressure—both stroking, massaging, and tapping. _____, (wife) note and talk about the sensations you have in response to your husband's exploration.

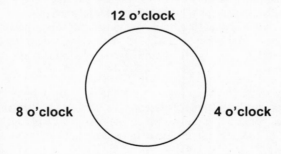

12 o'clock

8 o'clock   **4 o'clock**

Opening of vagina with four, eight, and twelve o'clock positions identified. These are often more highly sensitive areas in the vagina.

Step 4: Talk about the experience: what felt good, what you learned, what was uncomfortable about it. You may want to spend some time just holding and affirming each other. Write your reactions here.

Date:_____
Time:_____

Sexual Therapy Assignment 17
Nondemand Teaching

Step 1:   _____ will take responsibility to initiate this experience and set the atmosphere. Pillows against the head board of the bed usually work best. Design this for teaching, rather than romance.

Step 2:   Together, read these instructions and clarify with each other what each of you understands you are to do.

Step 3:   Bathe or shower together in a way that brings relaxation and enjoyment of each other's bodies, not touching for the purpose of stimulation or arousal.

Step 4:   _____ (wife) should start the actual experience by sitting in front of _____ (husband) in the nondemand position (See p. 158.) Then she places her hands over his hands and uses his hands to pleasure her face, breasts, abdomen, and genitals. The purpose of the exercise is for the one guiding the hands to discover what kind of touch he or she really likes. For the one being guided, his job is to let his hand muscles be relaxed and limp and attend to the kind of touch that he is being directed to give. He can learn what his wife really likes. This is a particularly good time for both to do a lot of experimenting and communicating about the kind of genital touch that brings pleasure. This is not likely to be an exciting or arousing experience, but a much more clinical and teaching kind of time. If arousal should occur, however, enjoy it.

When _____ (husband) guides _____'s (wife's) hands to discover and teach the touch he enjoys on the upper front of his body, he may need to slide down and use a modified version of the upper diagram of the nondemand position. For example, he may slide his head into his wife's lap. When _____ (husband) is guiding _____ (wife) in pleasuring his lower body, especially the genitals, we would encourage the use of the lower diagram.

Step 5:   Talk together both about what you learned in this experience as well as anything else that you have always enjoyed or has always been painful or difficult for you. You may write your reactions here.

Non-Demand Positions

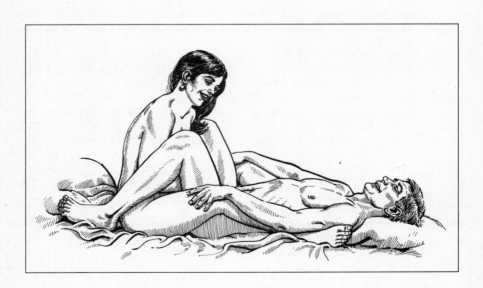

Date:_____

Time:_____

Sexual Therapy Assignment 18
Defining Your Sexual Experience

HOW IT IS NOW?   *HOW YOU WOULD LIKE IT TO BE?*

Desire:

What do you experience to indicate that you are sexually interested?

Initiation:

How do you express that desire for sexual intimacy?

Describe a typical process of initiation of sexual intercourse for you and your spouse (who does what and how does the other respond?).

Pleasuring:

What does or what would help the two of you bring your worlds together?

How important is it for you to talk during sexual activity?

What tends to stimulate you sexually (get you "turned on")?

What kind of touching is most pleasurable for you? (Describe the places, length of time, etc.)

When in the process does entry occur and who decides?

What inhibitions get in the way of the two of you freely enjoying the process of being together?

Letting Go:

Describe your sensations of sexual release.

For the woman: If you do not experience release, identify when your feelings start to lessen and what is happening at that point.

For the man: If you do not feel in control of ejaculation, describe when you ejaculate (at entry, how many minutes after entry, etc.), what triggers ejaculation, and what forms of control you have tried.

Affirming:

What do you usually do and feel during this time?

What do you sense from your spouse?

Date:_____

Time:_____

Sexual Therapy Assignment 19
Kissing Exercise

Step 1: _____ will take responsibility to see to it that the experience happens. Prepare a comfortable setting with lights low and soft music.

Step 2: Brush teeth, use dental floss, and gargle.

Step 3: Together read and discuss these instructions.

Step 4: Sitting on the couch, fully clothed, each or you describe to the other how you like to kiss and to be kissed. Use positive descriptions rather than listing what you don't like. Reflect back to each other what you understand from the other.

Step 5: _____, use your lips to experiment with kissing your spouse's lips. Pucker your lips and gently peck across your spouse's lips and cheeks from one side to the other, from top to bottom lip, etc. Take time to nibble on your spouse's lips, taking the upper or lower lip between your lips. _____, follow his or her lead. Be passive, but responsive.

Step 6: Reverse roles. _____, follow Step 5 in discovering how you like to kiss. _____, follow his or her lead. Be passive, but responsive.

Step 7: Take turns leading in experimenting with the use of your lips and tongue to find ways that you both enjoy, pecking, nibbling, licking, sucking, and in any other way interacting with each other's lips and tongues. Keep it soft and experimental.

Step 8: Allow the involvement with each other's mouths to become mutual, simultaneous enjoyment, if that is comfortable for both of you. Take turns inserting your tongues in and out of each other's mouths. If one of you becomes too intense or forceful feeling for the other, gently remind the intense one that you'd like to keep it soft, safe, and experimental.

Step 9: Talk about the experience. Did you most enjoy leading or being led? What felt especially good? What barriers did you experience? How would you like to enhance your kissing?

Date:_____
Time:_____

Sexual Therapy Assignment 20
You and Me

1. My first impression of you was

2. What I like about you is

3. My general image of you is

4. What puzzles me about you is

5. I am imagining that you

6. I think you see me as

Date:_____
Time:_____

Sexual Therapy Assignment 21
Creative Pleasuring

Step 1:   _____ will take responsibility to see to it that the experience happens and will set up the environment for your time together.

Step 2:   Together read these instructions and the Underlying Principles for Bodily Pleasuring. Tell each other what each of you understands the current assignment to be.

Step 3:   Bathe or shower together in a way that brings relaxation and enjoyment of each other's bodies.

Step 4:   Each of you should bring to the experience three items to use to pleasure your partner. Think of things that would feel pleasing and sensuous against the skin. Have these be a surprise for each other.

Step 5:   _____, start the actual pleasuring by having your partner lie on his or her abdomen and gently stroking his or her back with the first accouterment you chose for this event. Then do the same with each of the other objects. Together choose one object to continue pleasuring his or her entire body. When you feel finished, reverse roles and _____, do the same thing with the accoutrements you chose for pleasuring _____'s body. Stop when you have thoroughly enjoyed your partner's total body.

Step 6:   Talk about the experience. What did you enjoy? What you would have liked more of? What other kind of object could you imagine enjoying? What did you learn? Write your reactions here.

Date:_____

Time:_____

Sexual Therapy Assignment 22
Simulating Arousal Responses

Purpose: This experience is to help reduce self-consciousness and inhibition of the automatic responses of sexual arousal. It can become humorous, even hilarious.

Step 1: _____, select a setting that is peaceful, free of distractions, and protected from being heard. You may need to set up a sound barrier, like a tape or radio playing at the wall or door that might carry your noises. This should be in daylight or with the lights on.

Step 2 Lie side by side on the bed or on a comfortable surface, fully clothed.

Step 3: Take yourselves through relaxation: First, together take ten deep breaths, slowly in through your nostrils, hold and breathe out through your mouths. _____, lead in the deep, relaxed breathing. Picture yourselves in a beautiful, sunny, private garden. As you let out the air through your mouths, feel the tension in your bodies relax.

Step 4: Keeping in the same relaxed mode, _____, lead in taking five to ten deep breaths slowly in through the nose, then hold them and breathe out through the mouth with a sighing sound. Go to the next step when you feel natural and comfortable.

Step 5: _____, lead in the next five to ten breaths. This time as you breathe in, imagine the breath warming the inside of your body, all the way to your genitals. As you let it out, imagine the breath coming from your genitals, through your body, up your windpipe, past your vocal cords. Let out a relaxed rattling noise while you say, "Ah." Vary the pitch of the "Ah" with each exhalation. When you feel natural and comfortable with the noises and breathing, stop.

Step 6: Talk about your experience. Write your reactions. Take a break, if you wish. Then, take off your clothes and proceed with the next steps.

Step 7: Lie side by side on your back without any clothes on, with the lights on or in daylight. Imagine yourselves on a warm, sunny, private beach, totally secluded from anyone. _____, lead in taking three to five deep breaths in, holding and relaxing into the "warm sand" as you let the breaths out.

Step 8:   Now, imagine that you are doing your favorite sexual activity (each can picture something different). Breathe in and out slowly and loudly with the rattling "Ah" sound. _____, lead in five to ten of these.

Step 9:   Have the sexual activity continue to progress in your minds as you proceed with the noisy, loose breathing. This time speed the breathing slightly, making certain it continues to be deep and noisy. Tense the muscles in your body so that your foot extends outward, your facial muscles grimace, and you thrust with your pelvis. Imagine your body flushing as it does when you blush. If you have never experienced these natural arousal responses, simulate what your spouse is doing.

Step 10:   Repeat Steps 7–9 in the nude with _____ lying on his back and _____ sitting on top of him in the typical woman-on-top position. Do not insert the penis into the vagina.

Step 11:   Repeat Steps 7–9 in the nude with _____ lying on her back and _____ on top of her in the most comfortable male-on-top position. If this is uncomfortable, turn on your sides, face to face. Do not insert penis into vagina.

Step 12:   Switch to the position that is most comfortable to both, continue to build the breathing, sounds, and movements to intensify the simulation of the release of the orgasm. If you have never experienced an orgasm, imitate your spouse's acting out of what he or she usually does during an orgasm.

Step 13:   Rest together and hold each other closely.

Step 14:   Talk about and write your reactions to the various steps of involvement.

Date:_____

Time:_____

Sexual Therapy Assignment 23
Assigned Readings

The counselor/therapist selects and assigns readings that are pertinent to the couple's situation and the problem being addressed. The reference list at the back of this book can be used for suggested readings.

Date:_____
Time:_____

Sexual Therapy Assignment 24
Total Body Pleasuring Including Breast and Genital Stimulation

Step 1: _____ will take responsibility to initiate the experience and set the atmosphere with attention to temperature, privacy, and mood.

Step 2: Bathe or shower together. You may wash each other totally.

Step 3: _____ will be the first pleasurer. _____ will be the first receiver.

Step 4: Read the Underlying Principles for Bodily Pleasuring. Read and discuss the current instructions. Even with the addition of stimulation, the result of arousal is not expected. Sexual arousal is an involuntary response. Do not become concerned if there is or is not arousal.

Step 5: *Receiver:* Lie on your abdomen in a comfortable position.

Pleasurer: Place your hands on the back of your spouse. Enjoy pleasuring the back of your spouse's body in any way that is positive to you, giving and receiving warmth through your hands. Rely on your spouse to redirect you if anything you do becomes negative or demanding. Inform your spouse when you are ready for him or her to turn over.

Receiver: Turn onto your back. Soak in the pleasure.

Pleasurer: Sitting with your spouse's head in your lap, proceed with a facial caress. Then continue down his or her neck, shoulders, chest, arms, and hands. Enjoy stimulating his or her breasts for your pleasure, not for the result it produces. Incorporate the knowledge you gained from the non-demand teaching, as to the type of touch your spouse enjoys. Move to the side or between the legs of your spouse to pleasure his or her abdomen, legs and genitals. Again, enjoy stimulating his or her genitals for your pleasure, incorporating what you have learned as to the type of stimulation your spouse prefers. Inform your spouse when you are finished.

Step 6: You may want to rest or take a break before you reverse roles and repeat Step 5, but you are free to continue. _____ will be the pleasurer. _____ will be the receiver.

Step 7: Discuss the experience. Write your reactions.

Date:_____
Time:_____

Sexual Therapy Assignment 25
Sharing Love

Complete the following statements as candidly and honestly as you can:

1. When I love you I show it by _____
_____
_____
_____

2. I know you love me when you _____
_____
_____
_____

3. I know you are reaching out to me when you _____
_____
_____
_____

4. When you reach out to me I feel _____
_____
_____
_____

5. When I am "turned on" I _____
_____
_____
_____

6. I know you are "turned on" when you _____
_____
_____
_____

7. You "turn me on" when you _____
_____
_____
_____

8. I feel sexual pleasure when _____

_____

_____

_____

9. When you stimulate me physically, I feel _____

_____

_____

_____

10. Our sexual relationship makes me feel _____

_____

_____

_____

Date:_____

Time:_____

Sexual Therapy Assignment 26
Pleasuring Not Using Hands (Penis as a Paint Brush)

Step 1: _____ will take responsibility to see to it that the experience happens and set up the environment for your time together. The atmosphere should allow for playfulness and creativity.

Step 2: Together, read these instructions and the Underlying Principles for Bodily Pleasuring. Tell each other what each of you understands the assignment to be.

Step 3: Bathe or shower together in a way that brings relaxation and enjoyment of each other's bodies.

Step 4: _____, start the actual pleasuring by following the Underlying Principles for Bodily Pleasuring, except this time you may use any part of your body except your hands. Make it an experimental and fun time of discovering what parts of your body you really enjoy using to touch _____. You might use your hair, nose, eyes, tongue, ears, forearms, breasts, genitals, feet, or whatever.

When you have thoroughly enjoyed your spouse's total body, reverse roles and _____ will pursue the discovery of using various parts of his or her body to pleasure _____. Each of you may use your hands to hold the penis, whether erect or flaccid, to pleasure the wife's body and genitals. Stop when you feel you have thoroughly enjoyed your spouse's total body. Some attempts at using body parts may feel awkward. That is expected and not to be seen as negative.

Step 5: Talk about the experience. What felt particularly good? What new thing did you discover about yourself? About your spouse? What barriers were there for you? What got in the way of maximum enjoyment? You may write your reactions here.

Date:_____
Time:_____

Sexual Therapy Assignment 27
Shared Self-Stimulation

Step 1: _____ will prepare a comfortable, private setting.

Step 2: Read these instructions together. Discuss how each of you feels about this assignment.

Step 3: Bathe or shower together.

Step 4: Enjoy some mutual hugging and kissing without clothes on. You may proceed to some total body pleasuring.

Step 5: When both feel ready (let each other know), each of you get into the position that is most usual for you for self-stimulation.

Step 6: Either looking at or away from each other (whichever is most comfortable for both of you), each of you begin stimulating yourselves in the way that brings you the most pleasure. Continue as long as it is enjoyable. One of you will probably finish before the other. When you are finished, wait quietly without disturbing the other. Do not feel any need to rush to finish, once one of you has finished.

Step 7: When you are both finished, talk about the experience. Write your reactions.

Date:_____

Time:_____

Sexual Therapy Assignment 28
Total Body Pleasuring, with Mutual Manual Stimulation

Step 1: _____ will take responsibility to initiate the experience and set the atmosphere. You might want to vary from your past locations or choose one of the favorites you have already enjoyed.

Step 2: Bathe or shower together. Enjoy each other in any way that is pleasurable for both of you.

Step 3: Review the Principles of Bodily Pleasuring with each other. Remind each other of the guidelines that the two of you have found to be important in order to reduce demand and enhance freedom.

Step 4: _____, begin by pleasuring the back of _____'s body. Proceed just like you did for the Back Caress. Reverse roles. _____, pleasure the back of _____'s body. Spend some time taking turns leading each other in kissing while embracing each other's nude bodies. Take time to nibble, suck, lick, and thrust tongues. Proceed to mutually enjoying each other's bodies with any form of touch that has been positive so far. Do not have entry of the penis into the vagina. Spend some time manually stimulating each other's genitals. If it's more comfortable to take turns, that's fine. Use any part of your body to enjoy any part of your spouse's body. Have fun and vary the intensity.

Step 5: Talk about what you liked best, where you still felt inhibited, what you would like more of, and what you would not like unless you ask for it. Write your reactions.

Date:_____

Time:_____

Sexual Therapy Assignment 29
Principles Learned

Step 1: Each write down the principles you have learned during this sexual therapy process that would best enhance your ongoing sexual life.

Step 2: Share your ideas with each other, taking turns being the sharer and the active listener. Refer to the Communication Format.

Step 3: Work together with both lists of principles to develop one joint list. Number the principles in order of priority.

Date:_____

Time:_____

Sexual Therapy Assignment 30
Total Body Pleasuring with Entry

Step 1: _____ will take responsibility to initiate the experience and set the atmosphere. It will be important for this exercise to not only provide for mood, temperature, and privacy, but also birth control.

Step 2: Bathe or shower together. Enjoy each other's bodies in any way that is positive for both of you.

Step 3: Review the Principles of Bodily Pleasuring with each other. Talk about your feelings of being able to proceed to intercourse. Adjust for any concerns or demands that might arise.

Step 4: _____ will begin by giving _____ a facial, hand, and foot caress. Then spend some time mutually hugging, kissing, and enjoying the pleasure of each other's bodies in any way that is positive for both of you. Include breast and genital stimulation and using the penis as a paint brush to stimulate _____'s genitals. She may invite the husband to some poking of the penis into the vagina by adding a lubricant to the penis and between the labia, separating them as she does. With the woman in the top position, poke in a little at a time. Enter all the way when that is comfortable for both of you.

Rest together quietly without thrusting. Enjoy the closeness of each other's bodies. Kiss and pleasure as you desire. Then begin gentle thrusting. The woman should control the thrusting. Stop to rest every few minutes. Move around in any way you desire. When it is desirable for both, allow the intensity of the thrusting to build. Continue as long as that is pleasurable for both of you. If there is release for either or both, that is fine, but it is not necessary. Ejaculation and orgasm are reflex responses to the intense buildup of sexual arousal. When your body is ready for that and you can allow it, it will happen. That is not an expectation.

Step 5: Talk about the experience from start to finish. What was most positive? What got in the way? Write your reactions.

Date:_____

Time:_____

Sexual Therapy Assignment 31
Application of Principles to Home Plan

Step 1: Using the list of principles you have prioritized, individually write out a plan for your sexual relationship that would ensure that these principles will be followed.

Step 2: Share your plans with each other using the Communication Format.

Step 3: Work together, combining ideas from both plans, to make a joint plan that represents both of your desires for your ongoing sexual relationship. Be very specific. Define the different types of sexual experiences you would like to have, how preparation and initiation will happen, when and where the experiences will happen, how you will handle rescheduling if a scheduled time has to be canceled and how you will plan for scheduled and spontaneous opportunities.

PART II

DIAGNOSIS AND TREATMENT

SPECIFIC DIAGNOSIS OF THE INDIVIDUAL'S or couple's sexual dysfunction is necessary in order to adapt the general sexual therapy process to the couple's particular deficiency in sexual functioning. The careful assessment process described in chapter 8 will lead to the accurate placement of the sexual disorder into its correct category. The correct diagnosis will then give unique shape and direction to the general Sexual Therapy Plan described in detail in chapter 9.

Diagnosis of the sexual dysfunction takes into account much of the gathered data:

- The detailed description of the couple's dissatisfaction
- The effect the problem has on each spouse
- The duration of the difficulty
- What factors contribute to or alleviate the stress
- Whether the impairment is complete or partial
- The phase of the sexual response cycle in which the process is interrupted
- How the background history of each spouse contributes
- The physical and psychological elements related to the situation
- The results or relief desired by the couple.

When all of the above data are considered, sexual problems can be categorized into six problem areas:

1. Problems due to couple dissatisfaction
2. Problems of desire
3. Problems with arousal
4. Problems with release
5. Problems with intercourse
6. Sexual addictions

The first category has to do with relationship issues. The last category refers to sexual behaviors that have control over the individual. Categories 2 through 5 are technically considered sexual dysfunctions, which are defined by the *Diagnostic and Statistical Review, Third Edition, Revised (DSM-III-R)*[1] as disorders "characterized by inhibitions in sexual desire or the psychophysiological changes that characterize the response cycle." The earlier in the cycle the disruption occurs, the more difficult the relief of that symptom. The later in the sexual experience the problem occurs, the simpler and the more behavioral the treatment. For example, problems of desire often require more psychotherapeutic intervention, whereas problems with release are usually remedied with the traditional sexual therapy behavioral prescriptions.

CHAPTER TEN

TREATING PROBLEMS DUE TO COUPLE DISSATISFACTION

RELATIONSHIP DILEMMAS REGARDING THE SEXUAL experience may or may not negatively affect the sexual response cycle. Nevertheless, these chronic conflicts slowly deteriorate the sexual fulfillment of the husband-wife relationship in the same way that the friction of feet walking up a carpeted stairway wears the center of that carpet over time. One footstep alone will not show its deteriorating effect, but long-term use will destroy the carpet.

Similarly, relationship struggles over the frequency of sexual activity, initiation, boredom, or inhibition do not show their wearing effects immediately. In fact, the conflict the couple experiences may not even seem significant initially; but eventually, a couple's sexual life can be destroyed by what would seem to be minor wear and tear.

Frequency

When spouses differ on the frequency of their desire for sexual contact, conflict is likely to result. With time, the perception of their differences becomes exaggerated. If he desires sex once a day, and she is happy with it once a week, eventually he begins to believe she would only want sex once a month and she is convinced he would like it three times a day.

By the time a couple comes for sexual therapy and is asked how frequently each of them would like to be together sexually, each spouse is shocked by the other's response. For example, Earl came to the assessment process with the complaint that Marianne never wanted to be together sexually. Marianne said she never had a chance to experience her own need for sex because Earl always initiated it before she had a chance to feel that need. When Earl was asked how often he would like to be with Marianne sexually, he said two to three times a week would make him happy. When he was asked what he thought Marianne's desire would be, he said he suspected she would not care if they went two or three weeks without any sexual contact.

When the same questions were asked of Marianne, she said she would like sex once or twice a week and thought Earl would like it every day—or even twice a day.

Clarifying for Earl and Marianne that their desire for sexual frequency was not that far apart allowed them to negotiate a compromise. Earl realized that three times a week would probably be ideal for him. Marianne thought that once a week was more realistic for her. So they compromised and worked out a plan to be together twice a week.

They decided to schedule their experiences so that they would have quality times together. In this way, Earl was relieved of his concern that he might not be able to have sex as often as he needed, and Marianne could give herself more fully to their encounters because she knew sex was not expected every night. (We also see couples where the woman is frustrated because of her desire for more frequent contact.)

Resolution of the frequency issue is not always that simple. Some differences are much more extreme. In these cases, negotiation and compromise take more work. Other times, the extreme difference may be indicative of a deeper issue, such as lack of sexual desire. In this situation, the sexual dysfunction needs to be addressed.

Recently, the issue of lack of frequency has become more and more a joint concern, not a conflict issue. In many modern marriages, neither spouse is satisfied with the couple's frequency of sexually satisfying experiences. Both may have full-time jobs and a toddler who is in day care all day. When they come home from work, they share the responsibility of caring for their child, preparing dinner, and tending to household duties. By the time they have finished all this, they need to get to sleep. Weekends are their only social and church times, so there is little or no time left for the two of them.

Scheduling is the only answer to a lifestyle that does not leave room for the husband-wife sexual relationship. When the scheduling solution is suggested, one of the spouses will usually contest it by saying, "But how can you schedule sex? You can't schedule when you're going to be turned on."

To some extent that concern is true. Men and women cannot schedule themselves to be "turned on." But the scheduled block of time is saved and prepared for, so that life's demands do not snatch those moments away. The time is freed of distractions, as in the sexual therapy process, and designed for communicating and touching in the privacy of the couple's bedroom. This allows sexual interest, arousal, release, and/ or intercourse to develop; but the expectation or demand for anything more than physical and emotional connection is deliberately removed.

When a couple is satisfied with the quality and frequency of their sexual experiences, scheduling times to be physical is not necessary. But many couples find that planned times which can be anticipated and prepared for actually enhance the delight they enjoy together sexually.

Initiation

Initiation stress usually manifests itself as an approach-avoidance game. Typically, the man approaches and the woman avoids. This may be true even when the woman's desire for sex is as high or higher than the man's. This system goes back to the fact that women in our culture do not feel as comfortable displaying overt, assertive sexuality as men do.

What happens is that, over time, both spouses begin to experience their conflict as a frequency issue, similar to Earl and Marianne's. Because the wife does not show her interest in being together sexually, the husband begins to believe she has no interest in him sexually. His insecurity is triggered by her lack of display of interest, so he anxiously begins to initiate sex more often than he would want it if he were feeling sure of himself in relation to her. She feels the pressure of his initiation, so begins to avoid or pull away sexually. The more he approaches, the more consistent is her avoidance. The more frequent her avoidance, the more anxious is his approach. It becomes a negative spiral.

Sometimes the approach-avoidance cycle is not just a lack of comfort with overt sexuality, but is triggered by a difference in desire for frequency. When one spouse is always wanting sex, the other feels pressured, so he or she starts to avoid it; then the one with higher desire increases the frequency of approaching, working on averages. For example, if it is the husband who has the higher desire, he may believe if he initiates eight times, he's likely to get his wife involved once. She believes he wants it all eight times, so she feels all he ever wants is sex. Then she begins the avoidance behavior.

One spouse may avoid sex because it is a negative experience. If a man ejaculates prematurely or loses his erection, he will want to avoid the failure experience. His wife may increase her approach in response to his pulling away.

Sometimes one person is exhausted. The idea of sex might be great, but the energy does not seem to be available to initiate the activity. When that fatigue is ongoing, the other spouse may begin to experience the lack of initiation as avoidance and then pursue initiation of sexual activity more vigorously.

The approach-avoidance initiation pattern must be reversed by a simple problem-solving experience. The format we use is the following Problem-Solving for Initiation Problems outline. It can be given to the couple as a homework assignment.

PROBLEM-SOLVING
FOR
INITIATION PROBLEMS

Step 1: Each of you write how you experience your initiation process. What do you do and what do you feel in the process of sexual initiation?

Step 2: During a prescheduled two- to three-hour block of time:
Read each other's descriptions of your initiation process.
Provide feedback about how you understand the other's description.
Clarify and expand on what you wrote.

Agree on the need for a change.

Make a plan for that change.

Step 3: One suggestion for a plan is as follows:

A. Set aside a designated period of time, like one to two weeks. During this time:
 1. The usual initiator is to make no hints at sexual activity but is to be loving and warm.
 2. The usual avoider is responsible to initiate one sexual event of his or her choice.

B. At the prescheduled ending of the designated time period:
 1. Talk about each of your feelings that occurred during the experimental week(s).
 2. Talk about what actually happened sexually.
 3. Make a follow-up plan for the next week or two. Revise the previous plan to accommodate any difficulties that occurred.

The need to revise the previous plan may become evident at the follow-up talk if the sexually hesitant woman shares that she tried to initiate sex but he did not respond. Soon she discovers he was not even aware that she initiated; her sexual subtleness then becomes even more evident. The plan needs to include a clear understanding of how she will initiate on future attempts.

Boredom

Boredom with the sexual relationship usually sets in after a few years of the typical lovemaking experience in America. The scenario goes like this: The couple is in bed. The eleven o'clock news is on the television. He has the remote control. She is half-asleep. The news is over. He flicks off the television, rolls over, flops his arm over her breasts, and begins fondling her. She stirs and gets involved to some extent. He gets an erection. She may or may not get aroused. They have intercourse. He ejaculates. She may or may not respond orgasmically. Five to seven minutes later, it is over. They could both write the script. Their sexual experiences are totally predictable and primarily functional.

Scheduling quality sexual events again becomes the solution. When boredom is a problem, not only does the time need to be planned, so does the activity. The spouses can be assigned turns for creating the setting. Exercises like those listed and described in chapter 9 as part of

183

the Sexual Therapy Plan can be assigned. The couple needs specific guidance in expanding their sexual repertoire. They need to be given experiences that teach them how to be experimental and creative with each other. Experiences like the No Hands Pleasuring and the Creative Pleasuring assignments will be particularly stretching.

Inhibitions

The friction of inhibitions may cause wear and tear on a couple's sexual relationship fairly quickly. The inhibited one feels tenaciously bound by the inhibitions, while the other's frustration intensifies quickly because of the limiting control the inhibitions have on their relationship.

Inhibitions can be religious or personal. Religious inhibitions are just that; they are not biblical or Christian. The person may have been raised with rigid antisexual teaching in the home or church. Now in marriage, it is difficult to freely give his or her body to the spouse, or it is difficult to enjoy the spouse's body. The person carries a mental list of "shoulds" and "should-nots" into each sexual experience. It is very difficult for him or her to connect godliness and intense sexual freedom. As one man wrote to us, "Your book is convincing ministers in my denomination that sex is to be enjoyed. Sexual enjoyment *is of the flesh*. Husbands and wives are only to fulfill their duty to one another and produce children."

When such beliefs are deeply ingrained, the carrier of those beliefs may not be open to change. For those who are wanting to integrate their spirituality and sexuality, we promote an active process of inviting God into their sexual lives. We have them read all biblical passages teaching about sex in marriage. We encourage them to read parts of the Song of Solomon in a modern version as part of their preparation for lovemaking. We suggest they thank God every time they have a sexual feeling. We have them actively ask God to be present and bless them as they enjoy their sexual times together.

Sometimes, we as sexual therapists are seen by counselees as spiritually suspect. When this is the case, we enlist the help of their spiritual mentor. With the individual or couple's permission, we invite into the sexual therapy process the minister, minister's wife, Bible-study leader, or other religious authority. Before giving the invitation, we ascertain that the mentor understands and accepts a healthy, biblical view of sexuality. That person's presence in the sexual therapy setting can greatly assist the religiously inhibited in connecting their sexuality with their spirituality and give them permission to thoroughly enjoy their sexual relationship in marriage.

Personal inhibitions may have been triggered by a past trauma, situation, or teaching that rendered certain parts of the body or secretions or activities as aversive. Some men are repulsed by a woman's genitals or vaginal secretions. Often these men do not like messes or spills. For example, Alvin did not want to touch Susan's vagina. It made him feel "yucky." The Clinical Genital Exam (described in chapter 9) had to be assigned several times and done in small increments. He tried to look the first time, touch the second time, and actually stroke the third time.

Alvin was never allowed to be messy as a young child. Even now when his mother feeds Alvin's baby daughter, she constantly wipes the baby's mouth and hands, and controls her food intake so there will be no mess.

Women who were sexually abused may have difficulty or be unable to engage in the sexual activity that was forced upon them. Some of these women cannot look at or touch their husbands' penises. Others cannot allow their husband to fondle them.

When inhibitions restrict the fullness of the sexual experience, freedom from the bondage is desired. Often, inhibited clients have tried desperately to engage in the desired activity, but to no avail. They need to be informed that there is no way they can expect to jump from where they are to where they desire to be sexually.

Treatment for sexual inhibition is behavioral. The inhibited person is instructed to define in detail the inhibitions. These should be written on the top of a sheet of paper. On the bottom of the paper, the person writes the behaviors that would be desired and would indicate freedom from sexual inhibition. Next, the person fills in the many small steps that could be taken to get from the top of the paper (inhibitions) to the bottom (sexual freedom). Each step is a "just noticeable difference," from that step. An example is described in Table 10–1.

Whether the relationship issue affecting the sexual experience is dissatisfaction with frequency, stressful initiation patterns, boredom, or more difficult inhibition, the symptom must be dealt with behaviorally. The relationship patterns must be changed if the symptoms are to be relieved and mutual satisfaction enjoyed.

INHIBITION: UNABLE TO TOUCH HUSBAND'S PENIS

E			
	a		
		c	
			h

E
a
c
h

S
t
e
p

=

Just

Noticeable

Difference

Touch penis over undershorts and pants for 5 seconds
"   "   "   "   "   "   " 10 "
"   "   "   "   "   "   " 15 "
"   "   "   "   "   "   " 20 "
"   "   "   "   "   "   " 25 "
"   "   "   "   "   "   " 30 "

Touch penis over undershorts only for 5 seconds
"   "   "   "   "   " 10 "
"   "   "   "   "   " 15 "
"   "   "   "   "   " 20 "
"   "   "   "   "   " 25 "
"   "   "   "   "   " 30 "

Touch penis directly for only 5, 10, 20, 30 seconds.

Give penis a friendly name.

Thank God for husband's penis daily.

Daily pat and claim husband's penis as your friend.

Stroke and fiddle with husband's penis once per day,
then twice per day, 3 times, etc.

Mentally picture his penis being a warm, comforting,
pleasant gift from God.

Continue to affirm, enjoy, and stroke husband's penis in
longer and longer periods of time until the ejaculation occurs.

Freedom: Able to manually enjoy husband's penis while
stimulating him to orgasm.

Table 10–1

CHAPTER ELEVEN

TREATING PROBLEMS OF SEXUAL DESIRE

INHIBITED SEXUAL DESIRE IS a disorder of the appetitive, or pre-excitement, phase of the sexual response cycle. Both the desires and mental images for sexual activity may be impaired. The urge to be physically close, to be touched, to be aroused, and to have release is in some way inhibited so that the person is not drawn to his or her spouse.

Some people with inhibited sexual desire are not aware of any sexual feelings at all, not even a flickering. It would not be a problem for them if there was no possibility of future sexual activity. Others masturbate but have no desire to be with their spouses. Still others only feel sexual desire for someone they cannot have or someone who is destructive for them. And then there are those who feel sexual urges for their spouses, but only when there is no possibility of acting on those urges.

The sexual drive can be totally blocked, or it can be misdirected. Many times there is a barrier that keeps the energy from being expressed or experienced in the marriage relationship.

Although we are all born with a sex drive, about 40 percent of sexual therapy clients report disorders of sexual desire, (as reported from the clinical practice of Kaplan, and as we have found in our own practice). Men, as well as women, experience loss of desire. Problems of desire are usually deeper, more resistant problems than the dilemmas of the sexual response cycles.

FEMALE DESIRE PROBLEMS

Disorders of desire for women may be secondary to some other difficulty, or they may be the primary issue.

Secondary to Dissatisfying or Negative Experiences

When the sexual experience itself is in some way dissatisfying, over the years women will lose desire in being together with their husbands sexually.

Relationship Issues. If not resolved, the sexual relationship issues discussed in the last chapter eventually lead to lack of interest. More general relationship problems can also spill over and keep a woman from sexually desiring her husband. If she feels uncared for, she may believe the only interest her husband has in her is to have sex with her. He comes home from work, turns on the television, sits quietly at dinner, and watches television after dinner. Then at bedtime, his friendliness comes alive, and her anger sizzles. When relationship issues have resulted in loss of sexual desire, marital counseling is the first step. The underlying stress in the relationship must be resolved before positive anticipation of sexual activity with her husband can be elicited.

Unsatisfactory Sexual Response. The loss of sexual desire may also be a result of lack of sexual responsiveness. If a woman has difficulty becoming aroused or having an orgasmic response, with time the initial excitement of being together will lessen.

It was 9 A.M. Friday morning, and it clearly felt like the end of the week. The mixture of anticipation of involving ourselves in the lives of another couple and the fatigue of a week full of work and family responsibilities faced us as we began a three-hour evaluation process. The fatigue lessened, though, as the energy of unraveling the pieces of another couple's problems with desire engaged us.

Tim and Nancy were a striking Southern California couple—the "yuppie" stereotype. They were tanned, well-dressed, jeweled, confident, and beautiful people. They had been sexually active for the six months before they were married. That activity carried on into the marriage with continued excitement and more freedom. Nancy reported wanting sex as much as Tim. Initially, they were together four to five times a week.

Although Tim was usually the aggressor and more active in the sexual experience than Nancy, she would become very "turned on." Nancy would be so aroused she would beg for entry. But after entry, her arousal seemed to get stuck, and within a few minutes Tim would ejaculate.

At first, this was no big deal; but the frustration that Nancy experienced after entry began to intensify as the situation was repeated. Tim was working long hours, so he would fall asleep shortly after intercourse. Nancy, on the other hand, would lie there wide awake, feeling all stirred up, and not knowing what to do with the build-up in her body.

After three years, she noted that more and more often, they were having sex because Tim wanted it and very seldom was she getting aroused. Even when she did get aroused, it was not the intense arousal that had left her awake and frustrated earlier in their marriage. Now, more than four years later, Nancy was complaining of total lack of sexual desire. As far as she was aware, she had never experienced sexual orgasm in response to any form of stimulation.

Nancy's lack of sexual desire was diagnosed as secondary to inhibited sexual release. The graph of her sexual response from the beginning of their sexual intercourse experiences to now would be gradually declining until it was a flat line. It took longer for her to get aroused, her arousal was less intense, and eventually she did not let herself get aroused at all. By now, even the flicker of positive anticipation of sexual activity had left. Now she was having sex with Tim once a week out of duty, obligation, and guilt for not desiring him. The graphs of her sexual response from the time of their initial sexual activity until the time of the evaluation would look like the graph in Figure 11–1.

Lack of Desire Due to Sexual Conflict

For women, sexual desire may be inhibited due to sexual conflict, the inability to accept their sexuality, or the feelings of the sexual experience.

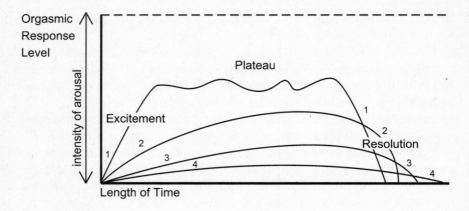

Fig. 11–1
Diminishing Sexual Response in Unfulfilled Women

When women experience conflict about being sexual, it may be because of rigid antisexual teaching, past sexual trauma, or ambivalence about being out of control and vulnerable with a man.

Rigid Antisexual Teaching. When rigid antisexual teaching is associated with religion (as it most often is) the approach to relieve the conflict—giving the woman permission to enjoy her sexuality and receive sexual pleasure—is the same as was presented in the previous chapter for reducing religious inhibitions. Deliberate, positive input regarding sexuality is necessary to counteract the lifelong subtle—or not so subtle—teaching that being sexual is to be avoided at all cost.

One of the most extreme examples of antisexual input was reported by Cindy, a beautiful young woman who, after three years, had not consummated her marriage. She had been raised in a warm, safe, but very strict Catholic home and school. In their home, they were not allowed to shower with the lights on or to ever be in the nude in a lighted room, lest they see themselves. They were directly taught to never use their hands to touch or wash their genitals, but to always use a wash cloth. Menstruation was handled with a "hush-hush" attitude and limited interaction.

At age sixteen, Cindy had to go to a sporting event. Because she was menstruating, she asked her mother about the possibility of using tampons. The horrifying, disgusting response of her mother totally confused Cindy. She thought she had asked a normal question; but after her mother's reaction, she felt she had committed a grievous sin to have even contemplated the idea. Her mother's response was, "You don't ever put anything there!" And at age twenty-five and after three years of marriage, she still never had. Nor had she given herself permission to be a sexual person with sexual desire and enjoyment of sexual pleasure. Attending our seminar was her first immersion into positive biblical attitudes about sexuality.

Sexual Trauma. Many adult women have had at least one sexual experience that left them confused, guilty, or traumatized. They usually blame themselves for these events and, thus, feel badly about themselves sexually. They do not feel worthy of receiving sexual pleasure, and have incredible conflict when they experience sexual feelings. Whether the event was something as violating as molestation or incest, or even if it was less traumatizing like having guilt about masturbating or fantasizing, sexual feelings have been paired with wrongdoing, fear, pain, and/or guilt. It is very difficult to disconnect that connection.

Usually the traumatic sexual event(s) will have been kept secret. Some victims grow up to believe that something terrible will happen to them if they tell. Others believe they have created the images in their minds which to them is one more indication of what nasty people they really are. In the case of abuse, the abuser may have warned the little girl not to tell, and given accompanying threats of what would happen if she told anyone. One woman shared that her rapist (who raped her at age ten) had told her she would be put in a mental institution because no one would believe her. They would know she was crazy, he had said. He was a strong leader in her church.

Another woman had gone to her mother at age six to try to tell her what the father was doing to her. Mother never even let her finish. Rather, the girl was reprimanded for thinking up such *stupid* ideas. It is easy to understand why women with such experiences and input would have difficulty enjoying their sexuality and their sexual relationship in marriage.

Guilt and shame are carried into adult life. The event may have been as innocent as discovering Dad's *Playboy* magazines and becoming aroused. Children feel responsible, not realizing they are innocent victims. They often believe they elicited or encouraged the abuse. Some little girls let the abuse happen because it was the only way they got Dad's love and affection. Yet, they grow up with the heavy burden of shame. They feel different from everyone else. They know that they know something that other children their age do not know. They have advanced sexual awareness.

Children who have experienced traumatic or negative emotions associated with sexuality may be withdrawn and shy, with low self-esteem, or they may become tough, act out aggressively, and become sexually promiscuous. In adult life, these women may have sexual phobias or aversions which are extremely tenacious resistances to being sexual. The panic reaction or avoidance may be to sex in general or to the specific sexual activities that were associated with the traumatic event. Some women do not want to have anything to do with sex with their husbands. Others who were forced to stimulate a man cannot look at or touch their husband's penis, but can enjoy all other sexual activity.

The woman who was fondled by her abuser may be able to freely enjoy her husband's body, but never allow him to touch her. Yet, these same women may need to fantasize the content of the trauma in order to become aroused and have an orgasm. This is the epitome of the conflict. The very activity that caused pain is necessary for the response. No wonder they do not desire sex.

There are women with lack of sexual desire who display many of the symptoms of having been sexually traumatized, yet have no recollection of any such experiences. Either they were too young to remember, they blocked out the event to protect themselves against the inner pain, or they experienced other trauma which produced the same conflict about sexuality as abuse.

The therapy to undo the sexual conflict that results when a sexual experience has elicited confusion, guilt, or trauma is multifaceted. The traumatic experience must be grieved and released; the sexual self must be developed (developmental tasks may need to be mastered); the guilt, shame, and trauma must be disconnected from the sexual experiences in marriage; and positive sexual feelings must be paired with safe sexual experiences (the sexual therapy process). This clearly calls for the combined effort of psychotherapy and sexual therapy.

PHASE I: Grieving and Relieving the Traumatic Experiences. In order to free themselves of the lasting effects of the sexually traumatic event, women need to talk about their abuse experiences. The details of what happened must be shared on numerous occasions. Writing down the memories is also necessary. Researchers have found that the discussion (in writing and talking) of traumatic events can help reduce adjustment problems that might result from the trauma.[1] Many women keep a journal or notebook in which they write any thoughts, feelings, dreams, or flashbacks. Writing helps them face the reality of what happened and helps them transfer the experience out of themselves onto the paper and put it on the shelf.

In addition to talking and writing, professional help is often needed. Women's sexual-abuse groups help the abused woman find support and begin to realize that she is not alone in her pain. If a woman has the symptomatology of past abuse, but no memory, being part of a group and hearing other women share their pain may trigger her memory. Reading about abuse can also open the awareness. Susan Forward and Craig Buck's book, *The Betrayal of Innocence*[2] has been the catalyst for a number of women to draw out their painful memories. We use this book as a diagnostic tool. If a woman has the symptoms of abuse, but no recollection, reading *The Betrayal of Innocence* will usually evoke intensely painful feelings, and quite often depression. This same reaction does not seem to happen for women without an abusive past, even though the reading is saddening.

PHASE II: Developing the Sexual Self. The sexual, and possibly the emotional, development may have been arrested when the abuse began or the traumatic event occurred. The psychotherapeutic process is necessary to aid the woman in defining how she sees herself sexually. It helps her develop her sexual self-esteem, so that one day she will be able to say, "Yes, I am a sexual person and I'm proud of it!" The Stages of Sexual Development depicted in Table 7–1 may be helpful in both identifying how she sees herself developing mentally and what the tasks are that need to be mastered.

PHASE III: Disconnecting Shame, Guilt, and Trauma from the Sexual Experiences in Marriage. In order to disconnect the negative feelings from sex in marriage, women have to go through a process of letting go of the pain. They have to recognize that what happened to them was not their fault. They were victims in those circumstances. Even if they were cute and "sexy," even if they did get aroused when they found their dad's magazines, they did not intentionally choose that event. The adults in their world should have protected them and should not have broken the trust and taken away their innocence.

These persons need to face the hurt, hate, and revenge for what happened. Then they can be helped to relinquish the pain and begin to forgive the adults in their world for violating them and not protecting them.

The possibility of confronting the abuser or the mother (for not protecting them) is usually raised. This issue must be considered most carefully so as to protect the victim from another abusive event. The counselor can help prevent further trauma by gathering as much data as possible about the current interaction patterns of the person to be confronted and by preparing the client for all possible responses or lack of response. Some women can let go after they confront, even if there was no response or a noncaring, hurtful response. Others are devastated if they do not receive a response that promotes healing.

PHASE IV: Pairing Positive Sexual Feelings with Safe Sexual Experiences. Finally, the woman will be ready to work on her sexual relationship with her husband—who must be a part of this sexual therapy process. It is most important that trust be established by the husband as he keeps to the boundaries of the assigned experiences and respects any requests from his wife during the experience.

The woman learns to verbalize or give her husband a prearranged signal when she has flashbacks of the abuse. Behaviors that cause phobia or aversive reactions are strictly avoided to begin with and then gradually desensitized during the process of therapy. This process of desensitization is the same as was described in chapter 10 for reducing personal inhibitions. The sexual therapy assignments are given in the order listed on the Sexual Therapy Plan in chapter 9, unless an experience to be assigned feels violating to the woman. In all touching exercises, the woman is encouraged to keep actively involved. She is to focus on the fact that it is her husband, that sex is good and of God, that it feels good to touch and to be touched, and that it will help to keep her mind actively engaged in positive pictures of the two of them enjoying themselves.

The goal is that with the trauma having been released, the sexual self-esteem being more positive, and the negative feelings having been disconnected from the husband-wife sexual encounters, then the process of sexual therapy will safely and gradually lead the woman to learn to delight in the sexual connection with her husband. This process often takes a long time.

Sexual Ambivalence. Another source of sexual conflict is ambivalence about being sexual. Even though these women can be very sexually responsive, they relentlessly resist being sexual. This is not a passive absence of interest in sexual activity. It is a persistent avoidance of sex. These women's sexual response graphs look like the graph in Figure 11–2.

These women come from alcoholic and dysfunctional homes. They struggle with control issues—and to be sexually responsive is to be out of control. Their homes were out of control, so they know well how to let go sexually; but they stubbornly fight losing control. The woman who lacks

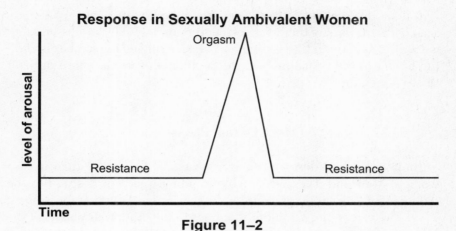

Response in Sexually Ambivalent Women

Figure 11–2

sexual desire because of ambivalence is an enigma to her husband. It is confusing to him to try to understand why she would resist when she seems so responsive.

Working with the sexually ambivalent woman requires a unique therapeutic approach. The first counseling task is to bring the woman to the place where she can make a decision to be sexual. This is very much like a conversion experience. She has been going one direction—fighting being sexual—and she decides to go the opposite direction—pursuing being sexual.

Second, her pattern of passively controlling the couple's sexual relationship through resistance must change to one of actively taking control of their sexual relationship by planning sexual times to be together. She needs active control. She has had passive control, but not by decision or to promote sex. She keeps the control, but now by deciding to be sexual.

Third, she will have to schedule and initiate the sexual encounters that she has planned. It is most difficult for these women to schedule without the feeling of desire. They want so badly to wait until they "feel" like having sex. Our experience suggests that it will be a *long* time until they initiate sex out of desire. We recommend that they plan to set aside time on their calendars to be with their husbands at least twice a week—the more often the better.

The fourth task is for the husband, who assumes a passive role. He no longer initiates or pursues. He allows her to take charge. This may feel wonderful to the husband, because sexual initiation has been completely his burden.

In addition to the unique therapeutic approach focused on the lack of sexual desire, these women benefit greatly from participating in an ACA (Adult Children of Alcoholics) group.

Inhibited sexual desire that is not secondary to other sexual disability is a challenge for any therapist. Psychotherapeutic skills are essential to work effectively with these women. As Helen Singer Kaplan has found,[3] the earlier in the sexual process the problem began, the more difficult the treatment.

MALE DESIRE PROBLEMS

Inhibited sexual desire in men is no easier to correct than it is in women. Men find it less acceptable to admit a lack of desire, but the dilemma may be almost as prevalent as in women. As is true for women, low desire can be the result of difficulties in the other four phases of the sexual response cycle. For example, if a man always feels like a failure because he ejaculates prematurely, his desire will diminish over time.

When the problem is not secondary to performance failure, men who lack desire to be with their wives sexually are either sexually naive, overly entrepreneurial and goal-oriented, emotionally and sexually blocked, or homosexually oriented.

The Sexually Naive Male

The sexually naive male may lack desire because of feelings of inadequacy and underdeveloped emotional expression. He never mastered the developmental tasks of the preadolescent years (see Stages of Sexual Development, Table 7–1). He was probably raised in an overprotective home or a home where emotional intensity and expression were not allowed. He may even have missed the usual childhood expressions of sexual curiosity such as exploratory play. His dating experience before marriage was probably limited. Thus, he entered marriage still feeling physically awkward with a woman. He may not even know how to kiss passionately. One man put it so aptly, "I feel like a junior-higher in an adult body. When I'm trying to make love to my wife, I just don't know what I'm doing. Nothing flows. When I try to caress her, I jab her with my elbow. Sex just feels overwhelming to me."

The sexually naive male is an extremely rewarding client to work with. He is like an empty sponge ready to soak up any help the therapist has to offer. Education can make a major difference. If he has a loving, cooperative wife, the process flows easily.

The Sexual Therapy Plan presented in chapter 9 is ideal in training this man to be a sexual adult. He must start from the beginning in learning to touch. Next, the teaching and talking exercises fill many gaps for him. The process can usually be completed with few changes from the therapy plan outlined in chapter 9. Full, confident sexual functioning is only weeks away. Once confidence and enjoyment are gained, desire surfaces rapidly.

The Entrepreneurial Male

The entrepreneurial or overly goal-oriented male has done a great job of courting his wife, who is usually an attractive, competent, and sensual woman. He has provided a beautiful home, maybe a child or two, and a well-managed life. His wife does not have to work, so she has time to pamper herself, take tennis lessons, etc. She likely can have a house-keeper. In other words, she has plenty of space to feel her sexual urges.

One of the entrepreneurial male's goals was to establish an ideal family and home. Now that that has been accomplished he is on to other goals. These may be building better and bigger companies, developing shopping malls, starting and building churches, or whatever happens to be his interest. He is the type who sees the potential in a project, works it well, turns it over to be run by someone else, and then is ready to move on to the next project—very much like he has done sexually with his wife.

Ellen had prepared a gourmet dinner for Jim (having just finished a French cooking class), had the children in bed, and was waiting in a candle-lit room. Jim said he would be home between 8:30 and 9 P.M. The clock strikes ten and he is still not home. At 10:30 P.M., Ellen gets a call that he had just finished the business negotiation on a big deal and he would be home in about twenty minutes.

This was not a surprise to Ellen. This same, disappointing call had come many times in their eight years of marriage. She had been looking forward to a sexual time together; it had been getting longer and longer between their times of physical closeness. A lonely pang bolted through her well-prepared body. But then the thought came to her that had kept her from complaining: *He has given me so much. I have a great life.* And she went to stretch out on the couch to enjoy the novel she was reading.

Unfortunately, Ellen is clearly being set up for an affair. All her needs are being met—except the sexual and intimacy cravings. Just like all other projects, the entrepreneurial male prepares his wife to be taken over and managed by someone else. He is goal-oriented. He sees the big possibilities. He cannot be bothered by such trivia as sexual needs, not his own, nor hers.

The entrepreneur can make changes, but the changes have to fit his approach to life. He must, by his decision, make his wife and their sexual relationship one of his priorities. She has to be scheduled in. Even then he may miss scheduled times because of business pressure. A matter-of-fact approach works best: If he misses their scheduled time, what are the consequences? Maybe he makes up the time before he leaves for work the next morning, or he gives her double time the next evening, or he takes her away for a day. Unfortunately, he will try to *buy* her something for the time missed. It must be made clear that lost intimacy must be replaced with intimacy, not gifts.

Some entrepreneurial men have actually chosen to give up their marriages rather than make these seemingly minor adjustments in their lifestyles. Others are very eager to find a system that works for both of them. Some find they can only allow their sexual-drive energy to surface when they are away with their wives or families. Fortunately, they can afford to get away on a regular basis and that makes both of them happy. The solution to the entrepreneurial lack of sexual desire is primarily one of problem-solving, priority-setting, and time management.

Emotional-Sexual Blocks

Deeper and more emotionally based barriers causing lack of sexual desire in men present a more difficult challenge to the sexual therapist/psychotherapist. In fact, psychotherapy definitely needs to be the basis for these more tenacious issues. Positive sexual anticipation may be blocked for a man because of lack of bonding in infancy, sexual trauma, rigid antisexual teaching, or a controlling, male-depreciating mother.

Lack of Bonding in Infancy. The capacity for intimacy is learned during the first year of life. It is from the maternal-infant bond that basic trust is developed.[4] During this critical learning period, the ingredient is acquired that prepares us to be able to be transparent with both our feelings and our sexual desires, to bond affectionately with our spouses, to be able to mutually give and receive pleasure from each other's bodies, and to responsibly and deeply care for each other. This is intimacy.

The fear of intimacy is present in both men and women. Thus, many of the issues that will be addressed here in relation to men's avoidance of sex because of fear of intimacy can also be applied to women. In our practice, it has been easier to isolate the intimacy / lack-of-bonding factor for men than for women, possibly because women also display the other issues of sexual conflict. Another speculation is that more mothers may have difficulty bonding with infant sons than they do with daughters because of their own fears of sexual feelings that arouse them when they are close with their baby boys.

Men who have been raised with an intimacy deficit (have not had their needs for closeness met early in childhood), are often as relentless in their resistance to behaving sexually with their spouses as are women who were raised in an alcoholic-type home. They have sexual drive, but they have no capacity for closeness and warmth with a woman. They may even verbally express their desire for what they unconsciously avoid or sabotage by their inappropriate behavior. They may roll away in bed when they notice they are aroused; they may watch television or be distracted in other ways to avoid connecting; they may pick a fight; or they may approach in a way that they have been told many times will be a "turn-off" rather than a "turn-on" to their wives, etc.

Many of these men have compulsive masturbatory habits that may be "boyish" in nature or be paired with a fetish. They are anxiously and guiltily meeting their sexual-drive needs while avoiding the intimacy of a sexual relationship.

James was adopted from institutional care after his first birthday. His adoptive home was adoring, but somewhat lacking in physical and emotional warmth and closeness. As an adult, James was verbally the one desiring more sex. Yet, when assigned sensate focus/touching exercises, he refused to do them because he said his wife was "just doing them out of obligation."

Later that day he would approach his wife Ann in their old pattern that was sure to be a disaster for both of them. He would often have an attack of rage before they were to go away by themselves for a romantic weekend. She was labeled as the one with lack of sexual desire; yet his behaviors indicated that, even though he had the sexual drive, he had incredible fear and avoidance of being sexually intimate with Ann.

Sexual Trauma. Sexual trauma produces the same phobic reactions to sex in men as it does for women. The abuse also leaves men with the negative feelings associated with themselves as sexual persons and with sexual feelings—shame, guilt, humiliation, etc. Thus, the man who experienced childhood sexual abuse or incest will suffer from a low sexual self-esteem. The same guidelines used for women should be followed in working with abused men.

Rigid Antisexual Teaching. Men may have aversive feelings toward sex with their wives as a result of rigid antisexual teaching or a very tight moral, restrictive upbringing. If his hand was slapped when he discovered his genitals in toddlerhood, if exploratory play was responded to with punishment, and if natural curious bumbling with the opposite sex was prohibited in junior high, the adult man is likely to feel restrictive and anxious about sex. If he also was strictly taught not to masturbate or was violently reacted to if he was found masturbating, the man will connect anxiety and guilt with being sexual.

Controlling, Male-depreciating Mother. If a boy grew up in a home with a mother who totally usurped any of his sense of power and independence as he was developing, he will be very hesitant to allow himself to be open and vulnerable with a woman. Having sex with his wife may elicit an overwhelming sense of panic at being swallowed up or controlled. In addition to being dominant and controlling, if the mother ridiculed his father, the boy's role model, the boy will grow into manhood feeling very unsure of himself and inadequate as a man. He will have a low sexual self-esteem. Fear of being vulnerable with a woman and a sexual sense of inadequacy are clearly components that lead to insufficient sexual desire.

Treatment. Treatment for men with emotional-sexual blocks requires a skilled, creative therapist who can adapt the therapy process to the level of intimacy the man can experience without feeling anxiety or aversion. Kaplan recommends that with some phobic avoidance situations a psychiatric evaluation may be necessary in order to prescribe medication and treat the case like other phobic disorders.[5] This treatment plan would be appropriate for clients who experience panic attacks, high anxiety levels, and such severe tension that they cannot proceed with any structured assignments.

Most men with blocked sexual desire can be treated with a combination of sexual therapy exercises, desensitization, and psychotherapy. The sexual therapy assignments listed in chapter 9 may demand too much intimacy and trigger the avoidance behavior. If this is the case, even less-anxiety-provoking assignments must be given. Kaplan says she "employed such tasks as lying near each other, first clothed, then unclothed, for several weeks, until this behavior becomes comfortable, before proceeding to more intimate behavior."[6] We have assigned taking daily walks together and holding hands, patting and affirming each other's genitals every night at bedtime, or hugging and kissing every morning for ten to fifteen seconds. The Guidelines for Sexual Therapy (Sexual Therapy Assignment 1A in chapter 9) must be adhered to rigidly so that demand experiences are stopped and negative feelings are verbalized.

The aversive sexual behaviors must be desensitized using the process described in the treatment of personal inhibitions in chapter 10. It is helpful if the counselee/client defines the small steps which he must take to move from his point of resistance to sexual freedom. He might also write out or verbally picture the physical contacts or events that would be positive for him.

When negative feelings are triggered by doing the sexual therapy assignments, or the assignments are in some way avoided or sabotaged, the sexual therapy must be interrupted and psychotherapy enlisted in order to work with the client to gain insight into the elements that are blocking his desire. To gain this insight, it is recommended the client talk with his wife about the negative feelings or write about them and then talk about them in the session. The man must talk through each experience in detail with the therapist, noting exactly what was enjoyable or free of negative feelings, and noting when the negative reaction occurred and what that felt like. Reviewing the client's dreams can help the therapist gain insight into unconscious reasons for the resistance.

Again, the goal is to relieve the symptoms of avoidance and gain positive connection with sexual feelings and an acceptance of himself as a competent sexual person.

Craig's mother was a distant, cold, society lady who had no capacity to radiate a warm, loving touch. She clearly let everyone in the family know that she was in charge and superior to her husband in almost every way. He was almost pathetic or disgusting in her eyes. Craig was raised with all the social skills; he was a dapper young man with high moral standards.

Before his marriage to Erin, he was appropriately physical with her. Erin did not sense his difficulty with sexual intimacy until the wedding night, when they were to have their first sexual intercourse. Craig kept avoiding. He wanted to go for a walk. When they got to their beautiful honeymoon suite, he turned on the television. He wanted to order a snack brought to the room. His negative anticipation of sexually bonding with his wife became very apparent.

When they did have sexual intercourse, it was a quick, genital act. He had no capacity to be passionate or intensely enjoy his wife's body. He resisted almost all future attempts that Erin made to engage him sexually. Sex only seemed to happen on rare occasions if she caught him off guard when he was partially asleep. Later, to her fury, Erin discovered that Craig had a masturbatory fetish that he practiced at least daily. His sexual need was high, but his desire for his wife was absent because of his never having experienced the warmth of a giving mother and his low view of men (thus of himself) in relation to women and his fear of losing himself to a woman. In his view, women control, dominate and put men down.

When assigning Craig and Erin sexual therapy exercises, his sabotaging had to be anticipated. The exercises had to be modified to start building intimacy gradually. Walking around the block holding hands was successful, and other exercises of controlled intimacy went fairly well. The first real avoidance came with the facial caress. Even after talking the experience through in the session with the therapists and anticipating the feelings, he still could not proceed when they were home together. Craig had limited ability to verbalize his feelings. All he could say was, "I just can't do it."

We, the therapists, started to verbalize for him with the help of his wife. We talked about the uncomfortableness of touching a woman's face, the very part one connects with one's personhood. The client's feelings of awkwardness and anxiousness were expressed for him. He could identify and even begin to expand on the feelings as they were expressed for him. We spent some time talking about the images of his mother and how Erin is different. The therapy process for Craig and Erin was slow. Appointments were often missed and assignments were not completed. In each step of the process, time was taken to get insight into Craig's resistance. At the same time, we had to empower Craig. He had to actively participate in the therapy decisions and in the experiences with Erin. To some extent, Craig will always have to consciously decide to have sexual times with Erin, but the experiences are now relieved of the helpless, anxious, inadequate feelings that were such a part of the avoidance of every sexual encounter before they came for therapy.

The Homosexually Oriented Male

Homosexual orientation will make it difficult for a man to positively anticipate sex with a woman, just as it would be difficult for a heterosexual man to picture himself positively with another man. A man may have always felt that he was more attracted to men than women, but never acted upon that attraction. He may have married to be socially and morally acceptable, and he may have been able to function sexually with his wife, but only by decision or felt necessity, not by desire.

Problems due to homosexual orientation are not our area of expertise for treatment, so we would highly recommend that counselors refer to books written by others.[7]

FEMALE AND MALE LACK OF SEXUAL DESIRE AS A RESULT OF EXTERNAL FACTORS

Both men and women experience lack of positive anticipation for sexual encounters at some time in their married lives. External circumstances can distract from the sexual-drive energy for each other. Relationship stresses can raise a barrier between the couple's positive physical anticipation of each other. Physiological factors can interfere. Illness can leave us still needing touching and closeness, but may drain most erotic energy.

Alcohol is a depressant; in small quantities, it can reduce anxiety and increase availability, but any more than a little usually takes away sexual-drive energy. Drugs, both street and prescription, can interfere with the autonomic nervous system which regulates the sexual response cycle. In her book, *Disorders of Sexual Desires*, Kaplan has an extensive chart of many types of drugs and their effect on the sexual response cycle.[8] This chart is an important reference for a sexual therapist to have available at all times. Hormonal changes can also affect sexual desire. Some oral contraceptives seem to cause loss of sexual desire for some women. Those with low testosterone activity that are prescribed for women with acne are more likely to have this affect (e.g., Demulen). Removal of a woman's ovaries removes her source of testosterone production.

Low testosterone may also be the reason for loss of desire in men. Other emotional stresses, such as depression or anxiety, will also lower sexual drive.

Whatever the cause of the dysfunction or the inhibition of sexual desire, and whether the woman or the man experiences the disorder, the most effective therapy is innovative and multifaceted. It is focused on reducing the symptomatology and regaining new, positive mental expectations of sexual encounters with one's spouse. Psychotherapy, problem-solving, priority-setting, scheduling, sexual therapy talking, teaching, and touching exercises, desensitization, and Christian pro-sexual teaching are all a part of the retraining process.

CHAPTER TWELVE

TREATING PROBLEMS OF SEXUAL AROUSAL

SEXUAL DESIRE IN MARRIAGE usually leads to the initiation of sexual activities that stimulate sexual excitement or arousal. Failure of the natural, involuntary bodily response of sexual excitement is usually due to anxiety, although physical, medical causes should be ruled out before assuming an emotional basis.

PROBLEMS OF AROUSAL FOR WOMEN

Lack of feelings of arousal

Inhibited sexual excitement for women, once negatively labeled frigidity, is usually experiential, not actual. In other words, the woman's body *is* responding with vaginal lubrication, nipple erection, and initial engorgement; however, she does not subjectively *feel* aroused. Her emotions are not connected with her involuntary bodily responses.

These women who lack the feelings of arousal are mentally disconnecting themselves from their bodies. They have not programmed themselves to be sexual persons or to enjoy the giving and receiving of sexual pleasure. They see sex as a duty they perform to keep their husbands happy and themselves from feeling guilty. They do not visualize themselves in positive sexual activities, nor do they view themselves as having sexual feelings. Usually they devote most of their energy and fill their minds with the tasks of life: their children, their household chores, their jobs, and their social lives.

Even in the actual sexual experience, they will be physically passive and mentally focused on everything but the sexual touching they are receiving. One woman reported that she would count the drops of the water dripping in the shower, trying to focus her mind on anything but sex.

This difficulty is interrelated with the sexual conflict that causes lack of sexual desire in women. Something has happened in these women's pasts that makes it difficult for them to positively associate sexuality with themselves. They have a low sexual self-esteem and certainly a blocked awareness of their sexuality. They are not receptive to sexual stimulation nor the arousal it produces.

The first task for women who lack feelings of arousal—even though their bodies are responding—is to shift to a positive mental sexual attitude, visualizing themselves sexually. The second task is to encourage positive bodily sensations while eliminating negative feelings associated with sexual touching. Through the accomplishment of the first, the positive sexual mental set, they can then learn to enjoy rather than block out the feelings of their bodily responses.

Women can best accomplish these tasks by: 1) Giving themselves permission to be sexual people and to feel sexual feelings, 2) Connecting sexual feelings with their actual responses, 3) Removing demands and the need to please, and 4) Actively listening to their bodies and vigorously going after sexual pleasure.

The first task is the most difficult. The mental images must change first, then the emotions; the pleasure follows. The reasons for the negative sexual images may have to be explored psychotherapeutically before they can be replaced with positive pictures. The programming of positive mental images works best if it is deliberate. Sometimes it is helpful for these women to picture themselves with their spouses in past positive situations. If they have never experienced positive sexual feelings under any circumstances, they may need to read examples like the Song of Solomon or watch educational videos of positive sexual encounters or imagine what would be positive for them.

Giving themselves permission to be and to feel sexual is an important part of the mental change. The woman needs to make an active decision that she is a sexual person and this is good and of God. A note inside the calendar that reminds the woman that she is a sexual person, verses from the Song of Solomon put on the refrigerator door, looking in the mirror and thanking God for creating her as a sexual person, are little daily ways of reprogramming her mental images and giving herself permission to be sexual.

The Sexual Therapy Plan in chapter 9 is the best process for helping these women with the second task of encouraging positive sexual feelings and eliminating negative ones. The Guidelines for Sexual Therapy in Sexual Therapy Assignment 1A must be followed precisely in order to remove all performance and response demands.

The touching exercises of The Sexual Therapy Plan allow these women to be able to receive and give pleasure for the sake of pleasure. If they resist, it is necessary to delve into that resistance and move ahead very slowly. Listen for their resistance. When reporting this completion of the assignments, one woman constantly pointed out that she had not felt anything in the exercise. We had to define neutral as positive. If she did not feel anything negative, then it was positive.

We developed a 1-to-10 rating system. Number 1 was no negative sensation, number 2 was comfortable, number 3 was warm, number 4 was relaxing, etc. She could not get herself to say that an experience had been positive, but she could rate the experiences with this numbering system that had very low expectations. She did regularly experience nipple erection and vaginal lubrication, even though she reported to have no feelings associated with these responses. Because of this, numbers 9 and 10 on the positive-rating system were labeled as nipple erection and vaginal lubrication. Hence, at whatever level of functioning is possible, the focus is on the positive aspects of the giving and receiving of pleasure.

Learning to enjoy their bodily responses begins with women's learning to know their bodies. The female self-exam is vital. Education is also important. Reading *The Gift of Sex* aloud with their husbands is helpful. Graphing of the Sexual Response, as explained in Sexual Therapy Assignment 13 in chapter 9, will teach the women what to expect and to know that what is happening in their body is sexual. We encourage these women and their husbands to note bodily responses and affirm them: "I am (You are) aroused!"

If sex can be changed from being an ordeal that the woman performs to please her husband to a pleasurable experience in which she feels the sensation of her arousal (and enjoys those sensations), then much has been accomplished.

Lack of Vaginal Lubrication and Engorgement

Emotions can interfere with the actual physical response of arousal for women just like they do in men. The lack of vasocongestion in women is the same as the inability to get or keep an erection for men. In women, this actual lack of physical arousal is rare, probably because women tend to be more passive sexually and arousal is a passive, parasympathetic nervous system response. The emotion of anxiety can, however, interrupt or prevent arousal for women. The sympathetic nervous system becomes dominant because of the anxiety and interferes with the involuntary parasympathetic nervous system responses.

Most women who lack arousal also do not have release. Nevertheless, there are some women who report being orgasmic, but not experiencing vaginal lubrication or nipple erection. The reflex of orgasm happens without all the enjoyable buildup. This could be compared to some men who learn to ejaculate without an erection. The treatment for this would be much like treating impotence in men, which will be discussed at the end of this chapter.

The most common reason for lack of physical arousal responses in women is lack of stimulation. This is usually due to sexual naiveté on the part of both the man and the woman. The couple is not kissing passionately, stimulating breasts, or fondling genitals. In fact, they are not engaging in much love play at all. They have intercourse when he has an erection and that is the extent of their sexual involvement. Other times, there may be love play, but there is no knowledge of or experimentation with effective stimulation of the woman.

The guidelines and exercises of the Sexual Therapy Plan are necessary to reverse this dilemma. The Nondemand Teaching exercise and the

Clinical Genital Exam in this plan are most helpful to counteract the naiveté and begin expanding awareness and learning effective techniques of sexual enjoyment. As mentioned earlier (chapter 5), lack of vaginal lubrication may also be due to a decrease in estrogen during and after menopause. Artificial lubricants are helpful and hormonal replacement therapy may be necessary.

PROBLEMS OF AROUSAL FOR MEN

Erection is the most significant response of arousal for men during the excitement phase; therefore, difficulty with excitement for men manifests itself physically as erectile dysfunction, or impotence.

Erectile Dysfunction

Impotence refers to a man's inability to achieve an erection or his difficulty maintaining an erection. Difficulty with erection can occur at various times during the sexual experience. Some men gain no erection at all. The usual kind of stimulation occurs, but the penis remains flaccid. This is usually due to anxiety about getting an erection. For others, an erection may occur in response to physical enjoyment, but the erection is lost as the love play continues. This loss is usually due to anxiety about maintaining the erection, or it is an anxious response to the normal ebb and flow of the intensity of an erection during extended pleasuring. When a man does not have the knowledge that it is normal to lose and regain erections during longer times of sexual enjoyment, the lessening of his erection triggers anxiety, and the anxiety interferes with the parasympathetic response of erection.

For others, the erection may be maintained very adequately up to the point of entry. When entry is contemplated or attempted, the erection dissipates. For some, the erection can be maintained beyond the point of entry, but it is lost after thrusting inside the vagina—again because the man is anxious about his response.

When impotence is the presenting problem, the assessment process should be used to differentiate 1) When in the process the loss of erection occurs, 2) What activity is happening at that point of the love play, and 3) What mental thoughts and feelings are associated with that event.

All men of all ages experience erectile difficulty at some time or another. The occasional inability to get or maintain an erection need not be an issue of concern; that is normal. Just because people may occasionally have a sleepless night, does not mean they have insomnia. Similarly, the occasional loss of an erection does not mean a man is impotent.

Causes of Erectile Dysfunction

Because impotence may be due to either anxiety or physical factors, a referral to a urologist is always important in the evaluation process. Also, tumescence evaluation at a "sleep center" can provide additional data. The man being evaluated by the sleep center will be monitored by various electronic devices to get a reading of his erectile and other bodily responses.

In addition, cardiac and vascular medical assessments are often warranted because impotence may be an early sign of cardiac or vascular impairment. An erection is a vascular response. The penis must be pumped full of blood, and the vessels must function to keep the blood trapped in the penis during sexual excitement. Diabetes, circulatory problems, and endocrine hormonal problems can interfere. All medications should be studied to determine whether impotence is a side effect. Antihypertensives, beta blockers, and alcohol are drugs to be suspected.

When the cause is emotional, the erection is interrupted at the moment the man becomes anxious or begins evaluating the state of his erection. The anxiety pattern has a definable sequence. The pattern begins with an experience in which the man does not respond with an erection like usual or he loses it during the process and does not regain it. This initial incident may be totally coincidental. It may be due to such things as fatigue, or alcohol or drug use. Or the loss of erection may occur in response to his wife. She might be critical, negative, unresponsive, or in some way set off feelings of anxious inadequacy. Guilt can also cause that initial difficulty with erection. Authentic guilt about an affair may cause him to be impotent in the affair or with his wife after the affair. Unauthentic guilt about being sexual in some way with his wife may also affect his erectile response. Other emotions of anger, depression, or anxiety about external factors such as finances can keep a man from focusing on the sexual pleasure and interfere with his arousal response.

Once anxiety about the erectile difficulty has occurred, it tends to perpetuate itself. This is true even if the reason for the original difficulty is removed. The man may no longer be fatigued, depressed, angry, or under the influence of alcohol. Yet, he is now anxious about his erectile functioning. It is the anxiety caused by anticipation of failure that perpetuates the dysfunction.

After the initial failure that triggers the erectile anxiety, subsequent failures occur due to the anxiety. The anxiety increases with each failure. As the anxiety increases, a preoccupation develops. The man becomes a spectator. He constantly monitors the state of his penis, almost like reading an ongoing computer printout. This may lead to frequent initiation of sex in an attempt to prove himself, or it may lead to loss of interest in sex because of fear of failure.

The stress may be so intense that he mentally dissociates his penis from his body as it loses all feelings, almost becoming numb, or anesthetized. General despair and depression often follow. Impotence severely attacks a man's self-esteem. It often makes him feel that he has lost his manhood.

The woman will also be affected. She may become anxious and stop any form of effective penile stimulation, thus perpetuating the difficulty with erection. Many women become angry when their husbands are impotent, which only exerts more performance demands and decreases the possibility of a reversal of the problem. Some women feel badly about themselves. They unrealistically believe that if they were more attractive or more sexual, this would not be happening. Feelings of rejection are also very common for the wife of the man who is struggling with erectile disorders

There are other causes for impotence besides this anxiety pattern that started with loss of erection in response to some external event or pressure. More long-term difficulties often wear on the man and lead to erectile difficulties:

1. Premature ejaculation leads a man to attempt to inhibit his sexual response so he will not ejaculate so quickly. Unfortunately, it is impossible to mentally and emotionally inhibit one response without affecting the other. The man with premature ejaculation starts watching his response. This spectatoring then interrupts the natural erectile response.
2. Being dominated or made to feel inadequate may eventually lead to the inability to get or keep an erection. This may have its origin with a dominant parent and then be perpetuated by a dominant wife.

3. Any long-term negative emotions connected with sexuality or the sexual act can eventually lead to erectile dysfunction. Rigid religious upbringing may cause a man to become uncomfortable and anxious when he is doing anything sexual. Fear of rejection may grow out of a long-term negative relationship. If his wife has gradually lost respect for him or constantly is in conflict with him, impotence could result from fear of rejection.

Whatever the original source of the impotence, the anxiety pattern described usually keeps it going. This is the pattern that must be interrupted in order to be successful in regaining erectile security.

Treatment of Erectile Dysfunction

Erectile disorders are reversible. As couples proceed through the therapy plan, the following components are necessary for successful treatment: 1) Distraction from the anxiety, 2) focus on the sexual pleasure without making demands of himself, 3) a wife who can thoroughly enjoy his body for her pleasure without putting any demands or expectations on herself to bring him an erection or on him to produce one.

The reversal process starts with open communication. A time of talking, confessing, crying, and forgiving will begin to diminish the hurts and disillusionment. This communication is crucial for the relief of the self-doubts, blame, anger, resentment, and frustration that have grown as the impotence has become the norm. Once the underlying feelings have been processed, the ingredients for treatment of erectile disorders are pursued.

Distraction from Anxiety. Distraction from the anxiety for getting or keeping an erection is begun by ruling out intercourse or attempts at intercourse. This limitation is the most powerful anxiety reducer for the man.

Almost as powerful is the acceptance of the reality that the touching exercises are not expected to produce arousal. It should be made clear that if an erection occurs during the pleasuring times, no attempt should be made to pursue that response. Rather, the sensations are to be enjoyed, allowing them to come and go. The ability to enjoy the increased and decreased engorgement of the penis is what eventually gives the man his erectile security.

Verbalizing performance anxiety or spectatoring to his wife is essential to distracting from the erectile anxiety. As soon as the man begins to focus on his response, or get into the spectator role, he must inform his wife that he is feeling anxious, self-conscious, or evaluative about his penile response. The verbalizing is necessary to interrupt the spectatoring. When the man verbalizes, he takes the emotions that are part of his right-brain function and moves that content into the left-brain. The integrative process of the two hemispheres of the brain is the reason for verbalizing the performance anxiety. The talking, which is a left-brain function, brings the feelings from the right-brain, where we have little control over them, to the verbal left-brain. Expressing the concerns about erections moves those anxious reactions to where they can be controlled rather than keeping them in the right-brain where they control.

Communicating anxiety is difficult for most men, yet it is crucial to regaining erectile functioning. Many men are concerned that telling their wives will only make both of them more discouraged and frustrated. There is a tendency to want to ignore the thoughts and feelings with the hope that they will go away and will not negatively affect the response. However, if the anxiety is not expressed (switched from the right-brain to the left-brain), it will become more overpowering. This is true with any fear. When a speaker finds his hands are shaking, his saying, "I guess I am anxious about speaking to you today. My shaky hands are certainly giving me away," will usually relieve the anxiety and stop the shaking. Thus, interrupting the anxiety by verbalizing it is absolutely necessary.

After the man has been able to verbalize his performance anxiety, and his wife has been able to receive it, the couple should change the focus of their sexual touching away from the penis or away from the activity that stimulated the anxiety and enjoy nondemand pleasuring. Usually it is necessary to switch the focus from pleasuring the husband to the husband pleasuring his wife. His being active distracts from the spectatoring. His enjoyment of her body takes him out of the spotlight where he feels the demand for a response.

Focus on Pleasure. The change of focus from preoccupation with the state of his penis to skin-to-skin contact and the fun of enjoying each other's bodies can only happen as all demands to attain and keep erections diminish and disappear.

To switch the focus off the erection (or the loss of it) and onto the enjoyment of pleasure, the Sexual Therapy Plan should be followed step by step. The touching exercises may be repeated several times; slow the process in order to establish securely the patterns of experiencing the pleasure of each other's bodies without demand to respond.

Specific steps for reversing impotence are listed on page 131 of the Sexual Therapy Plan. As part of the Clinical Genital Exam, the couple should be encouraged to name each other's genitals and claim them as their friends. From that point on, the couple is encouraged to pat and affirm each other's genitals every night before they go to sleep. This is to desensitize the anxiety and reduce demand for response that has become so connected with the wife's touching of her husband's penis. The patting and affirming is positive touch without any expectations. We call it "fiddling."

A Wife Who Enjoys His Body. The wife will need to be taught the ability to pleasure her husband's body, not for the response she can produce, but rather for the pleasure it brings to her. The more freely the wife can totally relax and delight in her husband's body and allow him to delight in hers, the more likely the natural response of erection will begin to occur. It is comparable to the biblical concept of losing our lives to gain them. When both husband and wife stop trying to produce an erection—when they let go and enjoy themselves—an erection is the most likely outcome.

When the sexual therapy progresses to include direct penile stimulation, this step must be handled most carefully. The wife is of critical importance. She must learn to practice keeping the penis hungry for more touch rather than touching too long and, thereby communicating a demand for response. It is great if she can be playful with her husband's penis, talking to it, naming it, and enjoying it, as well as learning to stimulate it in a way that is most pleasurable for him. She needs to be taught to build up the intensity of the stimulation and then move away from the penis to enjoying other parts of his body. Keep him off guard so he does not know what to expect and therefore cannot anticipate demands.

In all of the penile stimulation, there must not be an ejaculation without an erection. That is a firm and fast rule. Some men who struggle with impotence have learned to attain the release they want without making their penises do their part of the work. We call it the "lazy penis syndrome." A man will never interrupt his erectile dysfunction if he allows himself to ejaculate without an erection.

As the pleasuring experiences continue, honoring the prescribed guidelines, erections will come and go. They may be short-lived at first. But every response should be enjoyed without any pressure for more and without attempts to figure out what "made it work" so that the response can be reproduced. That is the demand pattern that we hope has been broken. As the couple learns to enjoy the penile responses without the demand to keep them or reproduce them, the man will gain confidence in his ability to attain, lose, and regain erections. He begins to rediscover that he *can* experience erections. If there is a dip in arousal that causes the penis to become flaccid, he will start to have the security that it will respond again. He will learn to interrupt any anxious or demanding thoughts as soon as they appear, without allowing them to interfere with their pleasuring times.

Before any attempts at entry are made, the penis and the vagina must become reacquainted. They need to be gently and gradually reintroduced to each other as friends, not feared objects. To help the penis become familiar with the vagina without performance anxiety, the husband and wife are both encouraged to use the penis, whether flaccid or erect, as a paint brush across the clitoris and opening of the vagina (refer to Sexual Therapy Assignment 26 in chapter 9). Through this activity, the man gains new confidence in his penis as a source of pleasure for himself and for his wife, without demand for an erection or entry.

After a number of sexual experiences that include positive responses to paint brushing, the poking into the vagina begins. The wife must manage these steps carefully so as not to trigger the demand of keeping the erection to have entry. In each pleasuring session, the penis is poked into the vagina just half an inch more (increments of "just noticeable difference"). The first time, the wife can insert the tip of the penis into the opening of the vagina for a few moments. The next time it might be for a few moments more. The following time she can insert it a notch further, but just briefly. Each time the penis is either left in a little longer or inserted slightly further. Eventually the couple will have had full entry without ever having been assigned that task.

Once entry has occurred, it should be enjoyed by resting together without thrusting ("quiet vagina" is the term used to describe this time of resting inside the woman) and allowing the erection to diminish inside the vagina. It is important that this is done intentionally to gain a sense of mastery. In other words, loss of erection does not happen to you—you allow it to happen.

In the next experience, mild thrusting is allowed after entry. Gradually, with each successive encounter, the thrusting is increased. Next, the couple is allowed to withdraw from the vagina and stimulate to orgasm manually. When the couple has gained a security with the sexual activity thus far, permission is given for them to decide, during the sexual experience, that they will allow the arousal to build to ejaculation inside the vagina.

In the total process of gaining security with erectile functioning, anxiety must be addressed and the therapy process adopted accordingly. The wife must be supported and encouraged, as well as provided with some private therapy time to vent her feelings. It is important that the focus on the pleasure be as much for her as her husband. When the husband pleasures a receptive and responsive wife, it is a great distraction from erectile dysfunction.

Because problems of arousal are an interruption of such a natural, ongoing physical response in our bodies, the treatment program is designed to eliminate the interruptions and allow the automatic bodily response. Difficulties with erections for men tend to become more of a concern than do problems with arousal for women. Intercourse cannot be successful without an erection, whereas, an artificial vaginal lubricant can be used if there is no physical arousal for the woman, and intercourse is possible even if a woman does not *feel* aroused. Nevertheless, therapists must address female problems of arousal with the same concern and helpfulness, as they do the male erectile disorders.

CHAPTER THIRTEEN

TREATING PROBLEMS OF SEXUAL RELEASE

MEN AND WOMEN TEND TO STRUGGLE in the opposite direction with orgasmic-phase disorders. Men often respond too quickly with premature ejaculation, whereas women inhibit their orgasms because they have difficulty allowing a release.

PROBLEMS OF RELEASE FOR WOMEN

Orgasmic Inhibition

Even though the reflex of orgasm is as natural as the foot jerk in response to the doctor's tap on the knee, many women have never experienced, rarely experience, do not know if they have experienced, or believe they have to work hard to experience that peak of physical release of genital vasocongestion. The fact that the vaginal and uterine contractions of the orgasm are eight-tenths of a second apart in all women does not make the subjective experience of an orgasm at all the same from woman to woman or even in the same woman from one time to another.

Women who have difficulty with orgasmic release may lack knowledge about their own bodies, the sexual response cycle, or effective stimulation. Some women have no expectation of receiving pleasure from the sexual experience, so mentally they do not connect with the building of the arousal response in their bodies. It is not uncommon for Christian and non-Christian women to feel they have no right to sexual pleasure. The biblical concept of mutuality in the sexual relationship in marriage has never had an impact on them. For these women, sex is something you do to please your husband. They never really grasp the idea that their enjoyment of sex is probably *the* most pleasing part of sex for their husbands.

Similarly, women may see themselves as passive receptacles of the man's aggressive sexuality, so they are totally passive during all sexual experiences. They become aroused because arousal is controlled by the parasympathetic branch of our autonomic nervous system, the passive branch. But their arousal stops at the end of the plateau phase right before the orgasmic response. It is as if they cannot make it over the hill. We believe that this is the point at which the involuntary control shifts from the passive (parasympathetic) to the active branch (sympathetic) of the nervous system. The heart rate increases, the breathing intensifies, and the involuntary thrusting starts. Overt, active sexuality has to kick in. If the woman is passive, those responses will not happen.

Women who were raised in homes that either lacked emotional expressiveness or were out of control emotionally may not know how to let go sexually or may fear the loss of control in letting go. Similarly, women who have difficulty with orgasmic release often feel embarrassed or self-conscious about the intense expression of an orgasmic response, particularly if they were raised with rigid antisexual teaching. Even their husband's orgasms may frighten them. It is important that these women not become orgasmic too quickly. Rapid success is likely to frighten them.

Lori was the sweetest young lady—rather frail and timid. She was obviously afraid of expressing herself verbally during the sessions. Her real father, who was an alcoholic, lived in their home until she was seven years old. The history suggested that her mother was emotionally unstable. A few years after her mother and father divorced, the mother remarried. Lori's stepfather was a strong, rigid, controlling man whose affection she attempted to win. He had clear antisexual rules for her dress and behavior. When she came out in the morning dressed for school, he would often send her back to change clothes because she looked too attractive. He said that her appearance would make boys look at her for the wrong reasons.

Unfortunately and unintentionally (from our perspective and hers), Lori had her first orgasmic response after the third sexual therapy session. She did not like it at all! It frightened her. It was wrong. She did not want it to ever happen again.

The process and goals of sexual therapy had to be readjusted. Time was needed for her to be able to understand her fear and dislike of emotional intensity and being out of control. She had to release the pain of her childhood. A number of months of psychotherapy were required before the sexual exercises could be resumed. During this time, Lori was helped to be able to ask for trust-building affection from her husband without expectation or pressure for her to experience erotic sexuality. In turn, she was able to agree to bring him to ejaculation manually on a regular basis. Even though his orgasmic response was somewhat uncomfortable for her, it was not aversive, and she wanted to be able to give him that pleasure while he was giving her space to unravel and heal her need to be in control.

Sometimes women's inhibition of their orgasmic response is secondary to some other sexual issue. Pain during intercourse increases women's tenseness, which inhibits arousal and then blocks release. They become so guarded in preventing the pain that they cannot relax, soak in the pleasure, and allow their bodily responses to build.

The husband's premature ejaculation may also keep the woman from an orgasmic response. If the husband ejaculates quickly from any form of sexual activity, she may not have time to respond, even from manual stimulation. If she is a woman who responds during intercourse and he ejaculates shortly after entry, she may not have enough time of intravaginal penile stimulation to become orgasmic. Unfortunately, many couples either lose interest in pursuing the woman's response after the husband's, or they are not creative in working out other ways for her to respond, like using manual intravaginal stimulation. Obviously, control of ejaculation needs to be the primary focus of change, but alternative means of orgasmic response for the woman may be employed in the meantime.

Relationship issues may also keep a woman from being orgasmically vulnerable with her husband. He may be her second-choice mate. She may have been engaged to be married and lost her fiancé either through his death, the parents' prohibition of the marriage, or his breaking the engagement. Perhaps the grief of that loss was not resolved before she quickly filled her sense of loss with her current husband. He became her second choice—not consciously, but by the fact that she was still wanting and grieving for her lost fiancé. The attachment is never the same and the ability to be vulnerable is inhibited. Anger, lack of respect, or outright dislike of a husband can also be a barrier to letting go sexually. These and other relationship issues must be resolved before orgasmic responsiveness is pursued.

Treatment of Orgasmic Inhibition

Orgasmic response is not a skill to be learned such as playing tennis, but there is the need to learn to be sexual, to learn about bodily responses, and to acquire techniques for deriving sexual satisfaction. To become orgasmic, a woman must be able to uncover and release the potential that is already inside of her. All women have a clitoris, that special apparatus designed to give and receive sexual stimulation and responsiveness. All women's bodies were designed with the ability to experience the intensity of the sexual response.

Sometimes barriers need to be removed through the process of psychotherapy or marital counseling before women will be able to actively pursue their sexual responsiveness. They may need to give themselves permission, reduce fears, resolve negative feelings toward the husband, build trust with him, or address any other inhibiting factors.

Once the underlying or interfering difficulties are addressed, the sexual therapy process is begun by assigning the exercises of the Sexual Therapy Plan (chapter 9).

Some sexual therapists[1] recommend that women learn to be orgasmic through self-stimulation before they become able to be orgasmic with their husbands. We have not found this strategy to always be necessary or even possible. For many women in our practice, the taboo of self-stimulation is much more difficult to overcome than it is to be able to be vulnerable orgasmically with their husbands. However, women who have difficulty being sexually free with their husbands may need to learn by themselves first.

Whether the efforts are initiated by self-stimulation or with her husband, the woman is encouraged to stop mentally focussing on the goal of orgasm, to refocus on the pleasurable sensations of touch and arousal, to reduce self-consciousness about the natural sexual response, and to take responsibility to actively go after her own sexual needs and desires. These are the ingedients of the sexual therapy process that are unique to treating orgasmic inhibition. They should be emphasized as the Sexual Therapy Plan is assigned.

Redefine the Goal. To stop mentally focusing on the goal of orgasm, women must redefine their goals. The therapist assists with this redefinition in the feedback session of the initial assessment. Rather than trying to have an orgasm, women are encouraged to allow longer times of arousal and more intense levels of arousal. Because the orgasm is an automatic reflex response, the "trying" prevents the orgasm from happening by putting the woman into the evaluative role of spectatoring or watching how she is doing. The intentional, goal-oriented "trying" actually inhibits the natural response. The new goals of longer periods of arousal and more intense arousal focus on the positive sensations of the vasocongestion in the genitals, as well as pleasurable sensations of the whole body. The woman is encouraged to extend her enjoyment of these sensations and the level of intensity with which she allows those to be felt.

Build Trust Through Learning to Give and Receive Pleasure. In order to refocus onto pleasurable sensations, trust must be built between the husband and wife so that the woman can freely enjoy the giving and receiving of pleasure. The talking, teaching, and touching exercises of the Sexual Therapy Plan are assigned for the purpose of building trust and learning to give and receive pleasure without a focus on the goal of orgasm. Because the exercises begin nonerotically and progress gradually, the focus on pleasure feeds the newly defined goals of longer and more intense arousal.

As part of the learning to give and receive pleasure, women must be willing to verbalize any spectatoring. The importance of the right-left brain shift that happens when we verbalize our mental processes which interrupt the sexual response cycle was discussed in the treatment of impotence in chapter 12.

Another way women keep the mental focus on the pleasure and off the evaluation of their response is by consciously listening to their body sensations while they are being touched. They also focus as they become active in pursuing what feels good, as well as communicating and directing their husbands in the kind of touch they enjoy.

Reduce Self-consciousness. Whether or not women with this difficulty report that they feel embarrassed about the active, expressive total-body responses that occur at the end of the plateau phase (see chapter 5), they are — for some reason—inhibiting the expression of this intense buildup. Therefore, all treatment of women with orgasmic inhibition includes the exercises designed to reduce self-consciousness. The Body Awareness-Mirror assignment, the Clinical Genital and Vaginal exams are preliminary exercises in the Sexual Therapy Plan that reduce self-consciousness. The Simulating Arousal Responses exercise is specifically aimed at reducing the self-consciousness of the breathing and sounds of a sexual orgasm. By practicing the expression of that response, the person becomes desensitized to his or her embarrassment with the expressions that accompany orgasmic release.

Once these women are in a sexual experience and the intensity of their arousal builds to a point that they would naturally be experiencing deep breathing, involuntary thrusting, grimacing, and noises, they are to notice if and when they stop these involuntary responses. When they become aware of the inhibition, they are to consciously do what they stopped their bodies from doing. In fact, they do best if they learn to exaggerate their natural bodily responses. When they feel like breathing deeply, breath even deeper. One woman felt like arching her body when she was in the top position, but that arching would cause her to look up and she had always felt like that was stupid. So she did not allow herself to respond with her body in that way. When she—with her husband's permission—made the decision to go for it, the intensity of her arousal built with each experience until the orgasmic reflex occurred. She was delighted!

Take Responsibility to Go After Sexual Needs and Desires. What does taking responsibility and going after sexual needs and desires mean? It means that women give themselves permission to be sexual. They decide that they are going to actively pursue sexual feelings, expressions, and intensity. They are going to allow their bodies to respond and enjoy those responses. And specifically, they are going to become active in helping their bodies switch from the passive, parasympathetic nervous system to the active, sympathetic nervous system.

Instead of being the recipient of touching, the woman becomes active in doing the touching. She learns to delight in her husband's body and to enjoy using her body to pleasure her husband. She kisses passionately with lips, tongue, and mouth. She uses her husband's body to bring pleasure to herself. She becomes an active pleasure seeker. She begins to accept that her husband's body is hers to enjoy for her pleasure. The husband usually loves it!

Specific exercises can be practiced to actively encourage greater intensity and longer periods of arousal. One of these exercises is a paired clitoral/vaginal stimulation that is timed. The couple is not assigned to continue the stimulation until the orgasmic response occurs (which would be sure to fail), but rather that the time of stimulation is limited by the timer. The husband and wife complete this exercise together with an electronic or kitchen timer by the bedside. They enjoy total body caressing, including breasts and genitals in a general sense. Then they set the timer. Graber and Kline-Graber suggest the timer be set for twenty minutes.[2] That may be too long, initially, for women who place demands on themselves to be orgasmic. When there is high performance anxiety, one minute may be plenty. The amount of time can be increased in small increments when there is greater ability to do the exercise without watching for it "to work."

The exercise that is practiced during the time allotted by the timer is clitoral/vaginal stimulation. The woman stimulates or strokes her clitoris while the man stimulates the PC muscle inside the vagina. If the woman is uncomfortable with self-stimulation, the man could stimulate both the clitoris and the vagina. The woman can tighten and relax the PC muscle as the man either strokes, taps, or in some way stimulates the PC muscle area (or the G-spot, the area just beyond the PC muscle toward the front of the woman's body). It is important that the woman direct the man to stimulate her in the way most enjoyable to her.

Once the couple has progressed in the sexual therapy process to the stage including the clitoral/vaginal stimulation exercise, this exercise should be repeated two to three times per week. Longer and longer periods of time should be allowed, up to twenty minutes. Eventually the reflex response of orgasm will happen.

The role of the helper is critical in keeping the balance between actively going after the stimulation so the orgasmic reflex will be triggered, and yet keeping the focus on the pure enjoyment sensations of the body, rather than the goal of the orgasm. The exercises designed as "going after" orgasm can easily become demands to respond. The focus can quickly switch to evaluating the degree of success in being able to be orgasmic. Thus, the redefined goals must be reviewed regularly.

Lack of Coital Orgasm

There is confusion for women regarding the need to have an orgasm during intercourse. More than half of all women (some studies report as high as 70 percent[3]) need clitoral stimulation to be able to respond orgasmically. Yet many husbands and wives place demands on themselves to elicit the woman's response from vaginal stimulation.

The demand for vaginally stimulated orgasms grew out of Freud's teaching regarding women. Freud believed the women who responded only to clitoral stimulation were immature little girls—that as little girls, they had learned to respond through self-stimulation of the clitoris and had never matured into women who could respond by receiving the man's penis into their vaginas.

Then in the 1960s, Masters and Johnson reported there was only one source of all orgasms, the clitoris. They claimed that whether from manual stimulation or intercourse, an orgasm was clitorally stimulated.

Since the Masters and Johnson findings, women who experience orgasm from both direct clitoral stimulation and from intercourse have reported there is a difference. Some prefer clitorally stimulated orgasms, some prefer vaginally stimulated orgasms, and still others delight in both. A clitoral orgasm is usually described as more intense because there is nothing in the vagina to hinder the movement of the PC muscle as it contracts. The vaginal orgasm is often described as deeper and more satisfying. The sensation that occurs with the contractions is one of bearing down, almost like the last delights of childbirth.

All orgasmic response brings relief of the vasocongestion of sexual arousal. There is no right or better form of stimulation to bring that about. It is not uncommon, however, for a woman to want to be able to respond orgasmically during intercourse. And this can be learned. There are two approaches.

One approach to teach the woman to be orgasmic during intercourse is called "pairing" or "bridging." The stimulation that already works is paired with or bridged to the response to stimulation that is desired. This is very similar to the clitoral/vaginal exercise described previously in this chapter. The woman stimulates herself clitorally during intercourse and alternately tightens and relaxes her PC muscle while her husband's penis thrusts inside her vagina. Thus, clitoral stimulation which has been effective in bringing orgasmic release is combined with the vaginal stimulation of penile thrusting and PC muscle contracting.

When the pattern of connecting intercourse with the orgasmic release from direct clitoral stimulation becomes ingrained, the manual clitoral manipulation can gradually be withdrawn. Initially, the pairing of the two should be continued until the woman's orgasm begins. Then she should stop the clitoral stimulation for a few moments before resuming it.

She should practice lengthening the time when she does not stimulate herself clitorally, as long as that does not stop her orgasm. If the orgasm does stop, she should immediately resume clitoral stimulation, then stop again. Eventually she will be requiring less time of clitoral stimulation. The clitoral stimulation during intercourse will only be necessary until the response pattern of orgasm from intravaginal stimulation is established.

The second approach to teaching women to be orgasmic during intercourse is taught in detail in *The G-Spot*, a book by Ladas, Whipple, and Perry. The G-spot, or Graffenburg-spot, is assumed to be an area located inside the vagina beyond the inner edge of the PC muscle toward the front of the woman's body. It is an area of tissue similar to the tissue of the prostate gland in men. The information about the G-spot is comprised of clinical data that have not been confirmed by research, but the information is validated by the help it brings to many women.

Using G-spot-area stimulation to discover intravaginal responsiveness takes both clinical discovery and the pursuit of pleasure of that discovery. In the Vaginal Exam (Sexual Therapy Assignment 16 in chapter 9), we give instructions for the discovery process. After the discovery, manual stimulation of this area can be enjoyed. During intercourse, various positions can be attempted that would put the penis at the correct angle inside the vagina to thrust up against the G-spot area. This can be fun if it does not become a demand for performance.

Although orgasm is the apex of the sexual experience, it is not the ultimate as far as the total sexual experience is concerned. Relieving the inhibitions of orgasmic release is important to a woman experiencing total fulfillment, but orgasm without pleasure and emotional and spiritual connection is not satisfying. The freedom for orgasm within the context of a totally fulfilling sexual relationship is the eventual hope for every woman.

PROBLEM OF RELEASE FOR MEN

Premature Ejaculation

The most common technical sexual dysfunction for men is premature ejaculation. This has been defined by Masters and Johnson as the timing of the man's ejaculation relative to the woman's response: ". . . the Foundation considers a man a premature ejaculator if he cannot control his ejaculatory process for a sufficient length of time during intravaginal containment to satisfy his partner in at least 50 percent of their coital connections."[4] This definition was derived to counteract the definitions that refer to premature ejaculation as inability to remain in the vagina for a designated period of time (i.e., thirty seconds or sixty seconds) without ejaculating. Still others define premature ejaculation as ejaculating prior to a certain number of thrusts (i.e., ten thrusts).

We define premature ejaculation as occurring when the man does not have control of his ejaculation—in other words, if the man ejaculates before he or his wife feel ready for him to do so. This definition grew out of our clinical practice in which we have found a great variation as to when ejaculation is desired after entry. Some couples are content with a few minutes inside the vagina. Others are frustrated with five to ten minutes. Some men have no need to be able to last until their wife responds because she prefers to be orgasmic before or after intercourse. Sustained intercourse may not be enjoyable for either of them. In essence, our definition is similar to Helen Singer Kaplan's definition:

> Premature ejaculation (*ejoculatio praecox*) is unmistakable, yet it is difficult to define precisely. Essentially, prematurity is a condition wherein a man is unable to exert voluntary control over his ejaculatory reflex, with the result that once he is sexually aroused, he reaches orgasm very quickly.[5]

The seriousness of premature ejaculation varies greatly. Some men experience so little control that they will ejaculate before entry or upon anticipation of entry. Even more extreme is the man who ejaculates as soon as his wife touches his penis. Others will ejaculate once entry is attempted or within a few seconds after entry. Probably the most common complaint is the inability to last more than a minute or two after entry.

Premature ejaculation seems to be a conditional reflex response. The man has learned to ejaculate quickly and has not learned to attend to the warning signs that precede ejaculation.

The conditioning of the premature ejaculation can be both implicit and explicit. In our culture, boys at early ages begin to participate in sports. (Today this is true for many girls, as well). In sports, scoring or the fast achievement of the goal is the reward. In sex, men even refer to "scoring" with a woman. The implicit teaching is that the faster you achieve, the better. Success in business and other male-dominated vocations similarly perpetuates this mentality: the sooner you reach your goal, the better.

More directly, the conditioning begins in early adolescence with the boy's first ejaculatory experiences. Because self-stimulation is a private discovery, frequently associated with restrictive admonitions and thus guilt, boys learn to stimulate themselves to ejaculation quickly. The focus in early masturbation is rarely on the good sensations and pleasure of the process, but rather on attaining the release. Premarital sexual stimulation to ejaculation and sexual intercourse continue the same pattern. These are often hurried events that take place in an unsafe setting. The male's body, again, is being taught not to heed the warnings of ejaculation as a reason to delay it, but rather to trigger the reflex as quickly as possible. The sooner the event is over (the faster he "comes"), the less danger of being caught. Kaplan refers to the lack of response to the warning signs as "inadequate penile sensory awareness."[6]

When men with this rushed pattern of ejaculation marry and commit themselves to a long-term relationship, they expect that the absence of hurried conditions will lead to longer love play and extended intercourse before ejaculation. Unfortunately, most of the time their bodies repeat their conditioned response patterns. Other men never realize sex should be any different. They have no intention or desire to postpone ejaculation once they are married.

For men who are sensitive, aware, and concerned with more than just a sexual release, ejaculating prematurely makes them feel inadequate sexually. Lack of control of their body functioning leaves them feeling unsure of themselves. Their pleasure is often decreased by the abrupt end to the sexual experience. Eventually their preoccupation with trying to delay ejaculation will hinder their ability to fully lose themselves to sexual pleasure.

As is common to all sexual disorders, premature ejaculation affects both the man and the woman. When a man is anxious, feeling inadequate and ejaculating unexpectedly, the woman is likely to be left unsatisfied. Her frustration will increase his anxiety, which in turn will increase his problem of lack of control. Some women reach orgasm only during intercourse and thus cannot be orgasmic when their husbands ejaculate prematurely.

However, premature ejaculation does not have to be a negative experience for the woman. The confident man who really enjoys the pleasure of a woman's body may engage in so much sensuous body play and manual intravaginal stimulation that his wife is well satisfied before entry and/or ejaculation occur. The couple may still both desire more time to be together after entry, but it is not a frustration for the woman. For other women, premature ejaculation is not a problem because they are quickly and easily orgasmic from entry, so they respond before or during their husband's ejaculation.

When the wife begins to feel used and unfulfilled, her frustration affects her husband and he becomes more and more concerned with his inability to control when he ejaculates. He usually tries to use mental games to distract himself from ejaculating. He may try to picture something sexually repulsive, imagine himself in unsexual situations or start counting backwards. These mental distractions may have short-term benefit, but soon are of no avail. Both husband and wife may begin projecting their frustration outward and blame each other for the struggle. "If only you wouldn't. . . ." are statements that begin to deflate the couple's joyful sexual anticipations. The woman begins to feel that if her husband really cared about her, he would control ejaculation. He knows it is not a voluntary action on his part, but he feels inadequate trying to communicate this lack of intention to his wife.

After a time, the couple may begin to withdraw from each other, not wanting to engage in a sexual experience that is bound to end up frustrating them. Soon the man doubts his masculinity and the wife has both anger toward her husband and decreasing confidence in herself as a sexual partner. If the pattern continues, the anxiety about ejaculating can lead to impotence for the man. Even if the consequences are not this extreme, there is likely to be hostility and discouragement about their sexual relationship.

Treatment of Premature Ejaculation

It is encouraging to report that learning ejaculatory control is most possible and not that difficult. Sadly, many couples never seek help and believe they have a difficulty they simply must endure. Some couples can learn ejaculatory control with no or minimal therapeutic guidance using chapter 29 in *The Gift of Sex*. When the habit is longstanding or connected with other marital discord or other sexual difficulties, ongoing therapeutic assistance is necessary.

As with any sexual problem, the resolution usually requires the active involvement of both husband and wife. If a single man wants to improve his ejaculatory control, it is possible for him to begin this process by himself. The principles would be the same. The activities would be adapted to self-stimulation, rather than stimulation by the wife. This

227

technique is taught by Brauer and Brauer in *ESO*,[7] by Helen Singer Kaplan in *Premature Ejaculation*,[8] and McCarthy and McCarthy in *Male Sexuality Awareness*.[9]

When premature ejaculation is a sexual difficulty within marriage, it is a "couple" problem, not just the man's problem. Both spouses are affected by it. Hence, we recommend that both husband and wife be actively involved in the treatment process.

Certain attitudes, commitments, and communication skills are essential to effective completion of this process.

First, the husband and wife must have a working relationship. They must be committed to each other and to the treatment process. If their relationship is fraught with distress and discord, marital therapy is necessary before the steps of learning ejaculatory control are pursued. If one or the other is resistant to the treatment process, this resistance must be understood and removed before beginning the specific therapy process. The man must desire control and believe it is possible for him. And he must be willing to allow his wife to participate with him. Similarly, she must believe that control can be achieved and be willing to work toward that goal. This requires the ability to enjoy her husband's genitals for her pleasure. If this is not already possible for her, she can learn it in the early steps of the therapy process.

Communication is also essential to the effective completion of this process. The couple needs to begin by talking about the problem. The Sexual Assessment communication exercise (Sexual Therapy Assignment 2 from the Sexual Therapy Plan in chapter 9) will guide the couple. In addition, the therapist helps each spouse to be able to express how the premature ejaculation has affected him or her. Each spouse needs to feel heard and understood by the other. Both must feel free to express their feelings about participating in the therapy process. Adaptations of the process may be necessary if there are personal issues that would interfere with the learning mode as prescribed.

The couple must be committed to following the Guidelines for Sexual Therapy (Assignment 1A in the Sexual Therapy Plan). In addition to not engaging in sexual intercourse, the man must refrain from all forms of sexual stimulation other than those prescribed, so that ejaculation is not a possibility unless it is allowed in the assigned exercise. If the couple is being seen by the therapist on a weekly basis, two to three pleasuring/squeeze technique exercises, one teaching exercise, and one talking exercise are assigned each week. If the couple is being seen on a daily intensive basis, one pleasuring/squeeze exercise, one teaching exercise, and one talking exercise are assigned each day.

It is important that the couple (or the man, if he is working on this by himself) realize that the more carefully the structure of the program is followed, the more rewarding the results. Exercises or parts of exercises must not be missed or approached carelessly. Methodical, deliberate assignments are essential.

The steps to learning ejaculatory control were first presented to the professional community as the result of the research by Masters and Johnson. At the present time, their basic principles are widely used by sexual therapists, along with adaptations of their original "squeeze technique." Other approaches are also being used. For the most part, we continue to use our version of the squeeze technique, which we find to be very successful when followed as directed.

In her book, *PE: How to Overcome Premature Ejaculation*, Kaplan promotes Seman's "stop-start" method, but refers also to the squeeze technique. Whatever the method used, her emphasis is to increase full sensual awareness, and thus gain ejaculatory control.

Learning to Give and Receive Pleasure. The first goal of treatment is for the man to learn to give and receive pleasure—total body and genital pleasure. This is what we utilize as the first step to correcting what Kaplan refers to as "the man's deficient sexual sensory awareness."[10] The first ten exercises listed in the Sexual Therapy Plan (through Sexual Therapy Assignment 10: Total Body Pleasuring, Excluding Breasts and Genitals) teach the focus on total body, non-genital sensual awareness. The plan's Guidelines for Sexual Therapy and the Underlying Principles for Bodily Pleasure (Assignment 1) need to be accurately understood and practiced by the couple to begin the process of the man gaining sensuous awareness and thus, ejaculatory control. In the feedback sessions after completing the touching exercises, the therapist asks questions of and listens carefully to the client to ascertain if he is learning to receive pleasure both when being touched and when touching.

Learning Ejaculatory Control—the Squeeze Technique. The second goal focuses directly on gaining ejaculatory control, our second step in correcting the man's deficient sexual sensory awareness.

This part of the process continues to encourage total body sensual awareness while focusing specifically on penile sensual awareness. The ability to enjoy (really soak in) penile pleasure without pursuing the ejaculatory response is taught by having the couple complete Assignments

11 through 17 in the Sexual Therapy Plan. The subsequent exercises may be used as they would enhance the couple's total sexual experience together.

PROCEDURE ONE: PLEASURING AND SQUEEZING
WITHOUT EJACULATION

Step One: Teaching the squeeze technique begins with the Sexual Therapy Plan's Assignment 24, Total Body Pleasuring with Breast and Genitals Stimulation. The man pleasures the woman first. Then the woman pleasures the man in the nondemand position (see Figure 13–1). It is important that the man be able to completely relax and focus on the sensations in his body. He must be able to experience pleasure rather than hold back or feel he has to do something for his wife.

Once there is a full erection from penile stimulation, the woman applies the squeeze (Figure 13–1). To do this, she grasps the penis with her thumb on the underside of the ridge around the head of the penis and her forefinger and middle finger above and below the ridge of the head on the front side of the penis. The squeeze should be firm but not hard and should be held for about ten seconds. The woman needs to be careful not to use her fingernails in this procedure.

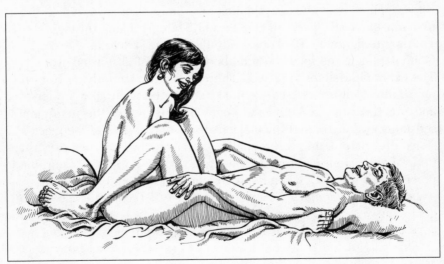

Fig. 13–1
Non-Demand Position

230

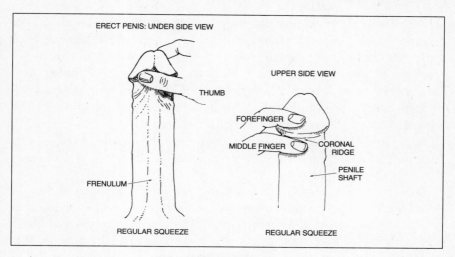

Fig. 13–2
The Squeeze Technique

After the squeeze has been applied, some men will probably lose their erections; others will not. The squeeze is effective whether or not the erection diminishes. Diminishing the feelings of the intensity of arousal while enjoying the sensations of the stimulation is what teaches the control of ejaculation. It is important that the man counteract his old habits of trying to hold back his arousal or being anxious about his ejaculation. This is best accomplished by his focus on the bodily and penile pleasure, and by verbalizing to his wife any thoughts that distract him from the enjoyment back to his concern about ejaculating too quickly.

The squeeze works most effectively if it is applied once there is a full erection but long before the man is approaching the point of no return (see Figure 5–1). This may take some time for the husband and wife to learn. If the man has been accustomed to ejaculating within seconds after a full erection, the woman will have to learn to apply the squeeze immediately when the erection is gained.

Step Two: Whether or not the squeeze results in loss of the erection, the woman is instructed to move away from the focus on the genitals to pleasuring other parts of her husband's body. His focus should move with her touch and the enjoyment of that touch, so that he does not mentally continue the stimulation of his penis after the squeeze, but rather soaks in the pleasure of the touch.

Step Three: After a few minutes of caressing other parts of his body, the wife moves back to penile stimulation and application of the squeeze once there is a full erection. He again focuses on the enjoyment of that penile stimulation, allowing the squeeze to interrupt the intensity, rather than feeling pressure to distract himself from arousal. He freely enjoys the arousal!

Step Four: The couple is to repeat steps one through three of the squeeze three or four times in one experience.

Step Five: After the last squeeze, encourage the couple to rest quietly together, affirming each other, talking about their feelings, and allowing the arousal to dissipate.

Procedure One may be repeated by the couple for several experiences until they have a good sense of how the process works and are able to allow longer and longer times of arousal before the squeeze is applied. The criterion for longer periods of penile stimulation is the man's ability to relax and focus on the enjoyment of the arousal without the reflex of ejaculation being triggered. Both the man and woman should be warned that an accidental ejaculation may occur. It is not a failure—only an indication that the squeeze needs to be applied a little sooner, and the man needs to enjoy his arousal without trying to hold back. The accidental ejaculation may have been the result of too long a time of stimulation or the man reverting to his old pattern of anxiety and trying not to ejaculate rather than being fully aware of and enjoying his sexual sensations.

Procedure Two: Pleasuring, Squeezing, and Pursuing Ejaculation by Manual Stimulation

The couple repeats steps one through four of Procedure One; but this time, they are encouraged to use a lubricant which will closely approximate the feeling that the man will have inside the vagina. We would recommend Albolene, a facial cleanser very similar in consistency to natural vaginal lubrication. Allercreme, a nonlanolin, nonallergenic body lotion is also effective, but it is difficult to find on the market. Probe, a new vaginal lubricant, is also not readily available. The couple may use whatever lubricant they have that keeps its slipperiness, but is not sticky or irritating.

After three or four times of repeating steps one through three of Procedure One, the couple is to decide that they will not utilize the squeeze, but will manually stimulate to ejaculation. The decision to pursue ejaculation does not mean there will now be rapid, vigorous manual stimulation so that the man quickly ejaculates. It is most important that the stimulation vary and have a playfulness to it with a very gradual building of the intensity (both vigor and speed). This is the woman's task to control. The man's task is to focus completely on the sensations of his genitals. He is to fully enjoy the building of the arousal, savoring it like he might savor his favorite ice cream—enjoying every stroke like he would enjoy every lick of the ice cream, rather than holding back the intensity. He is not to rush to finish quickly, nor to not really "taste" it because he is afraid it will be finished too quickly. The focus is on the wonderful sensations and wanting to receive the most enjoyment from them.

After ejaculation, the couple needs to be encouraged to have a time of holding, affirming, and sharing their feelings about the experience. If the woman can delight in the man's ejaculation and his new control, this is an additional benefit. The man encourages his wife's continued participation if he expresses his appreciation for her help in his gaining control.

PROCEDURE THREE: PLEASURING AND SQUEEZING WITH ENTRY,
BUT WITH EJACULATION OUTSIDE THE BODY

Step One: Using a lubricant, the couple is to repeat steps one through four of Procedure One.

Step Two: Once the woman applies the last squeeze in step four, she moves into the top position (Figure 13–3) and guides the husband's penis into the vagina. If the man has lost some of the fullness of the erection after the squeeze, she may have to stuff the penis in or stimulate it a little before inserting it into the vagina.

Step Three: After the woman has inserted the penis into the vagina, the couple is to lie quietly together for a few moments without moving (quiet vagina). If the penis tends to fall out of the vagina because of loss of erection, additional manual stimulation or a little thrusting may be necessary to keep it erect enough to proceed. The man must maintain focus on the sensation, not how the penis is responding. In other words, he is to focus on the touch and the sensation, not on the result of these. He is to thoroughly enjoy the feeling of having his penis inside his wife.

Step Four: After several minutes of lying quietly together and caressing each other's bodies, the woman may begin to gently move her pelvis

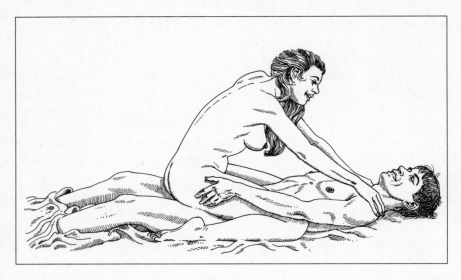

Fig. 13–3
Female Superior Position

in a mild thrusting manner. If the man gains a full erection quickly, she is to move off the man and apply the squeeze.

Step Five: The couple can rest together for a few moments while the intensity of arousal dissipates. Kaplan recommends that the couple not wait too long, though.[11] If 0 is no arousal and 10 is an ejaculation, the couple should wait until the arousal has come down to about 6 to 7 ½. Young men may even be able to allow it to lessen to a 5 or 6 level of intensity before resuming entry.

Step Six: The woman moves back on top of her husband and reinserts his penis into her vagina, thrusting gently until there is a full erection; then she withdraws and applies the squeeze.

Step Seven: The couple is to repeat three to four times the cycle of squeeze, entry, quiet vagina, thrust, withdraw.

Step Eight: After the third or fourth withdrawal of the penis from the vagina, the squeeze is applied. This is followed by body caressing and penile stimulation of varied intensity until there is an ejaculation.

Procedure three is repeated several different times, allowing longer and longer time within the vagina and increased intensity of thrusting before withdrawal and application of the squeeze.

PROCEDURE FOUR: PLEASURING, SQUEEZING, ENTRY,
AND EJACULATION INSIDE THE VAGINA

The couple repeats Procedure Three. This time, however, instead of withdrawing after the third or fourth time in the vagina, the couple decides to pursue ejaculation inside the vagina. Again, the mental set should be one of savoring and enjoying while varying the thrusting, including times of resting quietly together and caressing each other without thrusting. Gradually, the wife can allow the intensity of the thrusting to build to the point of ejaculation.

The couple is encouraged to take time to delight in the ejaculation event, each affirming the other's participation.

If the woman has not experienced an orgasm as a result of the process, and she desires that release, the husband can affirm her by delighting in the pleasuring and stimulation of her to orgasm.

The couple is instructed to continue practicing Procedure Four as their way of making love. They are to make this an increasingly mutual experience, taking turns and/or simultaneously pleasuring each other, hugging, and kissing.

As control is gained through the interruption of the stimulation and application of the squeeze, the man learns greater and greater awareness of the sensation of his body when he becomes aroused and approaches orgasm. Eventually, the couple may be able to just stop the stimulation and move to other closeness or just have a time of quiet vagina during intercourse, rather than withdrawing and squeezing.

The couple has achieved control of ejaculation when they can flow naturally in the pleasuring, stimulating, and intercourse experience without fear that the man is going to ejaculate unexpectedly. This may require the application of the squeeze every now and then as part of their sexual experience. They should be able to have periods of five to ten minutes of thrusting that varies in intensity. No man is able to thrust vigorously and intensely for an extended period of time and not ejaculate, unless he suffers from retarded ejaculation. Thrusting is designed to stimulate the reflex of ejaculation.

The more confidence that builds as the couple has regular times together when they feel that the ejaculation is in their control, the less likely they are to slip back into their old patterns. Once the man has learned the ability to thoroughly enjoy the sexual sensation and listen to his body's response, that ability will be with him forever. Times of anxiety or stress may cause an accidental ejaculation, but he now knows how to achieve control.

Retarded Ejaculation

Retarded ejaculation (also called ejaculatory incompetence or inhibited male orgasm) is the inability of a man to ejaculate, or the inability to ejaculate in some way that he desires. In this situation, the ejaculatory reflex is inhibited. The man may have sexual desire and be able to become aroused with a full erection; but even with 1) intense arousal, 2) felt need for release, and 3) more than sufficient stimulation, he cannot allow the reflex response of ejaculation. This inhibition is similar to what some women experience. They become highly aroused, but for some reason hold back or do not allow themselves to "let go." They enjoy the buildup of the arousal, but inhibit the orgasmic reflex.

There are different degrees of ejaculatory inhibition. The man may:

1. Have never ejaculated in any way, not even in a nocturnal emission (wet dream).
2. Have only ejaculated involuntarily—not ever by self-stimulation or with a woman, but only during sleep in a nocturnal emission. One man put a sock over his penis at night because of his fear of nocturnal emission. He had never ejaculated intentionally.
3. Have ejaculated by self-stimulation only—usually by himself, in secret.
4. Be able to ejaculate from oral or manual stimulation by his wife, but not during intercourse.
5. Have been able to ejaculate during intercourse, but now cannot (second wife, affair, physical injury); or he can with a certain woman, but not with another because of anxiety, guilt, or feelings of being controlled. Or he sometimes can with his wife, but not at other times.
6. Ejaculate without realizing he has. The emission phase is not impaired (the seminal fluid gathers in the duct system), but the ejaculatory phase with the eight-tenths-of-a-second contractions does not happen. Thus, the seminal fluid seeps out without the contractions and the feeling of orgasmic release. Masters and Johnson believe this partial ejaculatory incompetence occurs as the result of physical causes such as diabetes, prostatic disease, or damage to the urethra.

    Our experience, as confirmed by Kaplan, is that these men may have conflict about allowing themselves to feel the pleasure and intensity of the ejaculatory response, hence they have a psychological or "conditioned" basis for ejaculation, without the sensation of that response—similar to a woman who is aroused but does not feel aroused.

Once physical causes are ruled out, the treatment for partial ejaculatory inhibition is the same as that for complete ejaculatory inhibition.

By the time the men who are struggling with ejaculatory inhibition come for help, many of them are also suffering from impotence and/or lack of desire. Again, the men's reactions are very similar to those of women who are not orgasmic. Over time they become less aroused and less interested.

Causes of Retarded Ejaculation

Although physical causes need to be ruled out by a urological consultation, the cause of retarded ejaculation is usually psychological. The psychodynamics that may be present include the following:

1. A dominant, controlling mother or a strong bond with an overprotective, loving mother who may have been soft and servant-like in her control.
2. Fear of being out of control with a woman, which may be related to the controlling-mother issue.
3. Fear of being abandoned by a woman.
4. A strong need to control, with difficulty "letting go" in other areas. This is demonstrated by an inability to urinate in public restrooms, constipation, and difficulty with the expression of anger or other emotions.
5. A strict religious or moral upbringing connecting free expression of sexuality and guilt, anxiety, and conflict.
6. A traumatic experience—especially if sexual. This can cause the "ejaculatory response [to] become inhibited because of its association with a painful contingency."[12] Examples of this are that the man may have been beaten for masturbating, been interrupted by the police while having sex in a car, or been left by his wife through death or divorce.
7. Sexual naiveté or arrested development at the preadolescent stage associated with homosexual fantasies and fears.

According to Kaplan, whatever the psychogenetic basis, the ejaculatory response has become impaired by an involuntary, unconscious, and conditioned inhibition. Thus, the goal of treatment is "the extinction of this inhibitory process."[13]

Case Presentations

1. Marty and Carrie came to us after fifteen years of marriage and two adoptions. They had been through intense physical-medical workups and had gone through sensate focus sexual therapy which had taught them sexual pleasure without intercourse or ejaculation, with primary focus on Carrie's pleasure. They had been counseled for about five years.

Marty had never ejaculated in any way. His history revealed the following pertinent data:

- He had suffered an illness during late elementary school which kept him home and dependent on his mother, who was very caring, loving, and protective. This illness caused him to have a seizure, which was very frightening to him.
- He had felt socially and physically inadequate throughout junior high and high school.
- He had had a rigid religious upbringing.
- He reported homosexual fantasies and worried about being homosexual. He had been preoccupied with men's bodies since puberty.

Marty and Carrie had a committed and loving relationship. Carrie was clearly the stronger of the two in the relationship and in parenting the children. She was self-contained, assured, and not threatened by or affected personally by Marty's lack of ejaculation.

Marty would fit the judgmental stereotype of "the wimp." He had difficulty relaxing or "letting go" in all areas of life. The convulsion (seizure) he had had in elementary school seemed to cause him to connect "letting go" with pain and fear. His medical workup revealed no physical cause for retarded ejaculation.

2. Gus and Judy had been married five years when they came for help because of their desire to become pregnant. This inability, caused by Gus's inability to ejaculate, was the frustration that led them to seek help.

Gus had only ejaculated by nocturnal emission, never intentionally, despite his and Judy's many attempts. We discovered that Gus would stop effective stimulation. He would not allow Judy to stimulate the shaft of his penis, only the tip. Judy was naive and rather emotionally and sexually inhibited, so she did not know how to encourage him to receive more effective stimulation. Gus would also stop effective stimulation by getting headaches when his arousal intensified.

Like Marty in the previous example, Gus was troubled by homosexual fantasies. His fantasies had started in late junior high school; he had been approached in adolescence by a homosexual man. He had prayed for release from the fantasies with his pastor and a few committed friends. Gus had a dominant and controlling mother. Like Judy, he was sexually naive.

3. Mark and Susan were frustrated with the difficulty Mark had ejaculating during intercourse. They had been able to conceive and have a child because of the occasional ejaculations Mark had had with Susan during intercourse. He had no trouble ejaculating through self-stimulation.

Mark had been married previously and had experienced the same difficulty, but had not shared this with Susan. The reason he gave for not informing Susan of his problem was that they had become Christians so he had assumed his Christian marriage would allow him to respond freely.

Mark's description of his difficulty was much like the descriptions given by women who think they have to work hard to be orgasmic, but actually fight their own bodies with the work they do. In these cases, the natural, involuntary reflex of orgasm occasionally wins in spite of the voluntary "trying" to be orgasmic.

Mark was raised by a dominant, controlling mother who wanted him for herself and yet physically abused him. He was also sexually abused by a man when he was ten years old.

Mark also struggled with severe obesity. He had had medical workups for hormonal imbalances with negative results, although we continued to assess that possibility as a cause.

Treatment of Retarded Ejaculation

The treatment for retarded ejaculation involves desensitization through a gradual retraining process that reduces inhibition and allows the man to risk vulnerability in small, safe increments. Treating men with retarded ejaculation is rewarding. The therapy process begins with the regular sexual therapy format and the Guidelines for Sexual Therapy

(Assignment 1 in the Sexaul Therapy Plan, chapter 9). Intercourse, attempts at intercourse and ejaculation, or attempts at ejaculation must be ruled out. The couple is led through the teaching, talking, and touching exercises of the plan. Individualized treatment is incorporated into the program for unleashing the ejaculatory inhibition.

1. Assign, in order, all thirty-one assignments in the Sexual Therapy Plan in chapter 9. The teaching exercises are needed to reduce sexual naiveté. The talking exercises are to help build trust and bonding with the wife that allows the vulnerability of letting go. The touching exercises distract from the anxiety and pressures of ejaculation and teach the soaking in of pleasure for the sake of pleasure. All demands and the need to please are removed so that the man can "get with" his inner self. It is important to allow arousal to build gradually, so that it is not frightening. Start with a foot and hand caress, which is nonthreatening.

2. At the same time, assign the following steps for reducing ejaculatory inhibition:

A. Goal: Comfort in "letting go" with wife:

1) Urinate with wife listening.
2) Urinate with wife in room.
3) Urinate with wife watching.
4) Urinate with wife holding penis.

B. Goal: Comfort with self-stimulation to ejaculation:

1) Masturbate alone without wife knowing. With each masturbatory experience, the man is to increase the intensity and length of arousal. With time, this will eventually lead to ejaculation as he is able to focus on the good feelings. At the same time, he must be aware of conflict feelings and not allow those to distract from his pleasure.

It is important for the therapist to gather detailed data of exactly what happens in the man's masturbatory experiences. Deal with fears and barriers as they arise. During this feedback time, the therapist can reinforce any enjoyment of intensity and help the man gain insight into his conflicts about "letting go."

After the man becomes comfortable with and has confidence in his ability to ejaculate through self-stimulation, move to step 2.

2) Masturbate with wife knowing. He must tell her when he is going to masturbate. This step should be repeated until he is comfort-

able with and able to ejaculate through self-stimulation with his wife knowing.

3) Masturbate with wife outside the door.

4) Masturbate with wife in room.

5) Masturbate with wife watching.

6) Masturbate with wife pleasuring him and/or her hand over his. (By this time, the Sexual Therapy Plan will have proceeded through Assignment 17, the Nondemand Teaching exercise.)

When the man is able to comfortably allow ejaculation through self-stimulation in each of the six situations, the couple is ready to move to the next task.

C. Goal: Comfort with genital stimulation to orgasm by wife. (During the process of achieving this goal, the man is to limit his self-stimulation to orgasm to once a week or less.):

1) Total body pleasuring including genital pleasuring without focused stimulation (Assignment 14) is repeated in order to begin the connection of sexual pleasure with the possibility of release with his wife as the stimulator.

2) Total body pleasuring with genital stimulation (Assignment 24) is used to teach his wife to keep him hungry or tease him by stimulating his penis and then moving to total body enjoyment and then returning to the genitals. She is to vary the amount of genital stimulation, so he cannot anticipate the movement away. Playfulness is a helpful distraction from the fears of the intensity of the possible release.

3) As the intensity of arousal builds for step 2, and he is experiencing the desire for ejaculation, his wife brings him right to the point of ejaculation and then he takes over with self-stimulation. If this is too big a jump in the process, he may not be able to ejaculate the first time this step is attempted. If that happens, or if the therapy process reveals that step 3 is too big a jump, reduce this step into the following smaller behavioral increments:

a. Instruct him to leave the room to self-stimulate to ejaculation when his desire for ejaculation becomes evident.

b. Instruct her to not look while he self-stimulates to ejaculation. Perhaps this step could be completed in the dark.

c. Instruct her to be active in caressing his body while he self-stimulates to ejaculation (same as step 6 of Goal B).

4) Once the man is able to ejaculate by building right to that point with his wife and then switching to self-stimulation (step 3), he invites the wife to put her hand over his to bring him to ejaculation. This is after the pleasure of step 2.

5) Then he is to put his hand over hers to bring him to ejaculation.

6) Eventually the total body pleasuring leads to her bringing him to ejaculation by her hand alone.

D. Goal: Comfort with ejaculation from manual stimulation after intercourse. Moving to intercourse may raise the man's old conflicts about ejaculating with his wife. Therefore, the following steps must be honored:

1) Begin with Pleasuring, Not Using Hands (Assignment 26), using the penis as a paint brush and poking the penis into the vagina in small increments.

2) The next exercise is Assignment 24, Total Body Pleasuring, Entry by Invitation, followed by a time of quiet vagina to experience the feeling of being inside the woman without demand to ejaculate. Removing the demand increases the desire.

3) Assign the same exercise with entry while the woman is in the top position. She is in control of the thrusting so that she can increase rhythmic movement gradually. Then have the couple withdraw and stimulate to ejaculation. This step 3 may or may not need to be broken down into the more manageable steps of:
    a. Self-stimulation.
    b. Her hand on top of his.
    c. His hand on hers.
    d. Her hand only.

4) Assign the same exercise again, with entry while the woman is on top thrusting until the man feels as if he is going to ejaculate. Then the couple is to withdraw and stimulate to ejaculation.

E. Goals: Comfort with ejaculation during intercourse:

1) Repeat the preceding step 4 of Goal D; however, after withdrawal, have the couple proceed to self- and/or manual stimulation to ejaculation with entry just as ejaculation begins.

2) Have the couple move toward shorter and shorter withdrawal time until there is no withdrawal. This change must be managed so that it is almost unnoticed—"just noticeable difference."

3) Once the couple is able to stay together and the man is able to ejaculate during intercourse, manual stimulation of base of penis during coitus may be added.

If at any point there is ejaculatory inhibition, back up in the process until success is again secure.

Application of the Treatment Process to Three Cases

1. Marty, the man in our first case presentation who had never ejaculated in any way, was very eager for therapy. He had pursued medical treatment and other sexual therapy for five years, so he was coming to us as his last hope.

Because Marty and Carrie were from out of state, we initially began with telephone sessions. We did not assign the Sexual Therapy Plan because they were already practicing the pleasuring exercises. Although Marty was hesitant to attempt to "let go" with Carrie by urinating in her presence, he had no difficulty mastering those steps.

The second goal, comfort with self-stimulation to ejaculation, was more difficult for Marty. The first week he had masturbated three times. The first time he had had a lot of seepage (partial ejaculatory inhibition, that is, emission without ejaculatory contractions). This he reported as being *very messy*, which he did not like. The second time, it was painful; he felt he needed to ejaculate, but could not. The third time, he had difficulty maintaining an erection, so he gave up and stopped—and then the erection came. He did self-stimulate, but without ejaculation.

It was important to teach Marty that the first time he had actually ejaculated, but without the contractions. The critical observation was that his difficulty with "the mess" inhibited the ejaculation the second time, and then the pain of that inhibition (physically needing it, but emotionally not allowing it) kept him from even approaching ejaculation the third time. It was also important to gather the details of how he masturbated: where, how long, what went on in his thoughts and feelings. We discovered that he was self-stimulating only thirty to ninety seconds! To get as far as he had gotten in such a short time was incredible and this was reinforced.

The recommendation at the end of the therapy session was that the next time he self-stimulated he set the timer for ninety seconds. Each succeeding time, he should add fifteen seconds on the timer. Instead of regular fifty-minute sessions, the next two weekly sessions were fifteen-minute check-ins to hold him accountable. He had excuses why he had not had time to masturbate very often and that he had not been able to go as long as the timer. Thus, we dealt with his fear of success and emphasized the need to attempt self-stimulation daily.

The third week proceeded with the timed self-stimulation on a daily basis. By the third day, he began ejaculating with emission—a release of seminal fluid, but no feeling of release. He said, "Something comes shooting out the end of my penis, but I don't feel anything—then my erection gradually goes down." We reinforced the fact that he was now ejaculating and that the next step was to allow himself to enjoy the release of those sensations.

Throughout the therapy process with us, Marty and Carrie continued the pleasuring of Carrie. She was orgasmic from manual stimulation.

At this point in the process, Marty and Carrie came to Pasadena for an intensive therapy process. After more thorough assessment, we decided to use our sexual therapy format, even though they had had sexual therapy previously. Many of our exercises were new to them and they acquired new awareness and skills. The two most significant assignments for them were the Kissing Exercise (Assignment 19) and the Simulating Arousal Responses exercise (Assignment 22). The Penis as a Paint Brush exercise (Assignment 26) to pleasure Carrie without any demand was very arousing for Marty. Carrie became more active in the pleasuring of him. As a result, this was arousing for both of them.

They were able to move rather quickly to her manually stimulating him to ejaculation, but again without much intense feeling. Some regression occurred the first time he ejaculated in her presence. He lost his erection. But this was not the major barrier. The fear of "letting go" in a new way seemed to be more the barrier than the barrier of being with his wife. This was congruent with the fear of his seizure and its connection with "letting go."

They discovered that when he became excited, he tensed up; yet, when he was able to relax, he was able to attain his best release. So internally he was fighting what worked best.

Moving to intercourse with poking produced another regression. He would lose his erection. Consequently, we had Carrie manually stimulate him after a little attempt at poking to practice the principles of just noticeable difference. They got to the place of being able to enter, and then he would lose his erection. Thus, we recommended entry for only a moment, and then they were to withdraw and stimulate to ejaculation. Again, the time after entry was increased in a just noticeable difference, until longer and longer times in the vagina were possible without loss of erection.

Then male fantasies became an issue as a distraction to success. Marty resumed his fantasizing that he was with men. We dealt with this issue psychodynamically and then recommended they substitute fantasies between them. The next inhibition we discovered was that they were not thrusting after entry. They had to be verbally instructed how to move their bodies to have the penis move in and out of the vagina.

The final steps were to have intercourse with the timer set. Each time was to be a little longer. There were to be no attempts to ejaculate. When the desire or urge to ejaculate got so high, they were to withdraw and manually stimulate to ejaculation. His first resistance was that he did not think he could recognize the warning signs.

At the same time, we had them orally or manually stimulate almost to ejaculation and then enter as he was about to ejaculate. Eventually he did ejaculate, first without feeling and then allowing more sensation, but never with full gusto—as far as we know.

2. Gus and Judy represented a very standard retarded-ejaculation situation. We guided them through the process entirely as described in the treatment plan.

Gus had great success in learning to bring himself to ejaculation and was like a twelve-year-old who wanted to do it twice a day. His problem was much more associated with his dominant mother and, thus, he had more difficulty moving to ejaculation with Judy. He would sabotage her effective stimulation—actually stop her from doing what produced intense arousal—because he did not like it. Then when she was encouraged by us to continue effective stimulation even if he did not like it, he got intense headaches. We had to require him to stop his self-stimulation in order to be able to ejaculate with Judy.

Judy also had some hesitancies about being intensely sexual, so these also had to be a focus during the process. She, too, had to be taught to be orgasmic. Today, they have two children of their own and a fulfilling sexual relationship.

3. Treatment for Mark and Susan was simpler than that for Gus and Judy, or for Marty and Carrie; yet, they were not as committed to consistent involvement in the treatment plan.

Susan was a loving, alive, spirited gal who adored Mark and was game for anything. They worked well together. We took them through the sexual therapy process, ruling out masturbation which was an addiction for him. He was instructed to tell her if he did masturbate. They were to have intercourse, withdraw when he got near the point of ejaculation and manually stimulate to ejaculation. This was to be practiced every other day.

On the fifteenth day, he ejaculated inside her. On the seventeenth day, he ejaculated inside her with more intensity and feeling. On the nineteenth day, they came to our office for an appointment. He wanted to now add the rule that he could no longer ejaculate from her manual stimulation, but only ejaculate inside her. We were hesitant, but allowed it. Immediately he was unable to ejaculate inside her, so we changed back to allowing ejaculation from her manual stimulation. We have not seen them since, but Mark telephoned and said that all was going well.

Resistance to Treatment

Fear of success and sabotage of the treatment process is common to men experiencing retarded ejaculation. A typical dilemma is that the man will sabotage the stimulation which would make him ejaculate. For example, Gus would not allow Judy to effectively stimulate him. He would stop her because it gave him a headache, did not feel good, and he did not like it. Marty tended to sabotage also, but not so obviously. Our sense was that the amount of therapy he had undergone had taught him to be more subtle in his stopping of effective stimulation: he used some mental games and some restriction of body movement to inhibit his response. Mark sabotaged with his intense trying and not being regular in therapy appointments.

Lack of confidence that ejaculation is possible also serves as a common resistance to success in the treatment of retarded ejaculation. The feeling that "I can't" or that it is a medical problem and "if I got testosterone shots" (as Mark believed), then all would be well. The belief or fear that they may be homosexual was true for both Gus and Marty. This gave them the lack of confidence in their ability to ejaculate with their wives.

Our findings are that once ejaculatory inhibitions are freed, the men continue to ejaculate without difficulty. However, neither Kaplan, nor

Masters and Johnson report a cure with this degree of stability. They have dealt with more cases than we, but their cases have not been representative of such an absolute inhibition of ejaculation as ours have been. (Their reported cases seem more like that of Mark, who had occasional ejaculations and could ejaculate with self-stimulation.) That difference may affect the results.

CHAPTER FOURTEEN

TREATING PROBLEMS OF INTERCOURSE

PROBLEMS OF INTERCOURSE ARE problems which interfere specifically with the physical act of entering the penis into the vagina. These disorders include pain (or, more technically, dyspareunia); unconsummated marriages; and vaginismus, which is one of the causes of unconsummated marriages.

PAINFUL INTERCOURSE (DYSPAREUNIA)

Painful intercourse (dyspareunia) can be experienced by both men and women. However, in our practice, dyspareunia for men has been virtually nonexistent. In contrast, women frequently suffer from painful intercourse.

Men may experience pain upon gaining an erection, entering the woman's vagina, or ejaculating. Although the pain may be of psychogenic basis, it is more often caused by physical factors which are best diagnosed and treated by a urologist.

Pain for women during intercourse is often not regarded as a serious deterrent to satisfactory sexual enjoyment. Yet painful intercourse *does* seriously interrupt sexual fulfillment. Intercourse is supposed to be a pleasurable experience. If it hurts, it is not likely to be either eagerly anticipated or enjoyed. Thus, many times both the emotional process of lovemaking and all phases of the sexual response are interrupted by painful intercourse.

There are emotional and physical reasons for dyspareunia. Because the source of the pain may be physical, a medical consultation is always a necessary part of diagnosing and treating painful intercourse. For women, a gynecologist or gynecologist/urologist is usually recommended. However, some general practitioners work comfortably and effectively with dyspareunia, whereas occasionally a gynecologist may not be comfortable or knowledgeable in its diagnosis and treatment. Pain is often difficult to diagnose and treat.

TYPES OF PAIN AND THEIR TREATMENT

First Intercourse Pain. The first experience of intercourse for a woman may be painful. In addition to the breaking of the hymen, her vaginal muscle may be tight due to eagerness and anxiety. The combination of excitement and fear of the unknown interferes with the relaxation of the body. The sympathetic nervous system (SNS) overpowers the parasympathetic (PNS). This SNS dominance prevents the physiological changes of arousal from building and preparing the body for entry. Many times, the new bride who is a virgin wants so fervently to consummate her marriage that she cannot relax enough to enjoy the pleasure that would produce the parasympathetic nervous system responses of vaginal lubrication and the opening up of and flattening out of the labia.

If she and her husband force entry, there will be pain, which will interrupt any pleasure. That will increase her tension, which will increase her pain and prevent her from becoming aroused and responding. This can be a most disappointing first experience.

249

Such a negative scenario can be prevented. Premarital preparation should include the following recommendations:

1. That the couple read aloud together all but the chapters focusing on problems in *The Gift of Sex* or some similar book. This will give them a sound knowledge base biblically, emotionally, and physically, as well as break down barriers and help them talk openly about sex with each other.
2. That the woman begin stretching her hymen and the opening of her vagina by using graduated dialators or inserting first one finger, then two, and then three.
3. That the woman practice PC muscle exercises using the written instructions of Assignment 12 of the Sexual Therapy Plan in chapter 9. This is so she will learn to be able to tighten and relax her PC muscle voluntarily. Her focus should be on the relaxation part.
4. That the woman have a gynecological examination, including birth control management and testing for Sexually Transmitted Diseases (STDs) and AIDS. If the gynecologist is unable to do a vaginal examination because the opening of the vagina is too small, an additional consultation may be necessary to assure accurate diagnosis and treatment.

   In rare instances, the hymen is covering too much of the opening of the vagina, in which case a hymenotomy may be necessary. But the need for surgical intervention should always be confirmed by a second opinion. The woman may only need help in learning to relax her PC muscle, or she may need sexual therapy for vaginismus (which we will address in the next section). Surgery, when it is not necessary, only leaves more scar tissue and additional pain.
5. That the man have a routine physical examination, including testing for STDs and AIDS.
6. That both the man and woman individually complete the self-genital examinations (Assignment 11 in the Sexual Therapy Plan).
7. That they buy and use a genital lubricant for all of their sexual intercourse experiences, whether or not she is lubricating, until they unintentionally ease out of using the lubricant. As mentioned earlier, Albolene, a facial cleanser, and Allercreme, a nonlanolin, hypoallergenic lotion, are the two we recommend.

However, they are both petroleum-based products and should not be used with rubber condoms or diaphragms, because petroleum products break down the effectiveness of rubber-barrier methods of birth control. The most common water-based lubricants are K-Y Jelly and Lubrifax; but both have the disadvantage of drying quickly. A new product, Probe, is very effective and natural, but not readily available on the market. Natural oils (e.g., almond oil) and saliva can always be utilized for vaginal lubrication.

8. That they talk about their past sexual input to alert each other to any elements that might negatively affect their first coital activity. They might individually respond to and share their responses to the following questions:

    What did you learn about sex as you were growing up?

    What experiences have you had that may affect your first intercourse event? (The therapist should assist in making the judgment about sharing or not sharing hurtful data.)

    What do you think your parents' sexual life is/was like?

    What would you like your own sexual life to be like?

9. That they talk about their fears and anticipations of their first sexual encounter before the night of planned consummation.

10. That the couple plan to proceed to their first intercourse slowly. It is best that they take time to enjoy all the pleasure they have allowed before marriage, now adding the total body and genital caressing. Kissing is vital to their connecting and relaxing together.

11. That they place no sexual demands on themselves or each other, but completely delight in the enjoyment of each other's bodies.

12. That the woman invite and guide the initial entry, and that the couple have a time of resting quietly together (quiet vagina) before they begin a gradual and varied pattern of rhythmic thrusting.

The goal of therapy regarding pain during first intercourse experiences is prevention. Premarital teaching, examinations, communication, and preparation can make that first event comfortable and satisfying for both husband and wife.

Pain Due to Stress. All of us show tension in our own unique ways. Some women will tend to tighten up their genital muscles involuntarily. This tightening is an expression of their tension. They may not even be aware that the tensing is happening, yet the muscle tension is counterproductive to a comfortable and fulfilling intercourse experience. As a result of the tension, they experience pain.

Frequently the tightening will occur immediately before entry or as entry is attempted. This can make entry very painful. Sometimes, sharp spasmodic contractions occur after entry as the woman's arousal intensifies near or at the point of orgasm. It is as if she is having an orgasmic response, but the tension in her body keeps that muscle from responding smoothly. The spasmodic, painful contractions reflect her stress.

Treatment for relief of pain due to stress is aimed at reducing the stress that causes the pain and/or learning to relax and give and receive sexual pleasure in spite of the stress.

If the stress is due to external life issues—finances, children, moving, remodeling, job, etc.—then some stress reduction and coping techniques may be most helpful. If the stress is due to sexual conflict, psychotherapy may be required to uncover the woman's ambivalence about being sexual. Whatever the cause of the stress, a focus on pleasuring will always reduce the problem. Taking turns stroking and caressing each other's bodies simply for the sake of soaking in that touch can do wonders to relieve the pain due to stress.

Pain Due to Lack of Release. Lack of sexual release or orgasmic inhibition is another source of pain for women. When a woman does not experience orgasmic release even though she becomes highly aroused, she may sense painful fullness in her lower abdominal and lower back areas, especially after intercourse. As she becomes aroused, muscle tension builds as the whole reproductive system becomes congested with blood in preparation for an orgasm. The contractions in the lower part of the vagina and in the uterus are to relieve that congestion. When there is an orgasm, the draining of the blood from the genitals provides a great deal of pleasure. When the woman does not experience release, the whole pelvic area remains engorged, which may cause chronic pain. This pain is usually not intense, but is a dull, throbbing ache. It feels as though it is deep inside the body.

Obviously, the best remedy for pain due to lack of release is to teach the woman to allow herself to experience orgasmic release (see chapter 13).

Physically Based Pain. Infection of any part of the female genitalia, internal or external, will cause pain in that part when it is touched. The inflammation, irritation, and swelling of the infected part causes that tissue to be very tender.

Any infection should be treated immediately by a physician. Sexual activity should be limited according to the physician's instructions and be designed to prevent further negative painful experiences. These limitations provide an opportunity for the couple to focus on the total body pleasuring and other, often bypassed, special pleasures.

Vaginal irritations are troublesome because there often is no specific, identifiable disease present. Yet an irritated vaginal opening or vaginal barrel can cause as much sexual distress as an infection.

The generous use of a lubricant can help reduce the irritation, even though it does not treat the cause. The lubricant is especially helpful if the irritation is due to the thinning of the vaginal walls and the lessening of vaginal lubrication associated with aging. Women can help to slow the vaginal atrophy process. With menopausal changes, PC muscle exercises and hormonal replacement therapy can be of great help in actually keeping the vaginal tissues alive and functioning longer. Uterine contractions during orgasm may be painful after menopause due to the low estrogen level. Hormonal replacement therapy is also helpful in this circumstance.

When a young woman suffers from vaginal irritation, her diet, her birth control pills, and her reactions to her husbands' seminal fluid should be evaluated. Richard Dickey's book *Managing Contraceptive Pill Patients*[1] is very helpful in identifying the symptoms and selecting a different oral contraceptive that is not as likely to cause the irritation. Some women may need to work with their doctors to try a new pill each month until they find the one that works best for their system.

To help the couple determine if the irritation is a reaction to his seminal fluid, have the man wear a condom for several sexual intercourse experiences, and have the woman compare the difference in the pain she experiences without the condoms in contrast to with the condom.

Our own theory, which stems from biochemical and nutritional awareness as well as a high success rate for women who have tried diet change, is that change in diet can affect the pH balance in the body and reduce or eliminate the irritation. We think of adjusting the diet to affect the acid-base balance much like physicians often recommend it to help women prevent urinary bladder irritations. We recommend they eliminate all soda pop, sugar, caffeine, and citrus fruit; and that they eat yogurt, drink cranberry-apple juice, and take acidolphilus capsules with every meal and a multi-vitamin-mineral supplement designed for women. Some even find it very soothing to apply plain yogurt intravaginally. These recommendations should be confirmed with the client's physician. Although nothing recommended here should be harmful, it is always best to make certain that the therapist's recommendations do not in any way interfere with the physician's diagnosis and treatment of pain.

Physically based pain can also be the result of either tears in the opening of the vagina or small cuts (fissures) inside the vagina itself. Tears in the hymen usually cause pain upon entry. Pain due to tears or fissures is usually very sharp and specific. These women can pinpoint a specific spot inside the vagina that hurts when it is touched or thrust against. Continued sexual activity and the moist environment promote slow healing of fissures and tears. These must be treated medically.

Some women report a sharp, stabbing pain only upon deep thrusting. This most commonly is the result of tipped or retroverted uterus which causes the cervix of the uterus to be thrust against during deep thrusting. The cervix is sensitive to pain, so each thrust causes a sharp, stabbing pain. The woman may actually cry out or react with a jarring movement. Relief can be found immediately by a slight shift in position. The pain can be prevented by putting a small pillow or folded towel under the woman's upper buttocks if she is in the under position; or she can be in the top position and control the thrusting.

To correct the retroverted uterus, seek medical consultation. In addition, two exercises can do miracles for improving the uterine placement. The PC muscle exercise helps keep all the organs in place and the knee/chest position specifically adjusts the uterus into the desired location. The PC Muscle exercise is detailed in Assignment 12 of the Sexual Therapy Plan. The knee-chest position exercise should be done for five minutes once or twice a day. The woman positions herself on the floor on her knees and then rests her chest on the floor. While in that position, she separates her labia to let air rush into her vagina, and remains in that position for five minutes.

Other internal pathologies such as endometriosis, ovarian cysts, pelvic inflammatory disease, or a misplaced IUD can also cause pain upon thrusting.

Finally, physically based pain may be the outgrowth of childbirth trauma. One source of such pain is the sensitive scar tissue from the episiotomy, the incision that is made between the vagina and the rectum to assist the birth process. There may also be tears in the ligaments that hold the uterus in place, in the vaginal wall, or around the opening of the vagina. For those resuming sexual activity after childbirth, we encourage that they follow the same instructions as outlined in this chapter to prevent pain for the virginal first sexual intercourse. If pain continues, the woman should consult her physician or seek consultation from another physician.

Managing Pain

In the last section, specific treatment recommendations were given for each type of pain. Now we will suggest some general guidelines that are helpful for *managing* all types of pain:

1. Encourage the woman to talk with her husband about the pain. The couple can develop a signal system to let him know when she is feeling pain so they can change their activity to relieve it. Sexual activity associated with pain should never be continued.
2. The woman should identify exactly *when* in their sexual experience the pain is triggered and *how long* it lasts. She needs to note specifically *where* the pain is *located.* It is helpful if she can describe *what type of pain* she experiences: stinging, burning, stabbing, dull, rubbing, sharp, etc.
3. The woman should be given confidence to take charge of getting relief from her pain. She should seek medical help and describe in detail what she has already discovered about her pain (from completing step 2). She can boldly inform her physician that the pain is interrupting her sexual pleasure and she wants treatment to relieve that pain.
4. The couple can be inspired to use this time to discover what sexual activities are pleasurable and focus on that enjoyment.
5. After the reason for the pain is gone, the woman may continue her pattern of pulling away or tightening to avoid the painful sensation. The couple needs to identify this conditioned response and break the pattern by verbalizing the reaction and then correcting it by purposeful distraction and relaxation.

An increasing number of women, particularly young women, are reporting pain during intercourse. Pain does not have to be tolerated. In fact, pain *cannot* be allowed to continue if the couple is going to enjoy sexual pleasure.

UNCONSUMATED MARRIAGES

The absolute problem with intercourse is the inability to have it at all. When a couple has not been able to have intromission of the penis into the vagina, their marriage is unconsummated.

Couples may have been married three weeks or forty years and not been able to have intercourse. There are always stories floating around about some couple who lived together for fifteen years and never consummated their marriage because they did not know what to do. The humor of such a story is diminished quickly by hearing the experience of couples who are functioning normally in every other area of life, but have been unable to come together sexually, even though they know how and have been trying. One senses the pain and the shame they carry, making it difficult for them to even seek treatment.

A number of reasons cause the inability to have intercourse:

1. The couple does not know how. This may be difficult to believe in our sexually enlightened age, but it is a reality. These couples may have little education—education and intelligence are not the issue. Developmental naiveté has left both feeling awkward sexually. They bumble. They do not seem to be able to get their bodies in the right position at the right time and at the correct angle. They do not know to separate the woman's labia before entry. However, the sexually naive couple responds quickly to the sexual therapy process and education. The Sexual Therapy Plan can be followed in the order that the exercises are listed.
2. Obesity can prevent the possibility of the penis being able to enter the vagina. Creative positioning can help the couple be able to consummate, but weight loss is the preferred approach. A medical program for weight loss is usually recommended.
3. Physiological obstruction of the opening of the vagina due to skin growing over the opening, a rigid hymen, or any pathology of the pelvic organs will prevent entry of the penis into the vagina.
4. Psychogenic or physically based pain at any attempt at entry will prevent entry.

Sarah had been sexually active before her marriage to Tom, but they were unable to consummate their marriage due to extreme pain on attempted intercourse. She had been to several physicians, and surgery had been suggested. We began treating her for a conditional vaginismus while continuing to seek a more accurate diagnosis. A gynecologist/urologist who specializes in pain during intercourse finally discovered that Sarah had urethritis—a highly inflamed urethra. The treatment was painful and took long to take effect. After the urethritis was corrected, Sarah and Tom still needed sexual therapy to be able to consummate their marriage, because many negative patterns of sexual relating had to be reversed. The "pain effect" had had a negative impact on their entire sexual relationship.

5. Erectile dysfunction (impotence) may keep a couple from being able to consummate their marriage. If a man is not able to get or keep his erection, he will not be able to enter his wife. Treatment for impotence is discussed in chapter 12.
6. Panic attacks, probably caused by past abuse or rape, may keep the woman from allowing entry.
7. Vaginismus is the most common reason for unconsummated marriages and is clearly a problem with intercourse. It will be discussed separately.

The reward of treating an unconsummated marriage is so tangible there is no doubt when therapy has been successful. The couple either has been able to have intercourse or they have not. The success rate is high. This is the news that we hope couples will hear so that they will seek help within the first few weeks of the problem's occurrence. How sad it is that some couples wait for years before they do anything about this dilemma. Some go for help but are given an ineffective therapeutic approach. Fortunately, consummation is possible.

VAGINISMUS

Vaginismus is an involuntary, spastic contracting of the muscles surrounding the entrance to the vagina (the outer one-third), making penetration impossible. Negative feelings (fear, pain, violation, etc.) have been paired with the act or fantasy of vaginal penetration.

Some women's vaginal muscles only snap tightly shut with attempts at intercourse. Other women's vaginal muscles tighten at penetration attempts by the finger or any other object. The latter is most commonly the case.

These women will report never having been able to insert a tampon. They may have tried and become very nauseous. Or they may have incredible resistance to even trying.

The spasm of the vaginal inlet is usually associated with a panic fear of coitus or any vaginal penetration, even though these women may be very sexually responsive.

Many couples with unconsummated marriages have great pleasuring skills because they have learned to do everything but have intercourse. For others, all the intense pleasure they enjoyed in premarital necking and petting has dissipated with the stress of not being able to have intercourse.

When a couple comes to us, they may have seen several medical doctors, counselors, psychologists, and even sexual therapists, without having been given the treatment process that is written up and available in all standard sexual therapy manuals: primarily, the use of graduated dialators to release the spastic contraction of the muscle, along with therapeutic intervention for the cause of the condition. Our four-pronged treatment approach is presented in the last section of this chapter.

Causes of Vaginismus

What usually causes vaginismus?
1. *Misinformation:* As a young girl, the woman may have been warned never to put anything "in there," or never to let anyone else put anything in there. She may have received a message of hurt or disgust at the thought of something entering her vagina. She has not received the input that the vagina is an organ of accommodation, able to receive an erect penis. In fact, the messages have been quite the opposite.
2. *Emotional inhibitions:* These often come from rigid upbringing and negative conditioning to sex, based on religious orthodoxy. Cindy, the young woman mentioned in an earlier chapter, was raised in a strong Catholic home with very rigid instruction, and was taught never to look at herself or to touch herself. In fact, she and her sisters were required to turn the lights off in the bathroom when they showered so they would not see themselves. As adults, her two sisters also suffered from vaginismus.

258

One was able to have intercourse, but had extreme pain. The other, about to be married, was unable to use tampons or to complete her gynecological examination. Cindy had been married three years and her marriage was unconsummated.

3. *Traumatic sexual experiences:* We find that sexual molestation or abuse is most commonly the cause of vaginismus. The abuse may have been attempted penetration or actual entry. In response, the little girl protected herself by involuntarily tightening her vaginal opening. Physical abuse can cause a young girl to involuntarily and rigidly contract her vaginal inlet. An insensitive physician may have abused the young woman by performing a traumatic urinary tract examination or treatment.

Similarly, the evasive frequent use of enemas on a little girl can be the abuse that leaves her with vaginismus. In many cases, there has been multiple abuse. One woman had a ten-year unconsummated marriage. In the process of therapy it became clear that her father had had intercourse with her before age four. She was too young to differentiate the pain of vaginal entry from urinary functioning. Therefore, she always had difficulty letting go of her urine in public restrooms. She would never urinate during a school day. This led to intrusive urological procedures. She also struggled with constipation, so her mother gave her enemas and punished her for trying not to let them work. Her vaginismus was due to a combination of her perineal orifices having been abused.

4. *Excessive closeness to an overprotective mother:* Fearful mothers often instill many conscious and unconscious or nonspecific fears of life in general that can affect the sexual arena. These mothers project their own fears of the world or of sex onto their daughters. For example, mothers who survived the painful threats of the Holocaust were left with nightmare memories which they have communicated to their daughters. Dagmar O'Connor refers to these women who have a high incidence of vaginismus as "daughters of Holocaust survivors."[2]

Jeanie was born out of wedlock to her single mother—who had been raped. Her mother had a very unhappy and painful life; Jeanie was her only source of joy and meaning. When Jeanie was twenty-eight, her mother still sewed all of Jeanie's clothes. Jeanie needed to call or visit her mother daily. She had to constantly be thinking about making her

259

mother happy. Her mother indirectly and directly communicated to Jeanie a fear, distrust, and hatred of men, yet a desire for the white knight in shining armor to come and rescue her from her misery.

Jeanie could enjoy all sexual activity with her husband, except intercourse. With time, Jeanie's sexual desire lessened. Psychotherapy along with sexual therapy was necessary to reverse her dilemma.

Helen Singer Kaplan suggests that any adverse stimulus associated with vaginal entry may cause vaginal tightness, whether the stimulus is real or fantasized.[3] So whether the woman with vaginismus fantasizes trauma with vaginal entry because of the close protective association with her mother, the emotional antisex inhibitions, or misinformation about the vaginal function, or whether she experienced trauma because of rape, incest, or forced attempted entry, the result is the same. She experiences the rigid conditioned restriction of the muscles controlling the vaginal inlet—vaginismus.

Diagnosis of Vaginismus

Ultimately, vaginismus must be diagnosed by physical examination. Therefore, sexual assessment can only be used to speculate; then referral to a gynecologist for examination may be necessary. Often, though, the gynecological examination has taken place before sexual therapy is sought. The gynecologist may have referred the client for sexual therapy.

Sometimes the client has been misdiagnosed and has gone for a second opinion. If the second physician is uncomfortable telling the client her physician was wrong, he or she may refer the patient to us for an evaluation and to convey the hesitancy in regard to the physician's original diagnosis.

This was the case with Mary, who had been married seven years and had had entry one or two times with extreme pain. Now entry was impossible. She was told she needed surgery for removal of intracoital ridge, but was told to seek a second opinion. The second physician expressed some doubt about surgery and recommended sexual therapy. This physician asked Mary to have her sexual therapist call to discuss her case.

After the assessment, we called the physician and explained that Mary had a history of sexual molestation from her stepfather. She also had antisex fears which had been instilled by her mother because of the mother's alcoholic first husband—Mary's father—who ran around with other women and still held to many rigid antisex beliefs. She fit the pattern of women who have vaginal rigidity due to emotional reasons. The consulting physician was relieved, because there was no evidence upon examination of a need for surgical removal of an intracoital ridge. Our suspicion confirmed the second physician's finding of an inaccurate original diagnosis.

Other misdiagnoses that have been given for vaginismus are vestibulitis, vaginitis, and vaginal atrophy. Now these are all very possible diagnoses that could cause pain upon attempted entry—they may be accurate. When in doubt, get more than one medical opinion. This is especially important if the woman has a history of sexual abuse, or suspected sexual abuse, overprotective closeness with a mother who instilled fears of the world or antisex teaching or conditioning. Because these disorders are clearly connected with vaginismus, any other diagnosis needs to be validated or ruled out.

Is it a medical or emotional dilemma? Vaginismus is truly a psychosomatic disease. There are physical effects from psychological causes. Therefore, medical consultation is always necessary.

In referring to a gynecologist for examination, ask the physician to describe the procedure used in examining for vaginismus. A woman physician is usually preferred by the patient.

The examination should proceed as follows: First, the physician should ease the tension of the patient by talking with her. Then there should be a complete physical examination in which each body part is examined. All throughout the examination the physician is to inform the patient, "Now I am going to examine your_____; to do this I will use _____ [an instrument]. You will feel_____." Then, as each examination is completed, the physician should say, "Your _____ looks completely normal," etc. For the vaginal examination, the external genitalia should be examined first. Sometimes the involuntary tightening of the vaginal inlet is obvious from this external genitalia examination. In that case, insertion of finger or speculum should not even be attempted.

If a vaginal exam is necessary, the physician should:
1. Have patient's legs well supported, with more than only stirrups.
2. Show the patient the physician's gloved hand.
3. Coach the patient in breathing deeply.
4. Verbalize each step of what the physician is doing and perceiving in positive terms: "I am able to_____."
5. If the physician is able to insert a finger, the muscle will reflex and tighten around the finger. It may only be possible to probe with a cotton-tipped swab.

The vaginismic spasm or constriction of the musculature surrounding the outer portion of the vagina is usually detectable by vaginal examination. For some women, the tightening does not happen when examined by a physician. The husband may be needed to describe the clamping or pinching response to his finger or penis, attempting to enter or actually entering. When it is possible to have entry and the muscle relaxes after insertion, this is not complete vaginismus, but rather some degree of it. In partial vaginismus, the husband is able to insert with extreme difficulty and pain and then relaxation occurs. The vaginal examination will confirm or rule out the therapist's suspected diagnosis of vaginismus.

Treatment of Vaginismus

The treatment of vaginismus includes a multifaceted approach which begins with the therapist describing the diagnosis to the client and her husband. It is helpful to use a diagram of the internal female genitalia to show where the muscle is and what is happening to the muscle that is preventing entry. (See Figure 5–3.)

Telling the husband, "It must have felt like you were pushing against a brick wall when you tried to enter," often connects vividly with his experience. Likewise, the woman feels understood when her experience is verbalized: "You have probably believed it was physically impossible to get anything in your vagina and thought that something was physically wrong with you."

The helpfulness of having the diagnosis explained was expressed so well by clients of Dr. Dagmar O'Connor: "It was from the sex therapist that Larry and I finally learned that I had vaginismus, constriction of the vaginal muscles caused by fear when penetration is attempted. I was incredibly relieved to hear that my problem had a name . . . (and) that the cure rate for vaginismus was high."[4]

This woman's relief is representative of the feelings expressed by most women who seek our help for vaginismus. The women who come to us have been given tranquilizers, muscle relaxants, stiff drinks, been told to "grow up," "just relax," "fantasize some bizarre experience" or recommended to have surgery. When we describe their condition and its treatment to couples, they feel great relief. The description connects with their experience.

Therapy for vaginismus has four distinct tracks: 1) Releasing of the psycho-emotional conflicts associated with vaginal penetration, 2) Building trust to be able to give and receive sexual pleasure (not always necessary), 3) Gaining genital acceptance and voluntary control, and 4) Achieving vaginal penetration through reduction of phobic avoidance and desensitization.

Track 1: Releasing of the psycho-emotional conflicts associated with vaginal penetration. Although the source of traumatic association with entry into the vagina is not always evident, sometimes the cause will be revealed in the taking of the client's history. However, many times it will not. In the initial evaluation, Kathy was able to reveal the details of her rigid antisex training that had left her with extreme fear in response to anything being inserted into her vagina.

Likewise, Linda was able to tell us in the initial interview specifically how she had been trained to never allow anything to enter her vagina. Her mother had responded with horror and disgust, as though something terrible would happen to her if she used a tampon. Even the fact that she asked was an unforgivable sin.

However, it was not until several sessions that Kathy was able to tell us that when dating in high school, her boyfriend had entered her. She was naive and had not known what was happening. Being so frightened, she immediately pushed him out of her, got out of the car, and ran.

Mary was unable to tell us about the molestation by her stepfather until the third session. He was the "good Christian" and her only loving father. Her real father was the alcoholic who ran around with other women, spoke in vulgar language about sex around the home, and beat her mother. Yet her kind, loving stepfather was the one who fondled her breasts and genitals.

To uncover and release the conflict of this disorder, while proceeding with correcting the condition, have the woman read chapter 14, "Sex and the Unconsummated Marriage" in *A Gift for All Ages*. Then have her write her thoughts, feelings, and reactions. Also have her read Chapter 8, "Sexual Molestation and Abuse," in the same book.

If she feels she fits the description of someone who was abused, the chapter is emotionally difficult for her to read, or the awareness of being abused is identified; have her proceed by reading and writing her reactions to Susan Forward and Craig Buck's book, *The Betrayal of Innocence*, Rich Buhler's book, *Pain and Pretending*, and/or Ellen Bass and Laura Davis's book, *The Courage to Heal*.[5] (The last book includes references to lesbian activity, so read it first yourself and eliminate those sections or adjust them for your client before giving it to her. It is probably the most helpful book available, apart from the lesbianism presented).

Letting go of the emotional bondage and grieving the loss of healthy sexual openness may be a tedious process. The assigned reading stirs up the pain, and there will be a tendency for these women to want to avoid that. It may be so severe that they cannot continue with their ongoing responsibilities while they are releasing that pain. These women may need to segment their lives in order to confront their underlying conflicts at separate times from their life tasks.

One woman read, wrote, and cried about her pain (did her "grief work") from 9 A.M. to 2 P.M. Monday through Friday while her children were in school. Then she gave herself from 2 to 3 P.M. to put aside the pain and connect with her current world before her children came home.

Another woman, who had been severely physically beaten by her mother and who had an intense phobic reaction to *any* vaginal penetration, could not work on this issue while she was in graduate school. She would only work with us in confronting her pain while she was on vacation from school.

Another woman became so emotionally immobilized by the pain of her abusive past that she required short-term hospitalization with intensive daily individual and group therapy to be able to face the pain of releasing what had happened to her as a child in her home.

The fact is, in order to be cured, women suffering from vaginismus cannot continue to avoid their negative feelings. They must face the pain to release the hold it has on their vaginal musculature.

We encourage each woman to buy a notebook or journal, and use it to write her memories, feelings, reactions, dreams, thoughts, and fantasies. This helps to enable her to get with the pain, rather than avoid it, because she can release it by writing down all the facts. Some women find it extremely difficult to write about their past traumatic experiences. They feel too vulnerable putting their past on paper, saying, "Who knows who might read it?" Others find that writing about that painful past makes it far too real. But this is exactly what needs to happen in order to be cured. Still others resist writing because these events may not really have happened. "What if I just made them up?" These women should be reassured that whether their memories are of real events or fantasized events, they need to be released so that the events no longer have control over them. Instead, the women will have control over the effects of these happenings.

Eventually, in the process of releasing the pain, the woman has to be helped to 1) recognize the reasons for her tightening up her vagina, 2) accept that her fears of vaginal penetration are irrational, 3) choose to no longer allow her mother-instilled fears, father's abuse, or antisexual teaching to control her vagina, and 4) make a decision to stop resisting and to go after sexual pleasure and vaginal penetration. This last step occurs in a similar manner as a conversion experience. The woman has been using her energies to protect. She now turns the opposite direction and uses those same energies to engage.

Cheryl, whose story will be shared later, expressed this change so aptly: "Whatever they did to me, I'm not going to let them have control over me anymore. I am going to be able to have sex with my husband. Why should I allow them to keep me from that?"

Track 2: Building trust to be able to give and receive sexual pleasure. The exercises of the Sexual Therapy Plan in chapter 9 are assigned to teach couples how to give and receive sexual pleasure and to help the woman build trust in her husband—trust that he will not violate her sexually. As mentioned earlier, some couples suffering from vaginismus have developed all the skills of bodily pleasuring because they cannot have intercourse. These couples do not need this track of the therapy process. In this case, the woman is able to enjoy the giving and receiving of pleasure to the point of orgasm and trust her husband not to violate her. Her only barrier is the fear of vaginal penetration.

However, many couples have experienced much frustration and disappointment because of the vaginismus, and the woman cannot freely give and receive sexual pleasure or trust her husband not to violate her. These couples desperately need to be guided through the sexual therapy process, and the woman needs to build trust and learn to relax in the enjoyment of sexual pleasure.

Track 3: Gaining genital acceptance and voluntary control. Women with vaginismus have dissociated their genitals from their personhood. Their genitals have been a source of fear, confusion, conflict, and pain. An active process of genital acceptance must ensue.

We often refer to this process of genital acceptance and control as "naming and claiming." It begins with the Female Self-Exam (Assignment 11 of the Sexual Therapy Plan). The next step is the repetition of the Female Self-Exam, including the PC Muscle Exercise (Assignment 12). The woman is encouraged to watch the opening of her vagina as she tightens and relaxes the PC muscle, so that she learns that she can voluntarily control the opening of her vagina.

The couple is given the assignment of naming each other's genitals with fun and loving names. They are to pat and affirm each other's genitals every night before they go to sleep. This not only helps the woman gain genital acceptance, but it also continues the previous track of building trust with her husband.

Finally, the Clinical Genital Exam (Assignment 15) is assigned to continue the process of not only accepting her genitals for herself, but now being able to very openly share them with her husband. To connect her genitals as part of herself that is good, the woman is encouraged to praise God for his creation of her genitals and to ask for the healing of past pain associated with them. This may also be a time of giving her genitals to her husband for him to enjoy for his pleasure, with clear guidelines that she can interrupt his enjoyment anytime his activities become associated with violation or pain.

Gaining genital acceptance and the sense of control is vital to the woman's ability to pursue vaginal penetration.

Track 4: Achieving vaginal penetration through reduction of phobic avoidance and desensitization. Although Track 1 is the most painful part of the treatment process for women with vaginismus, Track 4 can be the most difficult. This is true when the woman has a phobic reaction to inserting anything into her vagina. Every stage of the therapy process may progress nicely, but the woman resists the task of inserting something into her vagina. Even a Q-Tip is overwhelmingly frightening.

During the first assignment, the woman must be sure of complete privacy and no interruptions. She is to take a leisurely bath and to pamper herself in any way that makes her feel special and relaxed (lotion her body, brush her hair, etc.). Then she is to prop herself up with large pillows behind her back and under legs so that she is in a reclined sitting position against the head of a bed with her legs bent and drawn toward her body. Have her repeat the Female Self-Exam and the PC Muscle Exercise while watching her vagina tighten and relax. She is to have a Q-Tip (or something even thinner that is clean), a hand mirror, and a lubricant available. As she breathes in, she tightens her PC muscle. As she exhales slowly through her mouth, she relaxes the PC muscle and inserts the lubricated Q-Tip.

This may sound as if it is a simple exercise. However, women have spent months not being able to do this. Women come back week after week having reasons why they could not complete the assignment. The woman who was physically abused by her mother spent forty-five minutes of shaking trying to get herself to do this exercise. This was true each time she tried. For her, we discovered it was easier for her husband to do the insertion. Some women can allow the physician or their husbands to accomplish vaginal penetration, but they cannot do it for themselves. Others are just the opposite. They need to be in control of breaking the vaginal barrier.

Ask the woman ahead of time whether she has a sense of whether it will be easier to accomplish vaginal penetration by herself or with the assistance of her husband.

Masters and Johnson are in a medical examination facility where they teach women to insert dialators into their vaginas by having the examining physician insert the dialator first. This can be a confidence-building experience for the woman. We do not have an appropriate setting for that; but on occasion, we refer the woman to a physician who is experienced in accomplishing this task with vaginismic women. The husband's presence during the examination and insertion is helpful—it brings him into the process. In most settings, the woman or her husband are verbally taught how to do the insertion as was just described.

When the therapy process cannot progress beyond this task, and all the above-mentioned approaches do not produce any movement toward insertion of even the thinnest object into the vagina, the phobic reaction must be dealt with. Each situation may require a creative approach. A psychiatrist's evaluation and medication may be necessary.

To reduce the patient's phobic avoidance of penetration, the woman writes a detailed description of what is to happen in the assigned vaginal entry exercises: the actual actions, what she will feel or think, and what will happen to her vagina.

Women are taken through deep relaxation exercises and then verbally guided through all the actions that will lead to and include insertion of the Q-Tip into her vagina. The verbalization is to be warm and positive, painting the picture of the vagina as open and receptive. This visualization may need to be repeated several times. In fact, it can be taped and sent home with the client to listen to daily. Obtain detailed feedback from the woman as to what thoughts, visions, or feelings come into her mind during the visualization.

The woman must be confronted with the fact that her phobia is not the reality about her vagina, and that until insertion into the vagina is possible, the therapy process cannot progress.

Once it is possible for the woman, her husband, or her physician to insert something into her vagina, the gradual desensitization process begins. A series of dialations, catheters, syringe covers, fingers, or any other objects which are graduated in size, and are clean and smooth can be used. The insertion of these objects serves to eliminate the involuntary spasms of the PC muscle controlling the opening of the vagina. These dilation exercises are necessary to the successful treatment of vaginismus.

The same circumstances that brought about successful insertion of the Q-Tip or a thin, rubber catheter into the woman's vagina are replicated as each of the next-size objects are inserted. If the woman was able to accomplish insertion by herself, this is how she proceeds. If her husband was effective and she was not, her husband is assigned to continue the exercises. If the physician was the only successful one, the transfer of this event from the physician to herself or her husband may need to occur in the physician's office. Transferring that ability to home often takes some change in the home environment. The dining-room table might be converted to an examination table, or the bedroom might be avoided.

In this same or similar setting (the one that is associated with success), the successful insertion is repeated daily until the woman is totally comfortable with the specific act. Depending on the individual needs of each woman, usually included in these dilation exercises are the following:

1. A warm, relaxing bath.
2. Pampering of herself or total body pleasuring with her husband.
3. Inserting the lubricated object (gradually increasing the size).
4. Leaving the object in the vagina for five to twenty minutes (start with five or less and increase gradually).
5. Reading *The Gift of Sex* aloud to each other while the dialator is in place.
6. Reading the Song of Solomon in a modern translation aloud to each other while the dialator is in place.
7. Tightening and relaxing the PC muscle while the dialator is in place.
8. Affirming the woman for her ability to allow this step of the process to be accomplished.

When changing to the next-size object, have the woman begin by inserting the previous size, waiting for the voluntary muscle spasm to relax, removing the previous size object, and then inserting the next larger size. Use objects of increasing size until the object being inserted is the size of her husband's erect penis. The couple can determine this. After the Q-Tip or thin rubber catheter, use larger rubber catheters, Haegar vaginal dialators, injection-syringe covers (start with the 2.5cc size), rounded plastic tampon inserters (start with the slim size), or her or her husband's fingers. (If you find a creative solution to dialators, contact us. We would love to know. Hegar dialators are very expensive).

If the woman has learned to relax her vaginal muscle by inserting the dialators herself, the next step is to transfer this learning to be able to occur with her husband. Start again with the smallest dialator; but this time have her husband insert it. If there is no regression of involuntary spastic contraction of the muscle or phobic reaction, the couple can proceed quickly to each larger size dialator.

Once the husband is able to insert the erect-penis-size dialator without any discomfort to his wife, the couple is assigned each of the following exercises in the order listed. These exercises lead to insertion of the penis into the vagina:

1. Total Body Pleasuring (Assignment 14) with the largest dialator inserted in the vagina.
2. Total Body Pleasuring with Breast and Genital Stimulation (Assignment 24) with the largest dialator in the vagina.
3. Pleasuring Not Using Hands (Penis as a Paint Brush) (Assignment 26)—this is to desensitize the woman to being able to have the penis pleasure her genitals without any demand for entry.
4. Total Body Pleasuring with the largest dialator in the vagina. Remove dialator, lubricate the man's penis, use it as a paint brush, and then, while the woman is in the top position, she pokes the head of the penis into her vagina about a quarter-inch.
5. Repeat step 4, increasing the insertions of the penis into the vagina by a quarter-inch each time.
6. When complete entry is accomplished, the couple is to lie quietly together. The woman should be in control of any intravaginal activity.
7. Repeat step 6, which is basically Total Body Pleasuring, Entry by Invitation (Assignment 30) until the woman can gradually increase the amount of trusting to allow enough activity to bring her husband to ejaculation. If she desires an orgasm from that process, she should go after it. She may be more comfortable with their familiar way of bringing her to orgasm.

Once penile entry into the vagina is possible, the tasks of therapy have basically been completed. For some, the barriers are broken once they make that decision to not let their past control their genitals. Others sail through all the behavioral tasks after they are able to insert the smallest dialator beyond the PC muscle.

Case Presentation. Cheryl was diagnosed as having vaginismus when she went for her premarital gynecological examination. Her physician referred her for sexual therapy. She came two months before her wedding. We had three premarital sessions and three postmarital sessions.

Cheryl came with no memory of abuse. But she clearly remembered both the rigid, religious, antisex training from her mother and her sister, and the promiscuity she witnessed in her home and extended family. She had never touched her own genitals and had never been successful in trying to insert even a slim-size tampon. She reported being easily orgasmic by manual stimulation from her fiancé.

After the first session of exploring possible abuse, she became highly anxious, unable to sleep and very uncomfortable around her family. At the second session, she reported she had been unable to insert the Q-Tip and feared remembering "something."

By the third session: 1) She had remembered hiding in her closet every time she was home and not washing her hair for weeks so she would not have to be in the bathroom very long for fear of her father. The picture of her father's sexual abuse of her never became as vivid as the fear and avoidance of that abuse. 2) After writing about her memories, she accepted her father's sexual abuse of her and the anger toward her mother for not protecting her, and realized that at twenty-six years of age, she was still totally under the control of her mother and father. 3) At this point, she made the decision that she was not going to let them control her any longer. She was going to be able to have sex with her husband. 4) She inserted the Q-Tip that evening, the smallest dialator the next evening, and came to her third session ready for the next-size dialators.

This rapid process has never happened in any other case. Our sense is that the timing greatly enhanced the progress. We usually do not have the opportunity to treat vaginismus until after marriage. Most women are not aware of this difficulty until they attempt to consummate their marriages.

Heidi and Mel had been married ten years when they came to us for help with their unconsummated marriage. Mel's father had sexually abused Mel's sisters, so he was very hesitant to push Heidi sexually. Heidi had an alcoholic father and a sexually abusive mother. Her mother would suggestively look at Heidi's body when she was undressing and pinch her nipples. At the time she came to us for therapy, her mother still insisted on being in situations with Heidi when Heidi had to undress. Heidi reported hating her body, yet she had a very attractive body and wore seductive clothing.

Heidi and Mel had a totally fulfilling sexual relationship with intense orgasmic response for both, great passionate kissing, and total body enjoyment except for manual breast and genital stimulation of her—and except for intercourse.

Heidi became nauseous and cried every time she tried to insert a tampon or when Mel would try to touch her genitals with hand, tongue, or the tip of his penis. She could rub her genitals on top of the shaft of his erect penis. In fact, that is what usually triggered her orgasmic release. She was very afraid of pain and had the vision that she would rip apart inside if he ever entered her with his penis.

The treatment process with Heidi and Mel required twenty sessions over a one-year period of time. Most sessions were with Heidi alone; Mel was included every fourth session. In the final sessions of moving toward intercourse, Mel was included in every session. Tracks 1, 3, and 4 were followed as defined. Track 2 was not necessary.

The turning point came for Heidi when she wrote a letter to her mother expressing her pain and anger. This letter was not to be sent; it was only for Heidi's benefit. After writing the letter, Heidi began having dreams of being about two or three years old and her father chasing her and raping her. She had always felt uneasy in her father's presence and had never been able to allow Mel to be in the top position during any sexual activity. Attempts at that position caused her to have a very sick feeling. These physical symptoms would be indicative that the behavior that elicited the sick feeling had occurred before she was old enough to have had complete verbal skills.

Heidi's progress with this track of the therapy process would fluctuate. One time she would have an easy time inserting the dialators and then the insertion would become difficult. This happened several times. When she began to believe that her father had raped her when she was very young, she cried intensely as though overwhelmed by the pain of a very young child.

The next session, she had made a decision similar to Cheryl's. She was so angry with her parents for having caused her such pain, she never wanted to see them again. She not only decided to stop allowing their weirdness to keep affecting her, but she was also able to say, "Yes, I am a sexual person. This is good and I am going to enjoy a total sexual experience with Mel." From that time on, her vaginal insertions rapidly progressed.

After that session, the therapy process moved along quickly. Heidi was able to rapidly increase the size of the dialators without eliciting regression, anger, or headaches. She was able to take charge of her sexual experiences positively, rather than keeping control to protect her from her sick feeling. Taking charge led her to allow herself to feel the nausea rather than avoid it, and thus, the nausea gradually lessened until it was no longer present. Penile vaginal entry went very smoothly. There was no pain. She felt almost let down that she had resisted so long over something that was so easy, even enjoyable. Their sexual experience flowed naturally from that time on.

For women with vaginismus the four tracks accomplish the following: The women recognize the reasons for the involuntary vaginal spastic contractions. They realize that their fears are irrational because there is no real danger associated with vaginal penetration. They make a conscious decision to let go of the negative, controlling force of their past, deciding to control their own sexuality positively by making a decision to accept their sexuality and to pursue sexual intercourse. And they learn to have control over their vaginal opening.

Vaginismus is correctable. There is no need for any couple to continue in an unconsummated marriage because of vaginismus. Masters and Johnson report 100 percent success. O'Conner reports 60 to 70 percent success. We find that any couple who stays with the therapy process will be successful. The problem is that many women's phobic avoidance causes them not to proceed with the therapy exercises or to stop therapy. This is probably the reason for the difference in reported results. Masters and Johnson's 100 percent probably refers to those who stay with therapy. O'Conner's 60 to 70 percent probably include those who start but then stop the process.

Problems of intercourse usually include medical involvement; but they are treatable. No couple has to live with painful intercourse, unconsummated marriage, or vaginismus. The treatment requires thorough physiological and psychological knowledge, as well as a sensitive and innovative therapist.

CHAPTER FIFTEEN

UNDERSTANDING AND TREATING SEXUAL ADDICTIONS

WE NOW COME TO ONE OF the most perplexing and difficult sexual dilemmas that ever confronts a Christian counselor—sexual addictions. The client's initial presentation of addiction comes in many forms. Sometimes the wife calls to say she is concerned about her husband's sexual needs, but feels that the situation is really her fault. She then expresses her guilt and even accepts a major portion of the blame because she is not interested in sex. When the story comes out, we discover that in fact the man has been seeing prostitutes the whole time they have been married and regularly masturbates to pornographic videos, which he watches after the rest of the family has gone to bed. Or we find that her desire has waned (or never even been felt), because of his persistent addictive pursuit of her sexually. She quickly became the sexual object to release his anxious addictive needs, rather than the mutual recipient of romantic, intimate, physical expression of love.

Another common presentation is that of the man calling and claiming that he is oversexed and unable to interest his wife frequently enough. This then forces him to seek sexual release through other means such as visiting topless bars or massage parlors. It may be presented first as a moral problem, which it certainly is. Another man is laden with guilt over the fact that he is the leader of the adult Sunday school department of his church, and yet he regularly views his stepdaughters through the keyhole in the bathroom while they are changing clothes or showering. He also uses every opportunity he can to have them discover him without clothes on.

Or we may first hear about the addiction from a mother reporting abuse in the family. Later on it is discovered that in fact the twenty-one-year-old son who still lives in the home has habitually abused all of the younger siblings for the last four years. He is unable to control his behavior. These real-life illustrations are but a small example, because sexual addiction displays itself with many different patterns.

DEFINING SEXUAL ADDICTIONS

Simply stated, when a person lacks control of sexual behavior, that person is struggling with a sexual addiction. The sexual addict feels controlled by the urge, similarly to the way an overeater is controlled by the eating disorder, or the alcoholic is controlled by the urge to drink. Even as we have come to think of alcoholism as an illness, so too should we think of sexual addiction as an illness. The sexual addict has a sexual preoccupation. If the addict is married, his preoccupation interferes with his marriage; he is unable to be satisfied by an intimate sexual relationship with his spouse. (Because the great majority of those struggling with sexual addiction are male, we will refer mainly to that gender even though obviously women, too, can become hooked on sex.)

The sexual addict may feel the urge to have sexual relations repeatedly in a short period of time with the same or different partners. When the sexual urge is pressing, the addict feels anxious. Before he acts out sexually, he is captured by the drive; but afterward he is guilty and ashamed. This pattern often takes an extensive amount of time away from the family or work as the addict pursues sexual activity or looks for the possibility of sexual activity. This secret drive escalates to become the major focus of living. It is a way of hiding from the realities of life that the individual does not want to face.

Sexual addiction is perpetuated by the mood-altering effect that comes from engaging in the experience. It can be an adrenaline addiction that is designed to give the momentary high that the addict seeks. The compulsion and the fulfilling of that compulsion become the predominant drive in life and the main source of self-nurture. This is no different than a drug addict who relies on the daily or nightly high from cocaine or the relaxation of marijuana. The sexual addict feels as though he no longer has the capacity to make choices about his activities, but is compelled to engage in them regardless of the self-loathing that follows.

Before we are too far into the chapter, we need to clarify what is not a sexual addiction. There is obviously a great range of sexual behavior that is considered normal. For example, having sex every day might be very normal for one couple. However, for certain individuals, it may be an expression of an addiction. So we cannot say that anyone who wants frequent sex is a sexual addict. For one man, visiting a prostitute may be something that he does when he is out of town every year or two, but he feels no great compulsion for it. As reprehensible as this may be, this would not be an addiction. Some men may masturbate on an intermittent schedule as they experience the urge to do so; but this does not comprise an addiction. There are men or women who on occasion will view pornographic material, whether that be in a magazine, movie, video, or topless bar; but they are not hooked on those activities, and hence would not be considered sexual addicts.

The emotional factors that distinguish various behaviors as sexual addictions are the obsessive and compulsive qualities that drive the person almost against his or her own will. Most sexual addicts struggle with other addictions as well. The sexual behaviors may be seen as a symptom of underlying emotional and relational needs that have not been met; hence the "addictive personality" will need to be addressed as the overall dilemma for the sexual addict. This addict does not choose to act on his sexual urges; rather, he tends to "zone out" or "split off" from his real self and take on a life separate from his usual personality. These emotional and mental qualities are radically different from the motivations of the couple going to a topless show in Las Vegas or Atlantic City, or a couple bringing home a pornographic video once a year. We are not implying that those are advisable or morally acceptable activities, but rather we are differentiating between a sexual addiction and choices about sexual activity.

Dr. Patrick Carnes of the Golden Valley Health Center in Minneapolis, Minnesota, has been the pioneer in this whole area of sexual addictions. Dr. Carnes first brought the subject into public awareness with his bestselling book, *Out of the Shadows*.[1] Since then, he has lectured extensively throughout the country, trained many professionals in both clinical and academic settings, and further defined sexual addiction in his latest book, *Contrary to Love: Helping the Sexual Addict*.[2] In addition, he has developed the Sexual Addiction Screening Test and many other publications on addictions. All that is written about in this chapter— from a systematic perspective—is borrowed from Carnes's work.

We have come to believe very deeply in Carnes's formulations because they fit so accurately with our clinical experience. We have also come to accept his treatment approach because it is the only one we have found to work. So as not to be pedantic, we will not specifically cite Carnes as the source of every important idea presented. But it is essential for the reader to understand that other than the clinical data, we are indebted to Carnes for virtually every concept that is presented here.

Addiction or Sin?

In the past, all activity that included lust or immoral behavior was simply labeled as a sin. The individual was seen as having violated God's rules, the devil had control of his life, and he needed to "get right" with God: repent, confess his sins, experience forgiveness, and go on his way, cleansed. While it is true that an individual is responsible for his own behavior before God, acknowledging this truth and giving over his life does not usually stop the compulsion. We are not questioning the severity of the sin; neither are we focusing on the immoral quality of these "sexual sins." Rather, we will deal with the compulsive nature of them and certain individuals' inability to overcome them. Hence, this should not be seen as an attempt to diminish the sinful quality of the action, but rather an attempt to understand the drive and how it can be controlled.

It is Thursday night. The minister has just completed his monthly board meeting with fifteen elders. These are the key leaders who are to determine whether or not to recommend a new building program. The church has grown from 250 to 1,250 since he arrived five years ago. He is weary in every way—weary from battles he has just gone through in the board meeting, weary physically from being out late every night so far this week, and weary because he knows his wife will be upset with him when he arrives home. Lately she has been complaining about how little time he spends with her. He reaches the intersection where a decision must be made. Almost as if by remote control, he turns his car away from home and heads toward that section of town where prostitutes loiter near a number of motels and bars.

As he nears his destination, the board meeting, the fatigue, and the wife quickly fade as his anticipation heightens and the addictive personality takes control. A couple of women are looking for business on one street corner, but he drives past because he only likes to deal with one at a time. Finally he spots a lone prospect coming out of a fast-food place. She smiles at him. He slows down. She comes over to the window, they negotiate, agree on a price, and then just as she is ready to jump into his car so they can drive to her place, he changes his mind. His real self snaps back into control. He remembers something he has to do and will need to be going.

This man is not interested in having sex with prostitutes, but rather is addicted to negotiating with prostitutes. His thrill or charge (or relief from life's stresses) is obtained from reaching the point of agreement on what they will do and for how much money. Once that is accomplished, his addictive urge is over. His next step is to bail out. Is this an addiction or a sin?

Addiction or Compulsion?

Some mental health professionals would argue that we are exercising overkill by using the term, "addiction" when in fact "compulsion" would be much more accurate and less pejorative. What is the difference between a compulsion and an addiction? When we speak of a compulsion, we are usually referring to a habit or behavior that an individual finds himself engaged in that can be cured and left behind forever. When we speak of an addiction, we are referring to a habit that has a lifelong hold on the individual and will be a lifelong struggle.

We used to treat sexual acting out behavior (perversions or deviations) as compulsions, only to find—several years later—the person would be back again going through the same dilemma with all of the accompanying turmoil and trauma. It was at that point that we began to see the addictive nature of the sexual behaviors that we are discussing here.

A specific illustration comes to mind: A man in his early thirties sought help about a year after his wedding date. His wife had discovered him peering into the apartment window next door where two single, attractive young women lived. He claimed he had sought help on two separate occasions over the past five years for this problem and each time felt he had worked it out so that it was never going to happen again. Yet here he was, two years later, again caught up in his voyeuristic activity.

His wife knew nothing about the hundreds of other times he had engaged in similar activity throughout the neighborhood. It just happened that she caught him this time. In the past, his voyeurism had been dealt with as a compulsion, but to no avail. The helpful way for this man to think about his struggle was to understand it as an addiction: He was hooked. He was going to be dealing with this struggle for the rest of his life, even as an alcoholic deals with alcoholism for his or her whole life.

He had repented, prayed, confessed, read his Bible regularly, and done all the spiritual disciplines that had been recommended to him; but still he found himself back in the throes of his peeping activity. It was most difficult for him to face the reality that this would be a life-time struggle. It was an addiction.

Addiction or Psychopathy?

It is not uncommon to diagnose addictive behavior as psychopathic or sociopathic behavior. The main way that psychopathic behavior is distinguished from any other behavior is that the psychopath behaves as if he does not have a conscience. He does not experience guilt. His behaviors may still have an addictive controlling quality to them, but they do not occur in the pattern of the addictive cycle described later this chapter. Ted Bundy, a convicted rapist and murderer, is a loud example of a psychopath who acted out addictively. Bundy attributes his severely perversive behavior to his addiction to pornography.

Fathers who sexually abuse their children may be acting addictively, yet have no conscience. Frequently, the psychopathology is not as blatant as in the case of Bundy. A situation comes to mind where a father abused several of his daughters—under the guise of helping them with their sex education. He wanted them to grow up sexually liberated, in contrast to their mother. This same man spoke about the Lord's will in his life and sought the Lord's guidance. He had no sense of his culpability in the abuse of his daughters, even after it had been reported and investigated by the state authorities.

To sum up these three perspectives: yes, virtually all sexual addictions would transgress the biblical guidelines, hence they are sin. All sexual addictions involve a compulsion, but they must be treated with an addiction model rather than a neurotic compulsion approach or the behavior will cycle back. And finally, the sexual acting out behavior may be psychopathic or addictive, depending on whether or not the violator experiences guilt.

How Addictions Develop

While no child or adolescent starts off his sexual life as an addict, history-taking usually reveals that there were early indications that the child was exposed to sexuality prematurely. One of the most prominent causes of this premature exposure is sexual abuse. In a high percentage of sexual addiction cases, one of the precipitating factors was childhood sexual abuse. For these victims, sexuality took on a neurotic meaning long before it was age appropriate.

In the normal developmental process, there is sexual experimentation with the same-age same-sex, same-age opposite-sex, or by oneself. This is natural. But the addict experienced something different than this innocent curiosity. In fact, innocence was lost when the erotic response was first triggered by the exposure, abuse, or addictive event.

A successful attorney told about discovering the pleasure that came from dressing in his mother's undergarments while looking at explicit sexual material that he discovered in his father's desk. This was at the age of eight. His disorder developed from this early cross dressing and enamoredness with pornographic magazines and progressed to a preoccupation with pornographic videos, then to a large collection of pictures of vivid, explicit, erotic pictures with various girlfriends as well as his wife. This particular individual had progressed to the place where the type of pornographic material that he was now interested in included some body mutilation such as nipple and penis rings as well as "boob battles" and other physically harmful activities.

It is not uncommon for an addiction to begin between age eight and twelve, if early childhood sexual innocence has been violated or the natural curiosities of preadolescence have been handled inappropriately.

During adolescence, most young people will experiment with sexual behavior. This experimentation, too, can move from normal to abnormal. The non-addict may have had an experience with peeping, exhibiting, experimenting with the same sex or the opposite sex, or viewing pornographic materials; but he made a choice about that behavior. He decided the activity was not beneficial and did not repeat the destructive behavior. In contrast, the addict became hooked on the behavior(s). The feelings that were set off by the activity met some emotional or relational need, and then a ritualized pattern for acting out developed. If the sexual addict was abused in the past, the experimentation will have elicited feelings of shame. He will repeat the activity to keep himself feeling shamed. He already views himself as an evil, shameful person; therefore, the activity serves to confirm his opinion. He needs that feeling of shame.

Even in adulthood, there will be those who engage in some sexual experimentation. For most, these experimental phases are brief and temporary. Some adults have responded to their curiosity about sexually explicit materials. Others have tried nudist colonies. Many have succumbed to an affair. None of this acting out means that a person is a sexual addict. If the behavior becomes a compulsion, with an established, secretive, ritualistic pattern, then we would identify the behavior as an addiction.

THE ADDICTIVE PATTERN

A Precipitating Event

Certain *precipitating events* may occur at critical times for some people, hooking them into a life of addiction. This fact is indeed frightening; we saw a clear example of it. At age fourteen, on his way home from a basketball practice, a young man innocently walked past a window where two teen-age girls were changing their clothes with the blinds up. He became highly aroused and proceeded home to masturbate for the first time. His first sexual response became paired with this event. It was as if he had been hooked, grabbed, captured. He returned many times after the first unintentional observation. In addition, he developed a whole system for discovering windows that would provide him with a repeat of that adrenaline-rush experience.

He had not been out looking for what happened on that first evening. He did not remember having looked into any windows prior to that point; but he also did not remember anything similar to the incredible rush he felt from discovering the women. When there is this kind of precipitating event, it may be some time before the individual feels controlled by the behavior. But in reviewing the history, it appears that he is controlled by it from the moment it happens. Obviously there were issues in his life and family that predisposed him to his response to this event. Not every fourteen-year-old boy who happened upon this site would have reacted and become addicted.

Frequently, precipitation of the addiction is connected with a mixture of emotional turmoil or neediness and some catalytic event. The circumstances that become fertile ground out of which an addiction can grow include any type of emotional stress where there is a strong need for nurture, affirmation, comfort, or control. In adulthood, the addiction may be set off after a death, a divorce, a separation, birth of a child, loss of a child, loss of a job, or added pressure at home or on the job. All of these life circumstances which provide extra stress may serve as the spark or initial nudge for acting out.

The behavior, the sexual acting out, offers the person an escape from emotional pain and problems in this life. It is the altered mood (the "zoning out" or splitting off) that often occurs as the person moves toward the addictive behavior, which provides escape from the pain, loneliness, or problems. In addition, the sexual activities may be associated with fantasies of being intimate, powerful, nurtured, or whatever the need is that is not being met in the person's normal relationships. Once this habit of dealing with stress has developed, the sexually addicted person will go through periods in life when the external stresses are greater and he uses the addiction to free the problems. This in turn worsens his pain and the negative vicious circle begins: the greater the stress, the more frequent the acting out; the more acting out, the greater the remorse and pain.

Paul was an aggressive businessman on his way up the corporate ladder. Yet he had a low self-esteem. This was in part due to the fact that his father had been hospitalized with tuberculosis when Paul was ten years old. Thus, Paul had been abandoned by his male role model at a critical age. He had never been that attractive as an adolescent or young man, and had always felt outside of the popular circle. This was true even though he had achieved admirably in academics and was editor of the school newspaper in high school.

In college, because he was a Christian, he did not feel he could participate with the fraternities and sororities, so again he felt inadequate even though he was looked up to as student body president at the large, prestigious private college. He could not let himself enjoy all the success, because the college women he really wanted to date were not a part of his "Christian world."

After college, he began climbing the corporate ladder. Suddenly, he was receiving much attention—not only from the secretarial and management group of women, but also from the wives of other business associates. Receiving such attention led into fifteen years of affairs with twenty or thirty different women. It finally came to a head when he was discovered by his wife at a hotel with another woman. He then sought help for the addiction that had plagued him. All the worldly success had never diminished his sense of inadequacy—even the high salary from his prestigious job with all the perks. He continued to carry the low view of himself as he went through the first twenty years of his marriage.

Carnes emphasizes that abandonment seems to be a particularly strong factor in the history of many sexual addicts, especially when they learned to bring relief to their empty, inadequate feelings through the captivating distraction of sexual acting out. But whether it is stress, abandonment, low self-esteem, a precipitating event, or a search for fulfillment or excitement, the addictive cycle becomes established once the behavior evolves from the precipitating event to an addiction. In both his books, Carnes describes the addiction cycle that follows the initial acting out. There are four stages to this cycle: preoccupation, ritualization, sexual addictive behavior itself, and finally, the reaction of despair. We will examine each of those in some detail.

The Addictive Cycle

The cycle usually has a distinct pattern that is unique to each sexual addict. For instance, there may be a period of time—days, weeks, months, or even years—in which life is lived normally and the person is not obsessed with his sexual acting out. Many even carry on a normal, fulfilling sexual life. Then some event occurs that trips off the addictive cycle. The event might be a particularly stressful time at work, inadvertently looking down a woman's blouse, driving through a certain part of town, or being criticized by his wife. Whatever the event, the cycle has begun.

Preoccupation. Once the cycle is triggered, preoccupation takes over. The individual's energy becomes focused almost totally on the sexual compulsion. The focus might be on planning how to carry out the activity, a fantasy imagining the activity, or a review of past experiences. How the obsession builds is determined by the pattern that has been established for this particular person, as well as the availability of the occasion, material, or people necessary to carry out the preoccupation. Some let it build slowly over days and weeks. Others begin their fantasy and feel compelled to carry it out within hours. For many, their preoccupation with the urge or plan to act distracts them from other life fulfillments.

Ralph was a middle-management person who had grown up in a rigid, religious home. His father was always working and mother was cold and distant. She had been warm with him until his younger sister was born. From that point on he never again remembered receiving a hug from her. After she died—when he was fourteen—he began dressing in her clothes for sexual gratification and comfort. He carried on with this activity for the first twenty-five years of his marriage without being discovered. He had a satchel full of women's undergarments, clothing, jewelry, and makeup which he kept hidden in the basement.

His addictive cycle would usually be set off by depression due to external stresses. Once the desire to cross dress was elicited, he would wait for up to several weeks before carrying out the behavior; the preoccupation would continue until he knew that his wife and their three children would not be in the house for several hours. During these weeks of preoccupation, he would be imagining what he would wear, wrestling with whether he might find a new garment and struggling to get the time alone. The preoccupation would continue until he was able to carry out his goal of dressing in women's clothing with all the preparatory ritual and accompanying excitement and masturbation.

The Ritual Phase. As the cycle moves into the ritual phase, it leads in the direction of the familiar. Addictive behavior can be differentiated from occasional behavior of the same sort by determining whether the activity has been ritualized or not. The minister who liked to negotiate with prostitutes always drove down the same road to get there. The rituals are often simple but completely predictable for each individual; they enhance the preoccupation to act. They may include visiting a certain bar or type of entertainment, driving to certain parts of town, selecting a video, buying some pornographic material, putting on a certain type of clothes that makes exhibiting easier, or getting ready to go for walks at night in order to fulfill the voyeuristic desires.

The ritual may also include specific behaviors that help thrust the addict in the direction of the addiction, whether that be getting into a fight with his wife or sabotaging sexual activity with his spouse to justify finding sexual gratification elsewhere. Other men overwork to deplete themselves to need the relief of the addiction. Still others engage in self-defeating behavior to make themselves believe they deserve the addictive behavior.

Melvin provides a helpful example of the latter. He had been married for three years, and his marriage was still unconsummated. Every time he attempted sexual intercourse, he would become so driven—so goal oriented—he had no capacity to love, caress, or prepare his wife. Because she had experienced some rejection in her past, she was highly sensitive to his cold, distant, non-intimate behavior. She would end up not becoming aroused and eventually had a severe case of vaginismus (see chapter 14). When she would not allow intercourse, Melvin would take this as permission to masturbate. He masturbated two or three times a day. Masturbating was his major addiction, but he also visited "adult" video arcades on a regular basis. Until he faced the reality that he was an active participant in sabotaging the consummation of his marriage, there was no possibility that this couple would ever be able to have intercourse.

As the ritualistic behavior moves the person closer to the action of the addictive behavior, it tends to become more intense—blocking out all other thought. This is the point at which greater risks are taken in regard to being discovered, being embarrassed, or being arrested.

By this time, the risk does not matter to the addict. His personality shift has occurred. He has "split off" or "zoned out." This aspect of the ritualization deadens the person against thinking about his values or about God. The only thing that matters is the anticipated high from the sexual experience or the relief from the anxiety or stress.

The Addictive Behavior. The third stage is the acting out stage during which the *compulsive sexual behavior* is carried out. There is no way to catalog all the possible addictive or compulsive behaviors that are practiced, but we certainly can refer to categories of behaviors. Almost all sexual addictive behavior includes sexual release through ejaculation, whether that be from masturbation, mutual stimulation, or intercourse.

Sexual release may result from no physical contact. Fantasy may be the only source of stimulation. For example, arousal and release might take place from indecent telephone calls, the reading of sexually provocative materials, or the viewing of videos or movies. These addictions could be carried out in isolation without any human contact whatsoever.

Next, there is the category of cooperative contact which includes massage parlors, the viewing of topless or bottomless dancers, a peep show where women masturbate for a collection of male clients who pay for viewing by the minute, men (or women) who have several affairs going at the same time, or the husband who wants to have sex with his wife three times a day because he is obsessed with being affirmed by her.

The final category would include violating contact which could range all the way from inappropriate liberties being taken on a crowded bus to voyeurism, exhibitionism, child abuse, or rape. All of these are part of the world of sexual addiction.

Despair. Once the addict has fulfilled his urge, *despair* is almost inevitable. The only exception is the psychopathic addict who may not allow himself to feel the despair or may have so deeply seared his conscience that no despair surfaces even after acting compulsively. For most addicts, relief is the first feeling after the peak sexual experience. It is as if whatever was controlling or driving the individual subsides. The relief is short-lived, however. It shifts almost immediately to the self-loathing response which floods over the individual as he moves back into his normal world and out of the addictive cycle. For the believer, this is usually the point of an intense focus on prayer, with vows to God and to himself that he will never again engage in this despicable behavior. At the same time, derogatory messages about himself flood his inner world. So while there is the peace from having experienced relief from his compulsion and the hope that this is indeed the last occurrence, there is also that nagging knowledge that this is but one more round in a never-ending cycle.

PERSONAL COMPONENTS OF SEXUAL ADDICTION

Carnes has listed four components that are foundational to the addictive system: the individual's belief system, his impaired thinking, his unmanageability, and the addictive cycle which has already been discussed.

In discovering the beliefs of the addict, it is essential to determine his view of women and his view of himself. The likelihood is that he believes he can only find gratification in the world through sex: No one is ever going to love him; he can only be gratified sexually if he goes after it for himself because there is no one who could really love him. He is such a shameful, despicable character. There are also common beliefs among sexual addicts.

> The shame and despair that come from the powerlessness and unmanageability help crystallize the core beliefs about sexual unworthiness that are part of the addict's addictive system.
>
> 1. I am basically a bad, unworthy person.
> 2. No one would ever love me as I am.
> 3. My needs are never going to be met if I have to depend on others.
> 4. Sex is my most important need.[3]

Although these beliefs seem to be common to all who struggle with sexual addictions—mild or severe—whether they be men or women, the addict may not be aware of these core beliefs. He may say that he comes from a very loving family, yet deeper exploration may reveal that his feeling loved is dependent on his being perfect.

Impaired thinking shows up in a variety of ways as the addict reframes his actions in such a way as to diminish the blame and avoid confronting the reality about his life, marriage, or work. It is not uncommon for rationalization or denial to take over as the addict's way of coping with his addictive behavior. He may justify his actions on the basis that his wife rejected him, does not like sex, is pregnant, is busy, or is preoccupied with the children. He may justify it on the basis that the person that he violated really wanted it, asked for it, and equipped it, so the incident really is as much the other person's doing as his. Or it may be that he denies that it was really that bad. "Everybody" has to "get it" somehow.

In addition to rationalization and denial, some use intellectualization, in which the addict stands back and treats the behavior as though it were some kind of experiment, helpful to the victim or necessary for the addict. Intellectualization serves to justify the actions, diminish the despair, and reduce the shame and guilt. Whether rationalization, denial, or intellectualization is used, the faulty thinking is a necessary part of keeping the addictive cycle going. This was the situation for a married man who violated a younger member of his wife's family. He was able to convince himself that his action was understandable because he had not been "getting much sex" from his wife and the person was asleep when he molested her. The impaired thinking is evident.

The component of unmanageability reveals itself as major portions of the addict's life become out of control. Life becomes unmanageable. This can affect almost any area of life: spending, sleeping, working, eating, drinking, and/or playing. When life is experienced as out of control and unmanageable, the addictive pattern is well established, and the addictive cycle will occur repeatedly.

How Addictions Progress

It is important to understand that as with every other behavior, sexual addictions vary in form, expression, and intensity. Some alcoholics only drink two drinks too much two nights every weekend. Other alcoholics drink twelve drinks too much every night. They both might identify themselves as alcoholics, but there is a major difference between the amount and frequency of the alcohol use that controls them. This is also true of the sexual addict. One man who masturbates two or three times a week to a pornographic magazine instead of having sex with his wife, who is sexually frustrated, might well be a sexual addict. Another man may feel the need for a new woman every day. He, too, is a sexual addict, but is acting it out in a much more extreme manner. As in all other diagnoses, it is vital that we allow for the variations from one individual to the next, recognizing that we can expect a whole range of sexually addictive behavior.

Sexual addicts also vary in the development of their illness. For some, the addictive cycle is established and repeats itself somewhat predictably. Others progress to "more intensity, more frequency, more risk, more unmanageability, etc."[4] Some of these addicts reach a peak and stay at that level, where the addiction continues to control their lives and the sexual acting out is limited only by opportunity. Whereas others of these, who escalate to a peak level of being controlled by the addiction, actually deescalate, maintaining the cycle at a low functioning level.

One of the helpful ways Carnes has broken down the behaviors of the sexual addict is to divide them into three levels. The first level includes activity that is widely practiced behavior in our society. This would include all addictive heterosexual relationships, from within marriage to involvement with prostitutes. It would also include such activities as masturbation in response to pornographic material, cross dressing, and homosexual activity. That does not infer that all homosexual activity is addictive activity, just as heterosexual activity can be addictive or non-addictive. But the man who has to be with five men an evening obviously is as much a sexual addict as a man who has to be with five women an evening.

Level two activities are mildly illegal, usually not violent in nature but involving the risk that discovery could lead to arrest—which adds excitement. Level two activities include such violating behavior as voyeurism, exhibitionism, indecent liberties, obscene phone calls, or fetish activities that involve stealing the objects necessary for the arousal. The fear of being discovered while stealing is part of the ritual and part of what brings the high.

The third level includes behaviors that clearly violate the law and are violent in nature. Example of level three are: rape, child molestation, incest, and some forms of sadomasochistic behavior.

There has been much talk about the progressive nature of sexual addictions. Our clinical experience has shown there are many male sexual addicts, in fact we would say the majority, who find one compulsive behavior and never progress to anything worse. So by listing three levels, we are not implying that everyone starts out at level one, progresses to level two, and then moves to level three. It is not uncommon for men to make obscene phone calls year after year after year, without ever engaging in any other inappropriate sexual behavior. The same is true for indecent exposure, voyeurism, and cross dressing.

The one situation where addictive behavior does seem to be progressive is in the area of pornography. It is relatively unusual to find someone who got hooked on mild pornography and then was happy just to settle with that. It is rare to find someone who is still satisfied with *Playboy* magazines after fifteen years of viewing them. They may have started there, or they may have started with the Sears Catalogue; but it is very likely that if someone is sexually addicted to pornography, he or she will progress to more explicit and often more violent material.

CO-ADDICTION

Common family patterns are present in the history of most sexual addicts. They were usually raised on one extreme or the other of almost any spectrum. They may have been raised in an antisex home or in a home where there were no sexual boundaries and sex was promoted almost as a means of control and communication in the family. Most addicts grew up in a shame-based system where there was a confusing mixture and overlap between what was seen as good and what was seen as bad. This only brought greater confusion, especially during the adolescent years when there was so much for the young person to struggle with inside himself.

The addict's current family may also be perpetuating the addictive pattern, especially if it includes someone who is in a co-addictive role. The co-addict is often the spouse who in some passive way participates with the husband in his addiction. Or, the parent might be participating with the child, subtly and unconsciously facilitating the addictive behavior. The blatant co-addict, the wife for example, engages with the addict in his sexual activity by "swinging," joining in on a threesome or whatever he might want. But most commonly, the co-addict is much more passive or unconscious in helping to perpetuate the system, often by not paying attention or responding to obvious signs of inappropriate behavior. Whenever the sexual addict finally comes to treatment, it is always necessary to work with the co-addict as well.

Religion is often used by the addict as a co-addict to perpetuate his addictive pattern. In the addict's view, God is a part of the addictive system because it is God—along with his father, mother, and society—who carries the big stick and makes him feel guilt and shame. This is true despite the fact that the great majority of the addicts we deal with in our practice come out of the conservative, evangelical community, and hold to its belief system. When the addict first comes for help, God is not seen as an ally but as an adversary. Prayer is not seen as a resource but a source of guilt. The Scriptures are not seen as a message of solace and hope but rather as one more authority telling him that he is worthless. The Holy Spirit is not experienced as a Comforter but as an accuser who keeps confirming from inside the addict that he does not measure up. Because the addict does not see his faith as an ally in the healing process, we often have to begin with restructuring and reframing his view of God, as well as his grasp of his disorder. The addictive belief system must be reversed. Any person or belief that perpetuates the addiction must be assessed and eliminated.

EVALUATION AND ASSESMENT

Careful, detailed assessment is essential when sexual addiction is suspected. How you evaluate what you hear will determine the path you take in treatment. A depressed man who has been caught in an affair and now is in a bind deciding whether he will go with his girlfriend or stay with his wife is in a very different situation from a man who has now been caught in his tenth affair and is working hard to avoid the grief and aggravation he knows he will have to put up with from his wife.

As in every other area of sexual addiction, we are again indebted to Carnes for his Sexual Addiction Screening Test.[5] This test is designed to evaluate the likelihood that the person is suffering from a sexual addiction. Carnes's Sexual Addiction Inventory is a fourteen-page questionnaire that assesses all aspects of the sexually addictive behavior. In his book *Contrary to Love*, Carnes provides us with a list of what he calls the key steps to assessment. These key steps are:

- Determine the extent of the sexual behavior or co-addictive behavior.
- Determine priority of obsession mode.
- Identify specific rituals.
- Determine catalytic events and catalytic environments.
- Check for life-threatening depression.
- Elicit rationalizations and distortions of reality.
- Search for evidence of out-of-control behavior.[6]

Most of these have already been discussed, so we will simply say a few words about each. A pattern of aberrant behavior is our first clue that there is more difficulty than merely an isolated sexual acting out. The acting out is usually backed up by the obsessive quality, frequently spoken about as "sex is all I can think about." Although the individual will blame this fact on his father who was antisexual, or the church which is antisexual, or the wife who does not want sex, if sex is the only thing on his mind, the likelihood is that he is struggling with an addiction.

To determine the priority of the obsession mode, the level of the preoccupation, as well as the content of the preoccupation must be clearly described. The ideal sequence of the activities the addict would like to act out will reveal the pattern of his thought processes. It is then important to identify for the counselee exactly how the preoccupation shifts into actual acting out of the specific rituals and what precipitating events occur as part of the pattern (Carnes calls these catalytic events and environments). Some addicts are in such despair over their actions when they come for help that they may be depressed or even suicidal.

The suicide risk needs to be taken seriously by an immediate suicide-potential evaluation and intervention.

It is also important to determine how the addict has made sense of his behavior and his obsessions in his own mind. How has he rationalized or distorted reality? How has he provided himself with justifications for what he is doing? How has he played down the impact of his behavior on others? All these steps are essential in determining not only whether he is struggling with an addiction but also the extent of it and the shape of it.

The final indication that the individual is indeed struggling with an addiction is the fact that his out-of-control behavior is obvious and bringing turmoil to his life. This is true for the female addict, as well as the male. A beautiful young woman in her late twenties presented herself as someone who had lost interest in sex. She had been married for three years and had been avoiding sex at all cost. As her story unfolded, we discovered that during her single years after her first marriage failed, she functioned in sexual binges. She would avoid sex for six months and then go on a rampage. She would seduce almost whomever she chose, have wild and free sex, and then go back "on the wagon," avoiding anything sexual whatsoever. These binges continued for three or four years after she became a Christian, and she had felt totally out of control.

Now she was married and could not let herself feel any sexual desire for fear she would act out her addiction. Thus, she controlled her behavior by shutting down all sexual awareness. But in fact, she continued to be an addict who fit all the patterns except that she was no longer acting out the behavior.

TREATMENT OF SEXUAL ADDICTIONS

It is crucial to understand that effective treatment, in addition to helping the addict stop the addictive pattern of behavior, must help bring about a shift in the core beliefs which led to the behavior and thus reduce the obsession and the cycle that follows. Again, we are highly indebted to Carnes for defining a framework for this treatment process. Usually, when a sexual addict presents him or herself for help in a counselor's office, there has been some crisis event that has precipitated seeking help. The addict has been caught by his wife, discovered by his children, confronted by his employer, or arrested by the police—or at least had a close call.

At this point, the addict comes for therapy with temporarily high motivation to change and to stop the addictive behavior. Because of this, change happens quickly. This quick change often leads the counselors to a false security that therapy has been helpful, even though the individual would have stopped the behavior for a time under the given conditions even if he had not come for help. This is why it is so vital that we make a careful and accurate diagnosis about an addiction and then go about helping to change the underlying impaired thoughts, feelings, and attitudes that are part of the addict's system. Even as Alcoholics Anonymous has been found to be tremendously helpful for alcoholics, so also it is being found that sexual addicts do best working in groups with other sexual addicts who follow the Twelve Step system of facing reality and coming to grips with their lives. AA is probably the best known of the entities using Twelve Steps, which is an international, lay-led, self-help program to assist addicts of all sorts to overcome their obsessive thinking and compulsive behavior. Several of these groups are available.

Sexaholics Anonymous
P.O. Box 300
Simi Valley, CA 93062
805–581–3343

Sexual Addicts Anonymous
Twin Cities SAA Intergroup
P.O. Box 3038
Minneapolis, MN 55403

Sex and Love Addicts Anonymous
P.O. Box 119
New Town Branch
Boston, MA 02258

Co-S.A.
Twin Cities Co-S.A.
P.O. Box 14537
Minneapolis, MN 55414
612–537–6904

An organization which helps spouses and family members of sexual addicts is:

S-ANON International
Family Groups
P.O. Box 5117
Sherman Oaks, CA 91413
818–990–6910

A professional organization that can provide information is:

National Council on Sexual Addiction Problems
22937 Arlington Avenue, Suite 201
Torrance, CA 90501
213–534–1792

It is in the process of individual counseling in conjunction with a Twelve-Step group that the greatest change is likely to take place. In the group settings, the belief systems can be challenged because the addict has the backup support of his individual counselor, yet he does not feel as alone as if he were only working individually, because he is dealing with others who are struggling with the same issues. Both individual counseling and the Twelve Step group process become places where the person is honest about his whole self. He is able to be his real self while he speaks honestly about his acting out behavior. This helps him integrate his addictive needs into his healthy self, so that the needs are met, rather than acted out.

One of the most difficult aspects of the whole process is the acceptance of the addiction as an illness that the individual will struggle with for the rest of his life. As has been true with alcoholics, this realization may not come until the addict has "bottomed out." We usually compare this scenario to that of the prodigal son who found himself in the pig sty, wishing he could eat what the pigs ate. The King James Version says, "And when he came to himself, he said . . ." (Luke 15:17). This moment of coming to oneself, of looking in the mirror, of facing the reality, of bottoming out is a vital part of reaching the point of acknowledging the first step that is necessary in the Twelve Step program—facing the reality that the addict is indeed helpless.

It is at this point that the message of grace and redemption can have its greatest impact. The Twelve Step program talks about relying on a higher power. We certainly understand this higher being to be God, the Father of our Lord Jesus Christ who has promised that he will be with us in whatever state we find ourselves. As we rely on him, he will give us the strength to gain control of our lives. That reliance on God and the reality of one's helplessness may be the beginning of a process of restructuring faith which can, indeed, bring the individual to a new place of joy, fulfillment, and control.

As the sexual addict faces himself, realizes he is helpless, and puts his trust and reliance on God, the work begins. It is crucial that the ritualistic patterns be thoroughly defined and action be taken to break them. For example, it may have been part of the pattern for a traveling salesman to always stop for lunch at a certain topless bar when he is out of town as a warmup for visiting a prostitute that evening. Then it is vital that he not only stop visiting the prostitute, but also stop the lunchtime event. It may be that to gain control he will have to stay in hotels that do not have the x-rated movies available in the room. In order to break the ritual, it is essential that the ritualistic behaviors be defined and clearly prohibited.

A common part of the whole recovery process and of working through the Twelve Steps will be the defining of celibacy. In the treatment of sexual addictions we look for abstinence, just as we do in the treatment of alcoholism. This may be one of the most difficult aspects of the treatment process, because sex has been the central and integrating factor in life. Although not all of the addict's sexual activity has been connected with the addiction, as treatment begins, all sexual activity is ruled out for a period of time—usually two to three months. This includes masturbation, intercourse with one's wife, viewing sexual material, all possible precipitating events, and any of the addictive behaviors. This may seem rigid and excessive, but until there is a shift in the underlying beliefs, attitudes, and emotions, it is too high a risk to engage in any sexual activity at all. In milder cases, the period of abstinence and celibacy can be modified. What the addict learns during this time is that he can survive without sex and that he can find other ways to resolve his problems and meet his needs other than his sexual acting out.

Keeping a journal can help the client keep with the abstinence rules. He can be assigned to write for ten minutes (or longer) right at the time he feels tempted or in the situations where the temptation is likely to surface. The writing should be in response to questions given by the therapists. These questions are to direct the person to healthy thinking and away from the addictive pattern.

Another term that has been borrowed from the Alcoholics Anonymous world is *sobriety*. Sexual addicts, too, will speak of having been sober for three months, or three years, or twelve years with the same kind of pride that the alcoholic expresses. They know the power their addiction has held over them, so their sobriety is a valid reason for celebration.

As we progress through the counseling process with the sexual addict, a reframing, reshaping, and rethinking of the self-concept is necessary. It is necessary because it helps the individual face the aspects of his history that he was not responsible for, accept responsibility for what he did have responsibility for, discover how he is an outgrowth of his family patterns, and rethink his faith as he grows into a healthier understanding of his relationship with God. Here again, the Christian counselor has that added benefit as he or she attempts to walk with the addict to a place of actually experiencing God's love. In all this, it is important to be specific in defining the exact goals the addict is working toward—how they will be measured, what will happen when they are accomplished, and what will happen if there is a relapse.

Slips or Relapses

We referred earlier to Melvin, who had an unconsummated marriage, had practiced addictive masturbatory activities, and had acted out inappropriately with other women. After initial treatment and determination not to slip back into his acting out patterns, follow-up treatment revealed that he was again rationalizing that because their marriage remained unconsummated, he could justify taking care of himself through masturbation and fantasy. So after four weeks of sobriety, he had slipped back into his old pattern, and had masturbated three times between sessions.

His wife was not wanting anything physical with him because their contact lacked intimacy and was again characterized by his "spacing out." This was most aversive to her. She felt like an object of his addiction. Immediately his old rationalizations and justifications were back. As is true with alcoholics, it is vital that these slips be seen for what they are, that the impaired thinking be clearly brought to light, and that a new plan be enacted. It is important to reassure the addict that such slips are not uncommon. Assure him that he is not a despicable person. A matter-of-fact approach which does not attempt to diminish or sidestep the reality of the relapse but that also does not condemn is the most effective approach.

The counselor's involvement with any co-addicts in the addict's life is essential to preventing relapses, because the co-addicts will have established patterns which participate in the addiction. New ways of living must be established for the addict and the co-addict. Where he drives, eats, and sleeps, who he contacts and all life patterns should be assessed carefully. It must be determined how all activities have participated in the addictive system and how the detrimental patterns can be changed.

Gaining Control

As the addict begins to manage his life, he will be living without secrets and sensing a control where there was chaos. He will be able to maintain control of his life without the counselor. Nevertheless, specific plans and guidelines will be needed for how to proceed if he finds himself shifting or plunging into old patterns of thinking, in old "neighborhoods," or in fact has a slip. In several situations, we have continued to see a counselee on an every-two-month basis as a way of providing accountability. Simply the fact that the addict knows the appointment is ahead on the calendar helps him stay on course. His accountability to his Twelve Step group also will be ongoing. The therapy process should assure a lifetime system of maintaining control.

In summary, sexual addictions can be controlled. Men or women do not have to be victims to addictive patterns all of their lives. The addictive tendency may be a struggle all of their lives, but they do not need to succumb. Recovery is most likely to occur when following the guidelines outlined briefly here, and in detail in Carnes's works. The recovery pattern has been found to be quite similar to that of alcoholics. Some addicts start the program and never look back; others go through a number of relapses. Still others make several false starts before they are able to manage long-term abstinence from the addictional behavior. And still others never recover and continue their addictive patterns. Your task is to help all clients face the true reality of their situation: that they are helpless and that they can only recover through the help of God and a daily commitment to managing their lives in the way they have learned from you and from whatever group they have joined.

CHAPTER SIXTEEN

THE RESULTS OF SEXUAL THERAPY

SINCE SEXUAL THERAPY IS DESIGNED to relieve the symptoms of unsatisfactory sexual experiences and to teach a couple to communicate and behave with each other in ways that reduce demand, enhance pleasure, and facilitate the natural physiological sexual response, the results are fairly measurable. The sexual therapy process is successfully terminated when the symptoms are relieved and the goals achieved.

Much change can take place in a relatively short period of time. Ten to twenty sessions are the average number needed to complete the sexual therapy process. How well that change is integrated into the couple's ongoing life depends upon their commitment to scheduling quality sexual experience times for themselves each week. Reviewing the principles that brought about the change and planning creative nondemand sexual encounters is vital.

Many couples have gained fulfillment and relief from difficulties through the sexual therapy process after years of frustration. What factors contribute to improvement in sexual functioning as a result of the prescribed teaching, talking, and touching exercises?

1. They alter a previously destructive sexual system. The secure ambience created by sex therapy provides the couple with an opportunity to learn to make love in freer and more enjoyable ways;
2. the resolution of sexual conflict is facilitated when the couple engages in previously avoided sexual experiences;
3. the tasks evoke the emergence of previously unconscious intrapsychic and dyadic conflicts which then become available for psychotherapeutic intervention and resolution.[1]

Kaplan has found that approximately 80 percent of sexually dysfunctional patients can be relieved of their symptoms by sex therapy.

We would like to review our observations with you by sharing the results we see in those who seek sexual therapy.

1. About 2 percent of the couples who come to us for sexual therapy receive the knowledge, feedback, or direction they need to relieve their symptoms from the three-hour assessment process.
2. Some couples never receive the help they were seeking because they abort the sexual therapy process.
   a. Some abort the process before they ever come for the evaluation because in the initial telephone contact: 1) We may redirect them; 2) they may discover the cost is prohibitive; 3) they discover they do not want what sexual therapy is; 4) the spouse who is calling may discover that the other partner is unwilling to participate.
   b. Some abort the process after the initial three-session evaluation process, because: 1) We redirect them for self-help, marital therapy, or individual psychotherapy; 2) one or both are avoiding confronting the problem; 3) there is a break in the couple's relationship. The evaluation may bring to light the severity of the problem or some secret data.
   c. Some abort during the sexual therapy process because: 1) The swift success of the process scares one or both. One may have another sexual partner on the side and have engaged in the therapy process only to prove that he or she could not be successful with

298

the spouse. When it starts to work, he or she bolts. Or there may be a deep conflict about being sexual which is set off by rapid success; 2) intense emotional barriers and resistances keep the couple from being able to complete the exercises; 3) the process reveals that, rather than sex being the struggle, other issues are the problem; 4) external circumstances interfere, such as a death in the family.

3. Some couples gain minimal benefits but the results are more difficult to measure because the couple never can commit to the process. They want the results, but they do not want the focus and work. These couples come sporadically, and cancel appointments frequently. Only occasionally do they complete the assignments between sessions. It would seem they relieve their guilt by being able to say that they are coming for help. They know that they have a problem—and this way they convince themselves that they are working on it.

About half of these couples actually attain their goals and relieve their symptoms with this long-term haphazard involvement with us. We have started asking these couples to keep individual journals of what happens between sessions. This has increased our success with these peripherally committed couples.

4. The sexual therapy process is sometimes utilized as a diagnostic process, rather than to attain sexual goals and relieve sexual symptoms. When this is the case, the couple is informed and given the choice to proceed for that purpose. When diagnosis is the focus of the sexual therapy process, that process is virtually 100 percent successful. This is usually done in a ten-day "intensive." There is no way a couple can be put together for ten days to do three experiences per day and see us one session a day and not have the troublesome issues surface. When the sex therapy is used in this way:

    a. Intrapersonal emotional problems are identified that require long-term psychotherapy before the couple will be able to have a fulfilled sexual relationship.

    b. Interpersonal patterns that are destructive to the relationship or to the sexual function become clear and may be corrected.

    c. Other sexual issues such as sexual addictions, homosexuality, or adultery become known as the real reasons the couple's sexual relationship has been stressed.

5. A large majority of our clients are couples who complete the following process successfully:

a. The three-hour assessment process,

b. The ten-session sexual therapy process,

c. Three to six follow-up visits, and

d. Attain and maintain the goals they and we had agreed upon.

6. The other large majority of couples (about equal to the number of couples in the previous category) successfully complete the process in the following manner:

a. The three-hour assessment process,

b. The ten-session sexual therapy process is only the beginning of attaining their goals,

c. Weekly or every-other-week sessions for three months to a year following the initial ten sessions.

d. Two or three six-month follow-up sessions, and they

e. Attain and maintain the goals they and we had agreed upon.

Follow-up sessions are necessary to make certain the couple has grasped and applied the principles and habits they learned.

For the most part, sexual therapy is most rewarding for the client couple, as well as the therapist(s).

Throughout this book we have emphasized the importance of careful attention to detail. The details of the couples' sexual experiences, emotional responses and beliefs, as well as the therapists' presuppositions, attitudes, and reactions are vital ingredients that make sexual therapy successful. In each chapter we have attempted to highlight those essential issues which can assist the therapist to intelligently and methodically guide his or her clients to discover sexual fulfillment in marriage.

BIBLIOGRAPHY

Barbach, Lonnie. *For Yourself: The Fulfillment of Female Sexuality.* New York: Anchor Books, 1976.

—————. *Women Discover Orgasm: A Therapist's Guide to a New Treatment Approach.* New York: The Free Press, 1980.

Bass, Ellen, and Laura Davis. *The Courage to Heal: A Guide for Women Survivors of Child Sexual Abuse.* New York: Harper & Row, Publishers, 1988.

Brauer, Alan P. and Donna Brauer. *ESO (Extended Sexual Orgasm).* New York: Warner Books, 1983.

Buhler, Rich. *Pain and Pretending: You Can Be Set Free From the Hurts of the Past.* Nashville: Thomas Nelson Publishers, 1988.

Carnes, Patrick. *Contrary to Love: Helping the Sexual Addict.* Minneapolis: CompCare Publishers, 1989.

—————. *Out of the Shadows: Understanding Sexual Addiction.* Minneapolis: CompCare Publishers, 1983.

—————. *A Gentle Way Through the Twelve Steps.* Minneapolis: CompCare Publishers.

—————. *Sexual Addiction Inventory.* Golden Valley, Minn.: Institute for Behavioral Medicine, 1988.

CompCare Publishers. *Hope & Recovery: A Twelve Step Guide for Healing From Compulsive Sexual Behavior.* Minneapolis: 1987.

Dickey, Richard P. *Oral Contraceptive User Guide*. Durant, Okla.: Infomatic Guides, Inc., 1987.

————. *Managing Contraceptive Pill Patients*. Durant, Okla.: Creative Infomatics, Inc., 1987.

Evans, Louis H., Jr. *Hebrews*. The Communicator's Commentary. Waco, Tex.: Word Books, 1985.

Forward, Susan, and Craig Buck. *Betrayal of Innocence: Incest and Its Devastation*. New York: Penguin Books, 1978.

Graber, Benjamin, and Georgia Kline-Graber. *Woman's Orgasm: A Guide to Sexual Satisfaction*. Indianapolis: The Bobbs-Merrill Company, Inc., 1975.

Greenwood, Sadja. *Menopause, Naturally*. Volcano, Calif.: Volcano Press, 1989.

Hancock, Maxine, and Mains, Karen Burton. *Child Sexual Abuse: A Hope for Healing*. Wheaton, Ill.: Harold Shaw Publishers, 1987.

Hite, Sheri. *The Hite Report: A National Study of Female Sexuality*. New York: Macmillan, 1976.

Hunter, Mic. *The First Step—for People in Relationships with Sex Addicts*. Minneapolis: CompCare, 1989.

Kaplan, Helen Singer. *Disorders of Sexual Desire and Other New Concepts and Techniques in Sex Therapy*. New York: Brunner/Mazel, 1979.

————. *PE: How to Overcome Premature Ejaculation*. New York: Brunner/Mazel, 1989.

————. *Sexual Aversion, Sexual Phobias, and Panic Disorder*. New York: Brunner/Mazel, 1987.

————. *The Evaluation of Sexual Disorders: Psychological and Medical Aspects*. New York: Brunner/Mazel, 1983.

————. *The New Sex Therapy: Active Treatment of Sexual Dysfunctions*. New York: Brunner/Mazel, 1974.

Kolodny, Robert C., William H. Masters, and Virginia E. Johnson. *Textbook of Sexual Medicine*. Boston: Little, Brown and Company, 1979.

Ladas, A. K., B. Whipple, and I. D. Perry. *The G Spot*. New York: Holt, Rinehard and Winston, 1982.

LaHaye, Tim and Beverly LaHaye. *The Act of Marriage*. Grand Rapids, Mich.: Zondervan Publishing House, 1976.

Masters, William H., and Virginia E. Johnson. *Human Sexual Response*. Boston: Little, Brown and Company, 1966.

————. *Human Sexual Inadequacy.* Boston: Little, Brown and Company, 1970.

Mayo, Mary Ann. *A Christian Guide to Sexual Counseling: Recovering the Mystery and Reality of "One Flesh."* Grand Rapids, Mich.: Zondervan Publishing House, 1987.

McCarthy, Barry and Emily McCarthy. *Female Sexual Awareness: Achieving Sexual Fulfillment.* New York: Carroll & Graf Publishers, Inc., 1989.

McCarthy, Barry. *Male Sexual Awareness: Increasing Sexual Satisfaction.* New York: Carroll & Graf Publishers, Inc., 1988.

McGinnis, Alan Loy. *The Romance Factor.* New York: Harper & Row, 1982.

McIlhaney, Joe S., Jr., *Sexuality and Sexually Transmitted Diseases.* Grand Rapids, Mich.: Baker Book House, 1990

O'Connor, Dagmar. *How to Make Love to the Same Person for the Rest of Your Life and Still Love It.* Garden City, N.Y.: Doubleday & Company, Inc., 1985.

————. *How to Put the Love Back into Making Love.* New York: Doubleday, 1989.

Pennebaker, J., J. Kielcolt-Glaser, and R. Glaser. "Disclosure of Traumas and Immune Function: Health Implications for Psychotherapy." *Journal of Consulting and Clinical Psychology.* (1988) 56(2), 239–45.

Penner, Clifford and Joyce Penner. *The Gift of Sex: A Christian Guide to Sexual Fulfillment.* Waco, Tex.: Word Books, 1981.

————. *A Gift for All Ages: A Family Handbook on Sexuality.* Waco, Tex.: Word Books, 1986.

Penner, Julene M. *Childhood Sexual Abuse: A Risk Factor for Addictive Behavior in Adulthood.* Honors Thesis, Harvard University, 1990.

Pomeroy, Wardell B., Carol C. Flax, and Connie C. Wheeler. *Taking a Sex History.* New York: The Free Press, 1982.

Smedes, Lewis B. *Forgive and Forget: Healing the Hurts We Don't Deserve.* San Fransisco: Harper & Row, Publishers, 1984.

————. *Sex for Christians: The Limits and Liberties of Sexual Living.* Grand Rapids, Mich.: William B. Eerdmans Publishing Company, 1976.

Stokes, Naomi Miller. *The Castrated Woman: What Your Doctor Won't Tell You About Hysterectomy.* New York: Franklin Watts, 1969.

Wheat, Ed and Gay Wheat. *Intended for Pleasure: New Approaches to Sexual Intimacy in Christian Marriage.* Old Tappan, N.J.: Fleming H. Revell Company, 1981.

Williams, Warwick. *Rekindling Desire: Bringing Your Sexual Relationship Back to Life.* Oakland, Calif.: New Harbinger Publications, 1988.

NOTES

Chapter 2 The Therapist: Are You Comfortable with Your Sexuality?

1. Clifford Penner and Joyce Penner, *A Gift for All Ages* (Waco, Tex.: Word, 1986).

Chapter 3 The Christian Component—It Sets You Apart

1. Louis H. Evans, Jr., *The Communicator's Commentary—Hebrews* (Waco, Tex.: Word, 1985), 243.

Chapter 5 The Body: Sexual Anatomy and the Physical Response

1. Alan P. Brauer and Donna Brauer, *ESO (Extended Sexual Orgasm)*, (New York: Warner Books, 1983).

Chapter 6 What Is Sexual Therapy?

1. Helen Singer Kaplan, *The New Sex Therapy: Active Treatment of Sexual Dysfunctions* (New York: Brunner/Mazel, 1974), 187.
2. William H. Masters and Virginia E. Johnson, *Human Sexual Inadequacy* (Boston: Little Brown and Company, 1970), 206.

Chapter 7 Why Sexual Therapy?

1. Barry McCarthy, *Male Sexual Awareness: Increasing Sexual Satisfaction* (New York: Carroll & Graf Publishers, Inc., 1988).

2. For other information on sex and the elderly, see "Sex and Aging" in *A Gift for All Ages*.

3. Dagmar O'Connor, *How to Make Love to the Same Person for the Rest of Your Life and Still Love It* (Garden City, N.Y.: Doubleday & Company, Inc., 1985).

4. Neil Warren, *Make Anger Your Ally: Harnessing One of Your Most Powerful Emotions* (Nashville: Wolgemuth & Hyatt, Publishers, Inc., 1990).

5. A. K. Ladas, B. Whipple, and I. D. Perry, *The G-Spot* (New York: Holt, Rinehart, and Winston, 1982).

Chapter 9 Sexual Therapy

1. If one or both of the spouses has shared past sexual activity that is unknown to the other spouse, the therapist should individually guide the spouses in sharing or not sharing the information. Many times, the revealing of past sexual experience is more harmful than helpful.

Part II Diagnosis and Treatment

1. *Diagnostic and Statistical Review, Third Edition, Revised*, 261.

Chapter 11 Treating Problems of Sexual Desire

1. J. Pennebaker, J. Keicolt-Glaser, and R. Glaser, "Disclosure of Traumas and Immune Function: Health Implications for Psychotherapy," *Journal of Consulting and Clinical Psychology*, 56, no. 2 (1988), 239–245.

2. Susan Forward and Craig Buck, *Betrayal of Innocence: Incest and Its Devastation* (New York: Penguin Books, 1978).

3. Kaplan, *The New Sex Therapy*.

4. Erik H. Erikson, *Childhood and Society* (New York: W. W. Norton, 1950).

5. Helen Singer Kaplan, *Disorders of Sexual Desire and Other New Concepts and Techniques in Sex Therapy* (New York: Brunner/Mazel, 1979).

6. Ibid., p. 98.

7. Elizabeth R. Moberly, *Psychogenesis* (New York: Routledge, Inc., 1983), and Elizabeth R. Moberly, *The Psychology of Self and Others* (New York: Routledge, Inc., 1985). See also, *Counseling and Homosexuality*, by Earl D. Wilson, vol. 15 in this Resources for Christian Counseling series (published by Word, Inc., 1988).

8. Kaplan, *Disorders of Sexual Desire*, 203–220.

Chapter 13 Treating Problems of Sexual Release

1. Barbach, *Women Discover Orgasm: A Therapist's Guide to a New Treatment Approach*, (New York: The Free Press, 1980), and Benjamin Graber and Georgia Klein-Graber, *Woman's Orgasm: A Guide to Sexual Satisfaction* (Indianapolis: The Bobbs-Merrill Co., 1975).
2. Graber and Klein-Graber, *Woman's Orgasm*.
3. Sheri Hite, *The Hite Report: A National Study of Female Sexuality* (New York: Macmillan, 1976).
4. Masters and Johnson, *Human Sexual Inadequacy*, 92.
5. Kaplan, The New Sex Therapy, 289–90).
6. Helen Singer Kaplan, *PE: How to Overcome Premature Ejaculation* (New York: Brunner/Mazel, 1989), 29.
7. Brauer and Brauer, *ESO*, 27–29.
8. Kaplan, *Premature Ejaculation*, 62–74.
9. McCarthy and McCarthy, *Male Sexuality Awareness*, (New York: Carroll & Graf Publishers, Inc., 1988), 196–206.
10. Kaplan, *Premature Ejaculation*, 46.
11. Ibid., 98–99.
12. Kaplan, *The New Sex Therapy*, 327
13. Ibid., 327–328.

Chapter 14 Treating Problems of Intercourse

1. Richard Dickey, *Managing Contraceptive Pill Patients* (Durant, Okla.: Creative Informatics, Inc., 1987).
2. Dagmar O'Connor, interviewed by Hornburg in "At Last I Have a Marriage," *Ladies Home Journal* (March 1983), 27–28.
3. Kaplan, *The New Sex Therapy*.
4. Hornburg, "At Last I Have a Marriage."
5. Susan Forward and Craig Buck, *Betrayal of Innocence: Incest and Its Devastation* (New York: Penguin, 1978); Rich Buhler, *Pain and Pretending: You Can Be Set Free From the Hurts of the Past* (Nashville: Thomas Nelson, 1988); and Ellen Bass and Laura Davis, *The Courage to Heal: A Guide for Women Survivors of Child Sexual Abuse* (New York: Harper & Row, Publishers, 1988).

Chapter 15 Understanding and Treating Sexual Addictions

1. Patrick Carnes, *Out of the Shadows: Understanding Sexual Addiction* (Minneapolis: CompCare Publications, 1983).

2. Patrick Carnes, *Contrary to Love: Helping the Sexual Addict* (Minneapolis: CompCare Publications, 1989).

3. Ibid., 87.

4. Ibid., 78.

5. "Sexual Addiction Screening Test," 1988. (Available from Patrick J. Carnes, Institute for Behavioral Medicine, 4101 Golden Valley Road, Golden Valley, MN 55422; 612–588–2771).

6. Carnes, *Contrary to Love*, 215.

Chapter 16 The Results of Sexual Therapy

1. Kaplan, *The New Sex Therapy*, 206.

INDEX

AASECT, 24
Abandon, 85, 237, 283 – 84
Abortion, 9, 100
Abstain, 84, 296, 298
Abuse, 6, 8, 13 – 14, 19, 54, 86, 89 – 90, 93, 105, 113, 191 – 94, 199, 257, 259, 261, 263, 265, 270, 276, 280 – 81, 287
Abused, 8, 11, 17, 19, 86, 89, 185, 193, 200, 239, 259, 263, 266, 271, 276, 280, 282
Abuser, 191 – 93
Abusive, 14, 89, 193, 264, 271
ACA, 93, 195
Acidbase, 50, 254
Acidolphilus, 254
Acne, 203
Addiction, 12, 17 – 18, 74, 76, 177, 246, 275 – 98
Adolescence, 10, 13 – 14, 18, 45 – 46, 54, 59, 64, 74 – 76, 89 – 90, 106, 113, 143, 226, 239, 281 – 83, 291

Adoption, 9, 72, 199, 215, 238
Adrenaline, 76, 91, 277, 282
Adultery, 6, 29, 32, 98, 301
Affair, 86, 197, 209, 236, 282, 284, 287, 291 – 92
Affection, 12, 16, 65, 79, 84, 142, 191, 198, 218
Affirmation, 27 – 28, 33, 65 – 66, 81, 93, 131, 134, 157, 161, 200, 207, 213, 232 – 33, 235, 266, 268, 283, 287
Aggressive, 14, 20, 39, 54, 81, 137, 189, 192, 217, 283
Aging, 46, 82 – 83, 253
AIDS, 50, 250
Albolene, 51, 232, 250
Alcohol, 107, 203, 209 – 10, 289
Alcoholic, 86, 93, 106, 194 – 95, 199, 217, 261, 263, 271, 276, 280, 289, 294 – 98
Alcoholics Anonymous, 294, 296
Allercreme, 51, 141, 232, 250
Allergies, 107

Ambivalence, 190, 194 – 95, 252
Anal intercourse, 50, 52
Anatomy, 44 – 45, 47 – 48, 51, 53 –54, 79
Androgen, 83
Anger, 9, 17, 40 – 42, 65, 87, 188, 209, 211, 219, 227, 237, 270 – 72
Anorgasmic, 81, 125
Anteflexed, 50, 66
Antibiotics, 50
Antihypertensive, 209
Anxiety, 4 – 7, 9, 51, 54, 56, 58, 69, 72, 76, 78 – 79, 82, 91 – 93, 96 – 97, 99, 104, 106, 124, 132 – 34, 147, 181 – 82, 199 – 200, 202 –04, 207 – 15, 222, 226 – 27, 231 – 32, 235 – 37, 240, 249, 270, 276, 286
Appetitive, 187
Areola, 57
Arousal, 9, 14, 16, 20, 46 – 48, 53, 55 – 59, 61, 64 – 65, 74, 76, 78 – 82, 86 – 88, 90 – 92, 101, 117, 125, 129 – 30, 133 – 34, 147 – 49, 155 – 58, 165 – 67, 174, 177, 181, 183, 187 – 89, 191 – 93, 199, 204 – 05, 207 – 09, 211, 214 – 15, 217 – 18, 220 –23, 225, 231 – 37, 239 – 41, 244 – 45, 249, 252, 282, 286, 290
Assessment, 19, 68, 87, 95, 99 – 106, 111, 116, 119, 121 – 27, 136 – 37, 177, 180, 208, 220, 228, 239, 244, 260, 291 – 92, 297, 300, 302
Assignment, 68, 122 – 26, 131, 134, 139, 141, 144 – 45, 147 – 51, 155 – 58, 160, 162 –68, 170 – 75, 182, 184, 194, 200 – 02, 206 –07, 214, 221, 224, 228 – 30, 240 – 42, 244, 250, 254, 265 – 66, 269, 301
Atmosphere, 10, 17, 115, 123, 132, 139, 144, 147, 155, 158, 167, 170, 172, 174
Atrophy, 253, 261
Attitude, 9, 11, 13 – 18, 20, 26, 37, 69, 74, 96, 111 – 12, 136 – 38, 190 – 91, 205, 228, 294, 296
Autonomic, 46, 62, 203, 217
Aversion, 12, 16, 89, 134, 185, 192, 194, 200 – 01, 218, 297

Bacteria, 50, 73
Barbach, Lonnie, 23
Bartholin, 61
Bass, Ellen, 263
Bathe, 29, 74, 127, 139, 141, 144 – 45, 147 – 48, 155 –58, 164, 167, 170 – 72, 174, 266, 268
Becoming one, 28, 34
Beta blockers, 209
Biochemical, 253
Birth control, 51, 59, 84 – 85, 108, 110, 174, 250 – 51, 253
Bitterness, 41
Bladder, 46, 48, 50, 53 – 54, 60, 63, 88, 109, 150, 254
Blocked sexual feelings, 104
Blood pressure, 61, 63
Body image, 8, 87
Bonding, 12, 14, 33, 35, 71 – 72, 77, 92, 198 – 99, 201, 237, 240
Boredom, 15, 44, 179, 183, 185
Brain, 212, 220
Brauer and Brauer, 23, 63, 101, 228

Breasts, 37, 52 – 53, 57, 89, 108 –
    09, 113, 117, 125, 128 – 29,
    147, 155, 158, 167, 170, 174,
    183, 207, 222, 229 – 30, 263,
    269, 271
Bride, 29 – 30, 249
Bridging, 223
Buhler, Rich, 83, 263
Bumblers, 75 – 77, 79, 200, 256
Bundy, Tedd, 280
Buttocks, 155, 254

Caffeine, 50, 254
Cardiovascular, 108
Caress, 58, 117, 123, 125, 127,
    134, 139, 141, 144, 147, 155,
    167, 172, 174, 196, 202, 222,
    232 – 35, 240 – 41, 251 – 52,
    286
Carnes, Patrick, 278, 284, 287,
    289, 292 – 93, 298
Carpopedal spasm, 61
Catheterizations, 88, 90, 268 – 69
Catholic, 190, 258
Celibacy, 296
Certification, 24
Cervix, 57, 62, 109, 254
Childbirth, 50, 55, 223, 255
Circulatory, 209
Clean, 50, 73, 141, 266, 268
Clitoris, 17, 51 – 52, 56 – 57, 62,
    66, 72, 101, 148, 156, 214, 219,
    222 – 23
Coaddictive, 291 – 92, 297
Compulsion, 277 – 82, 285, 287
Conception, 36
Condoms, 251, 253
Confront, 194, 264
Congenital, 8

Congestion, 59, 66, 252
Constipation, 237, 259
Consummate, 79, 90, 101, 103,
    190, 249, 251, 256 – 57, 271,
    286
Contaminated, 50, 73
Coronal ridge, 149, 156
Cross – dressing, 86
Curiosity, 12, 14, 19, 69, 74 – 75,
    196, 281 – 82
Cystitis, 79

Davis, Laura, 263
Demulen, 203
Depressant, 203
Depression, 106, 193, 203, 209 –
    10, 285, 291 – 92
Desensitization, 194, 200, 213,
    203, 239, 263, 266, 268
Desire, 6, 15 – 16, 18, 23, 27, 34 –
    36, 40, 46, 56, 63 – 65, 72, 76,
    78, 81 – 84, 86 – 87, 91, 93 –
    94, 103 – 05, 116, 124, 139,
    160, 174, 177 – 78, 180 – 82,
    185, 187 – 89, 191 – 92, 195 –
    205, 226 – 28, 236 – 38, 241 –
    42, 245, 260, 275, 285, 293
Despair, 210, 284, 287 – 88, 292
Developmental, 70 – 73, 75 – 77,
    89, 91, 192, 196, 256, 281
Deviations, 279
Devices, 209
Diabetes, 108, 209, 236
Diagnosis, 95, 97, 177 – 78, 193,
    249 – 50, 254, 257, 260 – 62,
    294, 301
Dialators, 131, 250, 258, 267 – 70,
    272
Diaphragms, 251

Dickey, Richard, 253
Diphasic, 47
Disorders, 23, 121, 178, 188, 200, 203, 210 – 11, 215 – 16, 226, 248, 261
Distraction, 42, 122, 134, 165, 181, 211 – 12, 215, 227, 241, 245, 255, 284 – 85
Distrust, 41, 260
Divorce, 218, 237, 283
Dominant, 33, 39, 48, 61, 65, 91, 200, 202, 207, 210, 237, 239, 245, 249
Douching, 50
Duct, 63, 236
Dyspareunia, 18, 45, 103, 248 – 49

Ejaculation, 25, 46 – 47, 51, 54, 58 – 60, 63 – 64, 78, 82, 86, 88, 91, 100 – 01, 103, 105, 108, 125, 131, 138, 151, 161, 174, 182 – 83, 189, 196, 207, 210, 213, 215 – 16, 218, 224 – 47, 249, 269, 286
Elimination, 72 – 73
Emission, 32, 108, 236, 238, 243 – 44
Empathy, 14, 18, 22, 98 – 100
Endocrine, 209
Endometriosis, 254
Enemas, 259
Engorgement, 56 – 57, 59, 61, 65, 80, 205, 207, 211, 252
Entrepreneurial, 196 – 98
Entry by invitation, 126, 130, 242, 269
Episiotomy, 255
Erectile dysfunction, 208 – 09, 211, 213, 215, 257

Erectile tissue, 52, 54
Erection, 18, 45 – 47, 54 – 55, 57 –59, 64 – 65, 78 – 79, 82, 90 – 91, 138, 182 – 83, 205 – 15, 230 – 34, 236, 243 – 45, 249, 257
Erect penis size, 269
Erotic, 15, 36, 46, 55, 72, 75, 78, 80, 85 – 86, 88 – 89, 203, 218, 281
Estrogen, 45, 82 – 83, 208, 253
Evans, Louis H., Jr., 34
Excitement, 15, 48, 56 – 59, 61, 64, 188 – 89, 204, 208 – 09, 249, 284 – 85, 290
Exhibitionism, 282, 285, 287, 290
Experimentation, 15, 112, 207, 281 – 82
Exploitive, 75
Exploratory play, 12, 75, 79, 112, 142, 196, 200

Facial caress, 125, 127, 141, 147, 155, 167, 202
Fallopian tubes, 48
Fantasy, 4 – 6, 48, 99, 113, 137, 191 – 92, 237 – 39, 245, 258, 260, 262, 264, 283, 285 – 86, 297
Fatigue, 106, 182, 188 – 89, 209 – 10, 279
Fear, 56, 76, 87 – 92, 106, 134, 198 – 200, 210 – 12, 214, 217 – 19, 235 – 38, 246, 249, 251, 258 – 60, 262 – 63, 265, 270
Female ejaculation, 51, 88
Femininity, 80 – 81, 83
Fertile, 283
Fetish, 199, 202, 290

Fiddling, 213
Finances, 39, 209, 252
First sexual experience, 18
Flaccid penis, 55, 80, 170, 208, 214
Flush, 58
Fondle, 31, 72, 183, 185, 192, 207, 263
Foreskin, 52
Forgive, 19, 28, 32, 86, 193, 211, 278
Forward, Susan, 193, 263
Frenulum, 149, 156
Frequency, 46, 107, 116, 138, 179 –82, 185, 289
Freud, 223
Frigidity, 204
Fulfillment, 9, 17, 23, 31, 33, 36 – 37, 40, 42, 66, 98 – 99, 136, 138, 179, 224, 249, 284, 295, 300
Fun, 82, 84, 124 – 25, 134, 170, 172, 212, 224, 266

G – spot, 51, 88, 157, 222, 224
Gastrointestinal, 50
Gender, 5, 122, 276
Genuineness, 22, 98 – 99
Germ, 73
Glans, 52, 56, 59, 61, 65, 148, 156
Goal – oriented, 59, 124, 196 – 98, 220
Graber and Graber, 222
Graffenburg spot, 224
Graphing, 124 – 25, 128, 151, 189, 194, 207
Grief, 8, 100, 192, 219, 264, 292
Group therapy, 122, 264
Guilt, 6, 9, 13, 17 – 19, 76, 86 – 87, 89 – 90, 100, 105, 189,
191 – 93, 199 – 200, 209, 226, 236 – 37, 275 – 76, 280 – 81, 288, 291, 301
Gynecological, 90, 250, 259 – 60, 270

Hegar Dialators, 269
Heterosexual, 77, 202, 289
History taking, 281
Holocaust, 259
Homosexual, 21, 98, 113, 202 – 03, 237 – 39, 246, 289, 301
Honeymoon, 18, 201
Hormonal, 45 – 46, 48, 52 – 53, 75, 83, 103, 108, 203, 208 – 09, 239, 253
Hostility, 227
Hugging, 56, 171, 174, 201, 235, 285
Humiliation, 199
Humor, 11, 98, 165, 256
Hurts, 8, 41, 211, 249, 254
Hymen, 249 – 50, 254, 256
Hymenotomy, 250
Hyperactive, 99
Hyperventilation, 61
Hysterectomy, 83

Identity, 11
Imbalances, 239
Immature, 75, 93, 223
Immoral, 5, 35, 278
Impotence, 18, 39, 82, 103, 105, 131, 207 – 11, 213, 220, 227, 237, 257
Impregnation, 36, 50
Impulses, 22
Incest, 191, 199, 260, 290
Infancy, 14, 70 – 72, 77, 198 – 99

COUNSELING FOR SEXUAL DISORDERS

Infection, 50, 73, 103, 108, 110, 253

Infertility, 109

Inflammation, 253 – 54, 257

Inhibit, 62, 74, 76, 78 – 79, 87 – 88, 91, 151, 210, 216, 236, 246

Inhibited sexual desire, 187, 196

Inhibition, 29, 84, 93, 105, 160, 165, 178 – 79, 185, 190, 194, 201, 203, 216, 218 – 21, 224, 236 – 40, 243, 245 – 47, 252, 258, 260

Initiation, 39, 41, 81 – 82, 93, 100, 116, 123 – 24, 132, 138 – 39, 141, 144, 147, 155, 158, 160, 167, 172, 174 – 75, 179 – 83, 185, 195, 204, 210, 220

Insecurity, 4, 40, 73, 181

Insensitive, 90, 259

Insomnia, 91, 106, 209

Interest, lack of sexual, 89, 138, 181, 188 – 97, 210, 237, 275 – 76, 293

Intimacy, 3, 5 – 7, 12 – 13, 39 – 41, 65 – 66, 68 – 69, 72, 80, 87, 93 –94, 160, 197 – 202, 276, 283, 297

Intromission, 256

Invitation, 126, 130, 184, 242, 269

Involuntary, 45 – 46, 51, 57, 61 – 62, 65, 70, 78 – 79, 90 – 92, 133, 147, 155, 167, 204 – 05, 207, 217, 221, 237, 239, 257, 261, 268 – 69, 272

Irritation, 40, 50, 253 – 54

IUD, 254

Journal, 131, 192, 264, 296, 301

K – Y Jelly, 51, 251

Kaplan, Helen Singer, 23, 47, 67, 101, 188, 196, 200, 203, 225 – 26, 228 – 29, 234, 236 – 37, 246, 260, 300

Kissing, 13, 48, 56, 79, 88, 100, 117, 125, 129, 162, 171 – 72, 174, 196, 201, 207, 222, 235, 244, 251, 271

Knee/chest position, 254

Kolodny, 88

Labia, 51 – 52, 57, 61, 66, 72, 148, 150, 156, 174, 249, 254, 256

Lack of bonding, 199

Ladas, Whipple and Perry, 88

LaHaye, Tim, 77

Lesbian, 264

Ligaments, 50, 255

Log, 122, 131

Loneliness, 197, 283

Lotion, 139, 141, 144, 157, 232, 250, 266

Lubricant, 45, 51, 83, 174, 205 – 08, 215, 232 – 33, 249 – 51, 253, 266

Lubricate, 38 – 39, , 45 – 46, 56 – 57, 269

Lubrication, 51, 54, 78, 83, 90

Lubrifax, 251

Lust, 35, 275

Male – depreciating, 198, 200

Male – dominated, 226

Manual stimulation, 48, 126, 130, 172, 218, 223 – 24, 227, (cont) 232 –33, 236, 242 – 44, 246, 270 –71

Marijuana, 277

Marital discord, 227

Marital therapy, 40, 228, 300

Masculinity, 54, 80, 83, 93, 227

Massaging, 157

Masters and Johnson, 23, 28, 47, 56, 68, 88, 101, 223 – 24, 229, 236, 247, 267, 272

Mastery, 70, 72, 214

Masturbation, 13, 21, 72, 84 – 85, 90 – 91, 100 – 01, 108, 112, 137, 142, 187, 191, 199 – 200, 202, 226, 237, 240 – 41, 243 – 44, 246, 275, 285 – 87, 289, 296 –97

McCarthy, Barry, 80, 228

Medications, 54, 103, 107, 200, 209, 267

Memories, 8, 142, 192 – 93, 259, 264, 270

Menopause, 45, 48, 51, 83, 208, 253

Menstrual, 32, 45, 109, 190

Mesh, 16, 134

Messy, 185, 243

Microorganisms, 50, 73

Mirror, 124, 127, 140, 148, 156, 206, 266, 295

Miscarriages, 109

Misinformation, 77, 80, 85, 98, 258, 260

Mmpi, 68, 103

Modesty, 7, 74

Molestation, 89, 191, 259 – 60, 263, 288, 290

Mood, 109, 155, 167, 174, 283

Mood altering, 277

Moral, 13, 15, 20, 22, 86, 200 – 03, 237, 276 – 77

Multiphasic, 68, 93, 103

Multiple orgasm, 63

Mutual stimulation, 286

Mutuality, 15 – 16, 33 – 34, 69, 133, 217

Mystery, 30

Myths, 9, 19, 26, 80 – 81, 83

Naive, 77, 79 – 80, 85, 100, 196, 239, 256, 263

Naiveté, 207 – 08, 237, 240, 256

Naked, 26, 28, 40 – 41

Nausea, 258, 271 – 72

Necking, 48, 54, 258

Negotiate, 180, 197, 279, 285

Nervous system, 46, 51, 54, 62, 65, 70, 91, 203, 207, 217, 221, 249

Neurotic, 281

Nipple erection, 57, 59, 79, 205 – 07

Nocturnal emission, 108, 236, 238

Noises, 78, 165, 221

Non – demand pleasuring, 130, 212

Nonaddict, 282

Nonaddictive, 289

Nondemand position, 158, 230

Nondemand teaching, 124 – 25, 128, 158, 167, 207, 241

Nongenital, 229

Nonverbal, 6

Nude, 12, 74, 82, 87, 113, 127, 140, 142, 144, 166, 172, 190

Nurture, 283

Nutrition, 50, 253

O'Connor, Dagmar, 87, 259, 262, 272

Obesity, 8, 239, 256

Obscene, 290

Obsession, 85, 277, 284 – 85, 287, 292 – 93
Oils, 51, 251
Ointments, 29
Old Testament, 29 – 33
One flesh, 28, 30, 34 – 35
Oneness, 33
Oral contraceptives, 203
Oral stimulation, 20, 48
Orgasmic, 5, 47 – 48, 61 – 65, 78 –79, 80 – 82, 86, 88, 91 – 92, 105, 130, 138, 151, 183, 188, 207, 216 – 27, 236 – 37, 239, 244 – 45, 252, 270 – 71
Orgasmic inhibition, 105, 216, 219 – 21, 252
Orgasmic platform, 61 – 63, 80
Ovaries, 48, 53, 83, 203, 254

Pain, 8, 14, 18, 40, 45, 50, 54, 56 –57, 62, 65 – 66, 75, 88 – 90, 95, 99, 100, 103, 105, 109, 138, 148 – 49, 157 – 58, 191 – 93, 218, 238, 243, 248 – 66, 271 – 73, 283
Pairing, 76, 90, 191 – 92, 194, 199, 223 – 24, 258, 282
Palpitations, 106
Panic, 89, 134, 192, 200, 257 – 58
Parasympathetic (PNS), 46, 48, 51, 54, 61, 65, 91, 130, 207 – 08, 217, 221, 249
Parent, 12 – 13, 39, 42, 48, 71, 73 –76, 79, 89 – 90, 111 – 12, 142, 210, 219, 238, 251, 272, 291
Passionate, 13, 21, 31, 35, 79, 84 – 85, 88, 94, 196, 201, 207, 222, 271

Passive aggressive, 40
Pathologies, 69, 254, 256
PC muscle, 45, 50 – 51, 55, 63, 80, 125, 128, 131, 150, 157, 222 –24, 250, 253 – 54, 265 – 66, 268, 270
Peeping, 74, 280, 282, 287
Pelvic, 33, 61, 166, 233, 252, 254, 256
Penetration, 56, 258 – 59, 262 – 67, 272
Penis, 16, 50 – 63, 65, 72 – 73, 78 –80, 82, 86, 90, 101, 108, 126, 129, 131, 148 – 49, 156, 166, 170, 172, 174, 185, 192, 208 –14, 218, 223 – 26, 229 – 34, 236, 239 – 45, 248, 256, 258, 262, 269 – 72, 281
Penners, 23, 98
Pentateuch, 32
Performance anxiety, 51, 64, 82, 91 – 92, 104, 134, 196, 205 – 07, 210 – 12, 214, 222, 224
Perineal, 52, 60, 259
Permission, 6, 9, 15, 81, 85, 97, 105, 184 – 85, 190 – 91, 205 – 06, 214, 219, 221, 286
Perry (Whipple and Ladas), 88, 224
Personality, 68, 93, 97, 103, 277, 279, 286
Perversions, 279 – 80
Petroleum – based lubricants, 51, 251
Petting, 48, 54, 90, 258
pH balance 50, 61, 253, 256
Phobias, 192, 194, 199 – 200, 263 –64, 266 – 67, 269, 272

Physician, 14, 54, 88, 90, 103, 253 –55, 257, 259 – 62, 267 – 68, 270

Pill (oral contraceptive), 253

Plateau phase, 48, 57, 59 – 61, 63 – 64, 217, 221

Playful, 170, 213, 233, 241

Playing "doctor," 142

Pleasure, 33, 36 – 37, 59, 69, 139, 141, 205 – 06, 211 – 15, 217 – 18, 220, 228 – 31, 251, 255 – 56, 263, 265 – 66, 299

Pleasuring, 117, 124 – 34, 144, 147, 155, 158, 160, 164, 167, 170 –72, 174, 240 – 44, 268 –69

PMS, 109

PNS, 130, 249

Pomeroy, 101

Pornographic, 6, 86, 112, 275, 277, 280 – 82, 285, 289, 290

Position, 224, 230, 233, 242, 254, 256, 266, 269

Postmarital, 270

Powerlessness, 288

Prayer, 34, 287, 291

Preadolescence, 75, 77, 196, 237, 281

Prearoused, 48

Preexcitement, 187

Pregnancy, 8, 31, 45, 61 – 62, 76, 85, 87, 89, 100, 238, 288

Premarital sex, 13, 90

Premature ejaculation, 25, 60, 105, 131, 210, 216, 218, 224 – 29

Preschooler, 74

Pressure, 33, 50 – 51, 58, 61, 63 – 64, 92, 157, 182, 198, 210, 213, 218, 232, 240, 283

Prestimulated, 48, 56, 65

Pretending, 263

Procreation, 15, 27, 51

Professional, 7, 9, 12, 21 – 22, 24, 97, 99 – 100, 103, 122, 193, 229, 278 – 79, 295

Progesterone, 45

Prohibited, 200, 219, 296, 300

Promiscuity, 84, 86, 89, 192, 270

Prostate gland, 53 – 54, 60, 63, 108, 224, 236

Prostitute, 31, 275, 277, 279, 285, 289, 296

Psychiatric, 22, 200, 267

Psychogenic, 249, 257, 263

Psychological, 93, 122, 136, 177, 237, 261, 273

Psychopathic, 280 – 81, 287

Psychophysiological, 178

Psychosomatic, 261

Psychotherapeutic, 67 – 68, 87, 93, 99, 178, 103, 121 – 24, 192 – 93, 196, 198 – 201, 203, 205, 218 – 19, 252, 260, 300

Puberty, 45, 48, 52, 238

Pubis, 80

Pubococcygeus, 150

Rage, 41, 199

Rape, 90, 191, 257, 259 – 60, 271 – 72, 280, 287, 290

Rationalization, 288, 292, 297

Rectum, 48, 63, 73, 108 – 09, 255

Reflex, 62, 64, 78, 174, 207, 216, 220 – 22, 225 – 26, 232, 235 – 36, 239, 262

Refractory period, 48, 64, 78

Regression, 244, 269, 272

Reinforce, 74, 240, 243 – 44

Rejection, 41, 65, 94, 210 – 11, 286, 288

Relapse, 297 – 98

Relationship problems, 93, 188

Relaxants, 262

Religious, 6, 13, 25, 32, 37, 83 – 84, 86, 115, 137, 184, 190, 211, 237 – 38, 258, 270, 285

Reproductive, 48, 53 – 54, 73, 108 – 09, 213 – 14, 252

Repulsion, 42, 72, 185, 227

Resist, 86, 90, 194 – 95, 206, 264 – 66, 272

Resistance, 8, 43, 124, 188, 192, 199, 201 – 02, 228, 245 – 46, 258, 301

Resolution phase, 48, 64 – 66

Respect, 36, 39, 41 – 42, 99, 125, 211, 219

Retarded ejaculation, 103, 131, 235 – 39, 245 – 46

Retroflexed, 50

Retrograde, 60

Retroverted uterus, 254

Rhythmic, 45, 144, 242, 251

Right brain, 212

Risk, 76, 90, 239, 286, 289 – 90, 292, 296

Romance, 29, 37, 75, 113, 158, 199, 276

Sabotage, 40, 87, 94, 199, 201 – 02, 245 – 46, 286

Sado – masochistic behavior, 290

School – age, 75

Scrotum, 33, 53 – 54, 58 – 60

Secretes, 51, 61

Secretions, 79, 185

Secrets, 6 – 7, 10, 17, 282, 298

Sedatives, 106

Seductive, 271, 293

Self – concept, 12, 296

Self – consciousness, 27, 29, 134, 165, 212, 217, 220 – 21

Self – esteem, 9, 192 – 94, 200, 205, 210, 283 – 84

Self – stimulation, 48, 79, 89, 92, 108, 129 – 30, 137, 151, 171, 219 – 20, 222 – 23, 226, 228, 236, 239 – 45, 247

Self – worth, 8 – 9, 17, 87, 94

Self – control, 34

Self – defeating, 286

Self – depreciation, 9

Self – disclosure, 40

Self – doubts, 211

Self – examination, 45, 84, 128, 148 – 49, 206, 250, 265 – 66

Self – help, 77, 104, 116, 120, 300

Seman's stop – start method, 229

Seminal fluid, 53 – 54, 60, 63, 236, 244, 253

Seminal vesicles, 54

Sensate focus, 67, 92, 123, 133, 199, 238

Sensual, 29, 52, 83, 85, 133, 139, 141, 144, 147, 164, 197, 226, 229

Sex education, 4, 24, 112, 280

Sex hormones, 45 – 46, 48

Sexual abuse, 8, 14, 54, 86, 105, 113, 193, 199, 261, 270, 281

Sexual Addiction, 12, 17 – 18, 177, 275 – 78, 281, 287 – 93, 295 – 96, 298, 301

Sexual anxiety, 91 – 93

Sexual arousal, 9, 14, 46 – 47, 53, 56, 58, 76, 78 – 80, 86, 90 –91,

133, 147, 155, 165, 167, 174, 204, 223

Sexual behavior, 21, 32, 34, 48, 69, 85, 89, 98, 100, 104, 137, 143, 276 – 77, 282, 286, 292

Sexual desire, 16, 23, 46, 56, 72, 76, 82 – 84, 86 – 87, 103 – 05, 178, 180, 187 – 89, 191 – 92, 195 – 96, 198 – 200, 203, 204 – 05, 236, 260, 293

Sexual development, 11 – 12, 14, 71, 73, 112, 125, 127, 142 – 43, 193, 196

Sexual drive, 16, 46, 72, 76, 83, 188, 198 – 99, 203

Sexual dysfunctions, 18, 67, 178

Sexual enjoyment, 19, 52, 77, 84, 184, 208, 249

Sexual feelings, 11, 17, 21, 48, 71, 76, 83 – 84, 89 – 90, 99, 104, 133, 136, 187, 191 – 92, 194, 199, 201, 205 – 06, 221

Sexual fulfillment, 9, 23, 98, 136, 138, 179, 249

Sexual identity, 11

Sexual intercourse, 16, 28 – 29, 48, 55, 79, 98, 105, 114, 132, 137, 160, 189, 201, 226, 228, 250, 253, 255, 272, 286

Sexual intimacy, 40 – 41, 69, 72, 160, 201

Sexual play, 50, 75, 82, 108

Sexual pleasure, 15, 17, 33, 36, 51, 76, 83 – 84, 91, 133, 136 – 37, 169, 190 – 91, 205, 209, 211, 217, 226, 238, 241, 252, 255 – 56, 263, 265

Sexual problems, 7, 23, 38 – 39, 41, 59, 93, 177

Sexual response, 15, 23, 46 – 47, 56, 62, 64, 67, 70 – 71, 78, 85, 91, 94, 124 – 25, 128, 136, 151, 177, 179, 187 – 89, 194, 196, 203, 207, 210, 217, 219 – 20, 249, 282, 299

Sexual stimulation, 46, 50 – 52, 54, 56, 81, 150, 205, 219, 226, 228

Sexual conflict, 68, 189, 192, 194, 199, 205, 252, 300

Sexual enhancement, 77, 80

Sexually transmitted diseases (STD), 108, 110, 250

Shameful, 282, 288

Simulating, 125, 129 – 30, 165 – 66, 221, 244

Simultaneous, 81 – 82, 137, 162, 235

Sin, 14, 19, 21, 28 – 29, 31 – 32, 35, 83 – 84, 86, 98, 190, 263, 278 – 79, 281

Single, 21, 76, 89, 96, 227, 259, 280, 293

Smedes, Lewis, 23

Sobriety, 296 – 97

Sociopathic, 280

Sounds, 166, 221

Spanking, 90

Spasm, 61, 63, 252, 257 – 58, 262, 268 – 69, 272

Spectatoring, 92, 130 – 31, 210 – 12, 220

Speculum, 90, 261

Sperm, 48, 53, 59, 62 – 63, 85

Sphincter, 60, 63

Spiritual, 22, 31, 33 – 35, 39, 77, 84, 92, 98, 134, 184, 224, 280

Squeeze technique, 229 – 30

Sterile, 50, 73

Stress, 17, 21, 41, 77, 177, 181, 185, 188, 203, 210, 235, 251 – 52, 258, 279, 283 – 86, 301

Suicidal, 106, 292

Surgery, 55, 83, 95, 106, 250, 257, 260 – 62

Sympathetic nervous system (SNS), 54, 91, 130, 207, 221, 249

Tampons, 190, 258 – 59, 263, 269 – 71

Taylor-Johnson, 103

Temperament, 103

Temptation, 22, 296

Tension, 59, 61 – 62, 65, 87, 98, 104, 114, 150, 165, 200, 249, 251 – 52, 261

Termination, 126

Testes, 53 – 54, 59 – 60, 108, 149, 156

Testosterone, 45 – 46, 53 – 54, 82, 203, 246

Thrusting, 50, 57, 61 – 62, 78, 131, 166, 172, 174, 208, 214, 217, 221, 223 – 25, 233 – 35, 242, 245, 251, 254, 286

Thyroid, 108

Ticklishness, 139

Time management, 198

Timing, 64, 224, 271

Tipped uterus, 50, 57, 254

Toddlerhood, 12, 72 – 73, 181, 200

Tongue, 162, 170, 172, 222, 271

Tranquilizers, 262

Transference, 96

Transparent, 198

Traumatic, 9, 14, 18, 75, 89 – 90, 143, 185, 190 – 94, 198 – 99, 237, 255, 259 – 60, 263 – 64, 279

Triad, 22, 99

Trust, 5, 26, 39 – 42, 69, 71, 89, 122, 130, 134, 193 – 94, 198, 218 – 20, 240, 263, 265 – 66, 269, 295

Tumescence, 209

Unaroused, 50, 56

Unashamed, 26, 29

Unauthentic, 209

Unclean, 32

Unconditional, 22

Uncongested, 65

Unconscious, 68, 85 – 89, 199, 201, 237, 259, 291, 300

Unconsummated marriage, 15, 79, 90, 100, 248, 256 – 57, 259, 263, 271 – 73, 286, 297

Unfaithful, 29

Unforgivable, 263

Unfulfilled, 81, 227

Unmentionable, 72 – 73

Untouchable, 72 – 73

Unworthy, 288

Urethra, 109, 236, 257

Urethritis, 257

Urinary, 48, 50, 54, 60, 63, 73, 80, 88, 90, 110, 148, 156, 254, 259

Urinate, 79, 88, 142, 150, 237, 240, 243, 259

Urological, 103, 237, 259

Urologist, 7, 54, 103, 209, 249, 257

Uterine tubes, 48

Uterus, 4, 48, 50, 56 – 57, 61 – 62, 66, 109, 217, 252 – 55

Vagina, 4, 16, 45 – 46, 50 – 52, 54 –
57, 59, 61 – 64, 66, 73, 78, 80,
82 – 83, 90, 101, 103, 109 – 10,
124 – 25, 128, 131, 148, 150,
156 – 57, 166, 172, 174, 185,
205 – 08, 214 – 15, 217, 221 –
25, 232 – 35, 242, 245, 248 –
70, 272
Vaginismus, 25, 90, 125, 131, 248,
250, 257 – 66, 268, 270 – 73,
286
Vaginitis, 261
Value, 7, 12, 20 – 21, 24, 27, 33,
76, 86, 286
Vas deferens, 53 – 54
Vasectomy, 53 – 54
Vasocongestion, 56, 61, 65, 207,
217, 220, 223
Vestibulitis, 261

Victim, 14, 17, 191, 193, 281, 288,
298
Violation, 21, 28, 32, 76, 86, 89,
258, 265 – 66, 281, 290
Virginal, 79, 255
Visualization, 205, 267
Voyeurism, 86, 280, 287, 290
Vulnerability, 40, 88, 96, 239 – 40

Warren, Dr. Neil, 87
Wet dream, 108, 236
Wheat, Dr. Ed., 36, 77
Whipple, Ladas and Perry, 88,
224
Withdrawal method, 59
Woman's orgasm, 64, 78, 224
Womb, 48

Yogurt, 254

Joyce J. Penner, R.N., M.N.
Clifford L. Penner, Ph.D.

Joyce Penner, a registered nurse and clinical nurse specialist, is in sexual therapy practice with her husband Clifford. A native of Minnesota, Mrs. Penner holds the B.S. in nursing from the University of Washington. Her master's degree in psychosomatic nursing and nursing education is from the University of California at Los Angeles.

Clifford Penner is a clinical psychologist and sex therapist. A native of Canada, Dr. Penner is a graduate of Bethel College (St. Paul, Minn.). He earned the M.A. in theology from Fuller Theological Seminary and holds the Ph.D. from Fuller's Graduate School of Psychology.

Together, the Penners have authored several books, including a classic in the field, *The Gift of Sex*, and *A Gift for All Ages: A Family Handbook on Sexuality*. They are active in leading sexual seminars in churches of all denominations. The Penners also lecture on college and seminary compuses and are seen and heard regularly on television and radio. They are the parents of three children: Julene, Greg, and Kristine.